D0973738

THE
DiMAGGIOS

THE
DiMAGGIOS

✳ ✴ ✳

Three Brothers,
Their Passion for Baseball,
Their Pursuit of the American Dream

TOM CLAVIN

An Imprint of HarperCollinsPublishers

HarperCollins books may be purchased for educational, business, or sales promotional use. For information please e-mail the Special Markets Department at SPsales@harpercollins.com.

A hardcover edition of this title was published in 2013 by Ecco, an imprint of HarperCollins Publishers.

FIRST ECCO PAPERBACK EDITION PUBLISHED 2014.

Designed by Mary Austin Speaker
Photograph on p. iv © Bettmann/CORBIS

Library of Congress Cataloging-in-Publication Data has been applied for.

ISBN 978-0-06-218378-1

14 15 16 17 18   OV/RRD   10 9 8 7 6 5 4 3 2 1

TO MY FAMILY

ACKNOWLEDGMENTS

It would have been impossible to write empathetically about the relationship between the three baseball-playing DiMaggio brothers without the information and insight offered by family members. I am grateful to the time given to me by Emily DiMaggio Sr., Emily DiMaggio Jr., Elaine Calloway DiMaggio Brooks, Joseph DiMaggio, and Joanne DiMaggio Webber and Paul DiMaggio, who were especially generous. My respect for the entire DiMaggio family grew because of my contact with them.

Also helping me enormously were the contributions of the people interviewed for this book who knew Vince, Joe, or Dominic during or after their baseball careers. My thanks go to Vic Barnhart, Matt Batts, Yogi Berra, Dean Boylan Sr. (and to his son, Dean Jr.), Dr. Bobby Brown, Larry Cancro, Ellis "Cot" Deal, Ike DeLock, Bobby Doerr, Dave "Boo" Ferriss, Dick Flavin, Dick Gernert, Lee Howard, Ralph Kiner, Ted Lepcio, Babe Martin, Sam Mele, Jimmy Piersall, Charlie Silvera, and Don Trower.

I also benefited greatly from the help of many people who provided research or contact information. A sincere tip of the cap to the Pacific Coast League historian Dick Beverage; Dick Bresciani and Sarah C. Coffin of the Boston Red Sox; Margie Cowan; Bill Francis, Pat Kelly, and John Horne at the Baseball Hall of Fame; Kathleen Iudice at the San Francisco Museum and Historical Society; David Kaplan at the Yogi Berra Museum & Learning Center; Doug Kelly; Sally O'Leary of the Pittsburgh Pirates; Mark Macrae; Bill Nowlin for his wonderful books on Red Sox players and history; Henry F. Scanell and Jane Winton at the Boston Public Library; Michael Tusiani and Alexandra Trochanowski of the New York Yankees; and the staff at the John Jermain Library and East Hampton Library. Deep thanks to Valerie Hanley for her transcribing skills and consistent support.

I am indebted to writers whose works proved to be strong sources of information about the DiMaggios or baseball in general. Topping that list are Lawrence Baldassaro, David Cataneo, Richard Ben Cramer, Harvey Frommer, Richard Goldstein, David Halberstam, Martin Jacobs and Jack McGuire, Roger Kahn, Kostya Kennedy, Barbara Leaming, Richard Leutzinger, Leigh Montville, John Snyder, George Vecsey, Fay Vincent, Donald Wells, Richard Whittingham, and Paul Zingg and Mark Medeiros.

This book would not have happened without the suggestion, guidance, and nudging of Bob Rosen. He would not take no for an answer, and I am grateful for that. Big thanks to the others at RLR Associates, especially Scott Gould and his smarts and infinite patience. It has been an inspiring experience to work with Daniel Halpern, Libby Edelson, and John Strausbaugh at Ecco.

Finally, the encouragement and steadfastness of family and friends enables me to survive the book-writing journeys, including this one. Leslie Reingold knows most of all what that journey is like and should be nominated for sainthood. Also on my team have been my children, Kathryn and Brendan Clavin; my mother, Gertrude Clavin; my siblings, Nancy Bartolotta and James Clavin; and John Bonfiglio, Heather Buchanan, Bob Drury, Michael Gambino, Phil Keith, Bob Martin, Ken Moran, Jacquelyn Reingold, Tony Sales, Lynne Scanlon, Bob Schaeffer, and David Winter.

THE
DiMAGGIOS

Prologue

THERE WERE 53 former players on the field at Fenway Park for Old-Timers' Day in May 1986, but most eyes were on the three men whose last name was DiMaggio: Vince, Joe, and Dominic, together for the first time in many years in a major league ballpark. The cheering crowd of over 31,000 people did not know that one of them was dying and that this would be the last time the DiMaggio brothers were together anywhere.

There were plenty of other luminary players with ties to Boston on the field—Carl Yastrzemski, Warren Spahn, Bobby Doerr, Johnny Pesky, and the greatest of all the Beantown ballplayers, Ted Williams. Many of those in Fenway Park had witnessed Yaz in the pennant-winning 1967 season when he won the Triple Crown, a feat that would not be replicated until Miguel Cabrera achieved it 45 years later. Some had seen Ted Williams, the "Splendid Splinter," roam left field and set records at the plate, and no doubt a few had been there on September 28, 1960, when a weary 42-year-old homered in his last at-bat, a godlike feat immortalized in a brilliant essay by John Updike. There was also the rare pairing of Ralph Branca and Bobby

Thomson, who had combined in a playoff game in 1951 between the Brooklyn Dodgers and New York Giants to produce arguably the most famous home run in baseball history. Less well known but still warmly embraced retirees included Tommy Holmes, Carroll Hardy, Tex Hughson, and Boo Ferriss.

And this wasn't just any Old-Timers' Day. The Red Sox were celebrating the 40th anniversary of their 1946 American League championship, which had been their first pennant since 1918. Since then, few men were more revered in Boston than Dominic DiMaggio. The 1946 season had been a brilliant one for Dominic and his teammates.

For Vince, however, 1946 had marked the end of his major league career. And Joe, after three years in World War II service, was back with the Yankees in 1946, but at 31 his greatness was waning. He hit .290, the first year he was below .300, and that October he had the disorienting experience of not being in the World Series. The Yankees had finished in third place, a startling 17 games behind Boston. Dominic had actually been the better ballplayer that pennant-winning year, with a .316 average, finishing in the top 10 in the MVP voting, well ahead of the brother routinely referred to as "the Great DiMaggio."

The Boston media had been promoting the festivities and the reunion of the DiMaggio brothers for a week. As he had been for close to a half-century, Vince still was compared unfavorably to his brothers. In one article, after describing Joe's and Dom's careers, the *Boston Globe* said of Vince that he "could hit the long ball but frequently struck out."

He probably hadn't read it, though. Vince was not one to dwell on negative things. In the clubhouse before the game, he and the other players greeted each other warmly—even though some of them, especially the younger ones, didn't even know that he had played ball. In his 10 years in the majors, Vince had toiled in the National League. His two years in Boston had been in the late 1930s, not with the Sox but on the roster of the Boston Bees, a team that only true aficionados of the game knew had ever existed.

Ted Williams and Joe DiMaggio, once great rivals, shook hands in the clubhouse. It was an awkward moment for Joe. Several of the others present knew that Ted had been more of a brother to Dominic than Joe had been—and still was. Over the years, Joe had exiled himself from the family. He hadn't visited Vince at all or Dominic in his home for a long time. Grabbing an infrequent meal together at a restaurant, including DiMaggio's Grotto on Fisherman's Wharf, passed for a get-together. Otherwise, they saw each other at the funerals of their sisters and other brothers. Vince and Dominic never knew where Joe was—New York, San Francisco, somewhere else hawking Mr. Coffee machines—so it was hard to visit him. He rarely picked up the phone or returned messages. Dominic, especially, kept trying, but Joe drifted further away, allowing himself to forget how close they once were as boys, when they shared a bedroom in their Taylor Street home in San Francisco.

Several years earlier, a frustrated Vince had told interviewer Ed Kiersh (who would later title his book on former ballplayers *Where Have You Gone, Vince DiMaggio?*), "Joe has always been a loner and he always will be. When the folks were alive, we were a lot closer. But I guess in the last four years I've seen him two or three times. What can I do? I'm Vince, he's Joe. It's only a shame we've gone different ways. That's real sad. Family should stick together."

Joe had heard about those remarks. He took offense, and added Vince to the list of people he wouldn't associate with—a list that had grown quite long after Joe left baseball in 1951. His sister Marie wasn't on it—he shared a house with her in San Francisco. Neither was Dominic. Joe still spoke to him, because Dominic kept trying. He was the one who had convinced Joe to come to Boston, and to be with Vince again. Dominic didn't know at the time what an act of kindness this was for both of his brothers, and for himself.

So far, it had not been a warm reunion. Vince had traveled east alone and was staying with Dominic and his wife, Emily, at their home outside Boston. Joe checked into a hotel in the city. When Vince and Dominic had dinner together on Friday, Joe wasn't there. When Joe and Dominic had breakfast on Saturday, Vince wasn't there.

In front of reporters that afternoon, Joe denied there was a rift among them. "It's not true as far as I'm concerned" was his curt response to questions.

Dominic knew telling the complete truth wouldn't help the brothers' relationship. So he implied that Vince was mad at him, not Joe. To do that he had to reach back to 1952, when he had been the American League player representative and it was decided that "any player who was on a major league roster in 1947 would be credited with all his previous activities," thus eligible for a pension. Vince had missed out by a year.

"Vince may still be bitter because he could not become a vested member of the players' pension plan and was ineligible for any benefits," Dominic explained. "His bitterness may be the reason why he made some harsh remarks to the press. If I were Vince, I wouldn't be here for today's Old-Timers' Game."

But Vince was there, though not in the best mood. A reporter asked him about the time back in 1932 when, as an outfielder with the San Francisco Seals, he'd persuaded his manager to sign his younger brother Joe. Vince replied, "Maybe if I had kept my mouth shut, I'd be remembered as the greatest DiMaggio."

Finally, the time came for the main events, and the brothers were introduced to the crowd. Vince received polite applause. Joe was used to receiving the loudest cheers from fans at such special events, where he insisted he be announced as "the greatest living ballplayer." But that wouldn't happen at Fenway Park, not with Williams there. He wasn't even the most popular DiMaggio on the field—the cheers for Dominic, dressed in his Red Sox uniform, easily outdistanced those for Joe. Arms around each other's waists, the brothers smiled for photographers and the fans.

They were becoming elderly men—Vince was 73, Joe was 71, and Dominic, the baby of the nine DiMaggio children, was 69— but those who had known the brothers long enough could still see in them the handsome, strapping young men who had come east from San Francisco in the 1930s to be major league baseball stars. Only Dominic would participate in the three-inning game featuring the former players, but it was good to see the DiMaggio brothers together on a baseball field. A handful of people knew it almost didn't happen.

"At the very last minute I got a call from Vince in San Francisco," recalls Larry Cancro, now a senior vice president with the Boston Red Sox, who had invited the three brothers in the spring of 1986. "He said he wasn't feeling well, didn't think he should come. Dom, worried about his brother's health, said, 'I want him to come because I want to take him to a doctor myself.' Between the two of us, we convinced Vince to make the trip."

Dominic, like everyone else at the ballpark that day, did not know that Vince was already in an advanced stage of stomach cancer. Every day it became more obvious to him, his wife, and his doctors that he would not survive. Vince had two daughters, and they didn't know his condition either.

"Dad didn't want to worry us, so he kept it to himself," says Joanne DiMaggio Webber, the older of his two daughters. "I found out because of that Old-Timers' Day. There was a photograph of the three of them in the newspapers, and when I saw my father in it, I knew something was wrong. I didn't know what exactly, but I *knew*. When he got back from Boston, I went up to see him. And he told me."

It was worse than anyone knew—Vince had less than five months to live.

After the Old-Timers' exhibition innings, Vince stayed at the ballpark to watch the Rangers–Red Sox game with Dominic. Joe didn't. He gave reporters the slip, a skill he had perfected as well as he had judged deep fly balls hit to center at Yankee Stadium. He was being driven back to New York, where he would have dinner at one of his favorite restaurants, alone.

When he felt tired before the game ended—an 8–2 Red Sox victory—Vince asked to leave. Dominic complied immediately, and they returned to his home in Marion, Massachusetts. He wanted his brother to get as much rest as he could, because he had scheduled a doctor's appointment for early the next morning. Whatever Vince needed, Dominic would take care of it.

That was what Dominic did. For him, it was all about family.

PART I

"I would like to take the great DiMaggio fishing," the old man said. "They say his father was a fisherman. Maybe he was as poor as we are and would understand."

—ERNEST HEMINGWAY, *The Old Man and the Sea*

ONE

Giuseppe and Rosalie DiMaggio believed in America. Like millions of other immigrants at the turn of the 20th century, they discovered that by working hard they could have a piece of the American Dream. More important, that dream would be available to their nine children—especially their three sons who would play baseball, the national pastime.

The couple had been born and raised in an area of Sicily that had the odd name Isola delle Femmine, Sicilian for "the Island of Women." It is not in fact an island, but a town of rocky hills facing the Tyrrhenian Sea. By one account, the town was originally populated by adulterous wives of Roman soldiers who had been banished. A more mundane and reliable account of how it got its name is that in the 19th century, when a plague broke out in nearby Palermo, some of the city's women and children were sent to Isola delle Femmine to wait it out. As the town grew in subsequent decades, it consisted mostly of fishing families.

Giuseppe was the son of a fisherman, and inevitably he became one too. Rosalie was the daughter of a fisherman, and her future was to become the wife of a fisherman and raise his children in Isola delle Femmine. Surely, in the 1890s, anyone who told her that she would live most of her life on the other side of the world and that her son would be one of the most famous athletes of all time would have been considered mad.

It was Rosalie, however, who started the DiMaggios down the path to America. A member of her family had managed to escape the relentless routine of Isola delle Femmine and emigrate to the United States, settling in Collinsville, California, a rural community east of San Francisco in the Sacramento River delta area. This relative wrote Rosalie in 1898 describing the wonders of America, the trains, the electricity. A hardworking man like her husband, the relative suggested, could make a better living there.

After his wife read the letter to him—Rosalie had spent some time as a schoolteacher—Giuseppe thought hard about such an adventure. He could not speak English. He could not read. His wife was pregnant. Who knew how long he would be gone before he could send for his wife and child, or if he could indeed make a living at all? As harsh as the life on the storm-battered Sicilian coast was, it was familiar. A young man knew what to expect.

Whether or not Rosalie encouraged him to seek a better life for them is unclear, but in any case Giuseppe set off on the journey. He wound up in Martinez, 35 miles northeast of San Francisco. There he acquired a boat (later, he could afford an engine too) that he named the *Rosalie D*. With the exception of Sundays, he rose at 4:00 A.M. every day and went out to fish. He sold his catch and saved his money. After four years, he had a house and sent some of that saved money back to Isola delle Femmine for his wife and child's passage to America.

The Bay Area that Rosalie was sailing to in 1902 would not have been totally alien territory. In 1870, 2.2 percent of the population of San Francisco was Italian, and overall 29 percent of the city's residents were immigrants from Europe. By 1900, the Italian population had tripled and was larger than the Chinese and Japanese communities. The acceleration of Italian immigration during the DiMaggios' early years in the Bay Area is demonstrated in the 1930 census, which found that the population had almost tripled again, to over 16 percent. Most of the immigrants lived in San Francisco itself, while others headed inland, to the Alhambra Valley.

The Karkines Indians, part of the Costanoan Indian group, had been the original inhabitants of that valley. In 1824, when California was owned by Mexico, the government gave 17,000 acres that included the Alhambra Valley to Don Ygnacio Martinez as thanks for his military services. Twenty-five years later, his son, Don Vicente, built an adobe house, beginning the Martinez settlement. Its only distinction at the time was a ferry service across the Carquinez Strait between Martinez and Benicia.

By 1849, California was no longer a colony of Mexico. The United States had coveted California for some time, and the administration of James Polk had actively encouraged separatist movements. The explorer John Fremont led the Bear Flag Revolution in the Bay Area in 1846, and in May of that year war against Mexico was declared. Three months later, the first American government in San Francisco was formed. When the war ended in 1848, California was a territory of the United States.

The humble ferry service became much in demand in May 1848 when a man named Sam Brannan announced that he had found gold dust during a visit to the American River south of San Francisco. The ferry provided one of the few means of transportation from that city to points south for the eager prospectors wanting to get to the gold fields fast. (This ferry service would operate continuously until 1962, when it was replaced by the George Miller Jr. Bridge.) Houses and other structures were built around the ferry landing site, and Martinez became the first town in the District of Contra Costa. It was designated the county seat in 1851.

Those not interested in seeking gold were joined by those who had failed at it to establish hundreds of farms in the Alhambra Valley, as well as in the nearby Reliez and Diablo Valleys. As it happened, most of these farmers were from Massachusetts or Missouri, and soon they were writing home encouraging friends and family members to head west and share in the fertile fields and generous climate. They grew wheat, peaches, cherries, pears, figs, and walnuts. The harvests were hauled to San Francisco, where they were sold and put on ships.

In 1869, John T. Strentzel (whose son-in-law was the naturalist and Sierra Club founder John Muir) invented a method of carting fruits in containers packed with carbonized bran that allowed them to remain fresh while being transported to distant markets. After a railroad line arrived in Martinez eight years later, even more crops could be sent on their way. In 1899, the year after Giuseppe DiMaggio arrived, the Atchison, Topeka, and Santa Fe Railway began running trains in and out of Martinez.

Fishing became the other main industry in the area. The waters of the Carquinez Strait teemed with an abundance of sardines, salmon, and other fish, and initially there were not enough men to harvest them. Beginning in the late 1870s, fishermen from Portugal and then Sicily and other parts of Italy came to Martinez. They worked long days and sold their catches to canneries, to be shipped to San Francisco and from there to the eastern United States and Europe. The fishermen constructed serviceable docks for their boats and shacks for sleeping. As they made a few dollars and realized that they would be staying indefinitely, they sent messages home to wives and brothers, similar to the ones the farmers were writing to relatives back east.

According to *Martinez: A California Town* (1986) by Charlene Perry and others, the Italians "brought the age-old style of their former homes in Sicily and on the coast of Italy. All saved their earnings to send for families left behind. They lived by the special calendar of the fisherman, the two straits seasons of spring and fall and the

Alaska salmon season of early and mid-summer. As soon as the fishermen could afford to send for their families, houses were bought or built for them in the area north and west of Alhambra Avenue and Main Street. Families settled near other families from the same old-country villages making Martinez a microcosm of parts of Sicily and mainland Italy."

It had to have eased Giuseppe's transition from Sicily to the Bay Area that just about all of the fishermen who lived in nearby shacks and tied their boats to Granger's Wharf and other docks in Martinez were from Sicily too. No doubt there were Sundays when Giuseppe sat outside his own shack enjoying a thin cigar and a cup of wine, closing his eyes to listen to the voices and dream that he was home.

Rosalie arrived with their daughter in 1902. She could not have come with many expectations, since her husband had been uncommunicative about his experiences. But probably she was pleasantly surprised. Though a relatively poor community, Martinez had electric streetlights. Many fishermen's boats had engines, those who didn't fish worked in the town's factories, and for much of the year the weather was more congenial than in storm-tossed Isola delle Femmine. She was reunited with her husband, and they had a house. Already it was like a dream had come true.

Living the dream was not easy. For Giuseppe, the six-day weeks continued, week after week, month after month, year after year, as there were more mouths to feed. Though he was a short man, the generations of fishing in his family had given him an especially strong neck and powerful shoulders. He could lift fish-filled nets out of the water into his boat with the best of them. He wore a fedora, a custom from the old country, to keep the sun out of his eyes. With his strong constitution, robust health, and the moderate weather of the Bay Area, Giuseppe rarely missed a day on the water. At the end of the day, after selling his catch to the agents waiting on Granger's Wharf who represented San Francisco fish brokers, he tied up his boat on Alhambra Creek and trudged home to his wife.

It would be 47 years before they were separated again. Giuseppe was devoted to his wife, and Rosalie to him. He was not an articulate or charismatic man, but he was unquestionably the patriarch of the family. His priorities were always family and hard work. For the DiMaggios in America, that would be plenty.

The house had just two bedrooms to go with a kitchen and living room. Still, it had to be spacious for a family of three in their early days there. The bathroom was an outhouse perched on the bank of Alhambra Creek. Their next-door neighbors were Salvatore DiMaggio, Giuseppe's brother, and his wife Frances, Rosalie's sister. Everyone in the community spoke Sicilian because there was really no reason to speak or read English. The children would take care of that.

TWO

TWO GIRLS CAME FIRST. Adrianella had been born in Sicily (her name was later shortened to Nelly), then Mamie in Martinez, the first of the DiMaggio children born in America. On the third try, Rosalie gave birth to a son for Giuseppe. They named him Thomas. Marie (born Mary) was the fourth child; then came Michael and Frances. Vincent was born on September 6, 1912. Giuseppe Paolo DiMaggio Jr. was born on November 25, 1914. Though the fourth son, he was the one named after his father because in the Sicilian tradition the grandparents had to be taken care of first. Giuseppe and Rosalie were even less creative when giving their sons middle names—Gaetano and Michelli were given to Thomas and Michael, but it was simply Paolo as a middle name for the other three boys. Eight children are plenty for any family, especially one depending on the precarious income of a fisherman, but a ninth, the third son in a row, was born on February 12, 1917. Dominic would be the last DiMaggio of that generation, and like his eight siblings, he was born at home.

It was around the time of Dominic's birth that the family of eleven, clearly having outgrown the house on Alhambra Creek, moved from

Martinez to San Francisco. After a short stay at a place on Filbert Street, Giuseppe and Rosalie rented a house at 2047 Taylor Street in the North Beach section. Below them was Fisherman's Wharf, the new home for Giuseppe's boat. Joe was to write in *Lucky to Be a Yankee* (1946)—though published while he was still playing, it is the closest there is to an autobiography—that "my earliest recollections are of the smell of fish in San Francisco, where I was brought up."

San Francisco had been growing by leaps and bounds since its emancipation from Mexico and the 1848 announcement of the discovery of gold. For the remainder of the century, the Bay Area became the destination of emigrants from two directions. First were the gold seekers, many from east of the Mississippi, who arrived first by horse and wagon via new extensions of the Oregon Trail, then on the newly constructed transcontinental railroad, thus lending some credence to the "manifest destiny" of America. Later came the Asians and the Europeans like Giuseppe and Rosalie DiMaggio, who sought opportunity more than gold. Only two years after the end of the war with Mexico, in September 1850, California was admitted into the Union, becoming the 31st state.

In 1850 the population of San Francisco was 35,000. That year the first theater and the first free public school opened. A chamber of commerce for the city was organized. The Bavarian-born Levi Strauss arrived with a supply of clothing and dry goods to open up a business. There was a seamy side to growth too. The so-called Barbary Coast, the red-light district centered on Pacific Avenue, led from the wharf area to the city center and was known for gambling, violence and other crimes, and prostitution—of the 300 women living in San Francisco in those gold rush days, two-thirds were ladies of the evening. Despite occasional reform efforts, the Barbary Coast thrived for decades.

In 1853 San Francisco could count twelve daily newspapers, six weeklies, and two triweeklies, one in French and the other in German. More people arrived by clipper ship after the completion of the Panama Canal, which sped up travel from the East Coast to the West Coast by way of Central America. A literary movement that began in 1860 boasted Mark Twain, Bret Harte, and Ambrose Bierce among its notables, and by that year the city's population had nearly doubled from a decade before. Relatively untouched by the distant Civil War and the Reconstruction in its aftermath, the population of San Francisco in 1870 was 137,419. Twenty years later, that figure was at almost 300,000, and San Francisco ranked as the largest city in California and the eighth largest in the United States.

The city attracted high-profile cultural and sports events, like the world boxing championship held in September 1892, when native son "Gentleman" James J. Corbett knocked out John L. Sullivan in the 21st round. Five years later, gold was discovered in Alaska, introducing another boom period for San Francisco. In 1898, when Giuseppe DiMaggio arrived from Sicily, the United States was at war again, this time with Spain. By order of President William McKinley, San Francisco was the base for the country's Pacific operations and the embarkation point for ships and troops heading to fight in the Philippines. The year Rosalie DiMaggio arrived, 1902, San Francisco was lighted by electricity. Two years later saw the formation of the Bank of Italy (to become the Bank of America), the largest private bank in the world.

The DiMaggios had to have felt the Great San Francisco Earthquake of 1906, but Martinez was spared any significant destruction. The quake struck at 5:12 A.M. on April 18. By noon, fires had spread throughout San Francisco. By the time they were brought under control three days later, nearly five square miles had burned, over 28,000 buildings had been destroyed, and 311 people were dead, with 252 reported missing.

The immediate impact on the DiMaggios and other fishing families in the area was the destruction of portions of the city's waterfront and weeks of interruption of commerce. "Thousands of men who went to bed wealthy last night awoke this morning practically bankrupt," reported the *Evening Daily News*. Yet when reconstruction began that summer, San Francisco was on its way to becoming one of the most famous and exciting cities in the world. Sports played a part in that. It was a special place for the athletic DiMaggio boys to grow up after the family moved there during World War I. Not long after they did, in 1920, the population of San Francisco passed the half-million mark.

The DiMaggio family was moderately poor, an income level that was typical for the large family of a fisherman who had emigrated from Europe as recently as the turn of the century. In the years before and during World War I, the waters in and around the Bay Area offered a steady supply of fish and shellfish. If a man like Giuseppe was willing to work long hours to tap that supply, he could put food on the table.

It made a big difference that he and his equally hardworking wife were frugal. For example, only Nelly and Tom, the oldest daughter and son, would know the experience of wearing new clothes. The rest of the DiMaggio children were on a regular cycle—after two years, the clothes of the two oldest were handed down to Marie and Mike, and two years after that those same (much-mended) clothes went to Frances and Vince, and so on. Joe and Dominic were at the end of the line. It's no surprise that as an adult with spending power Joe would always appear in public dressed impeccably.

The DiMaggio daughters helped their mother keep house and care for the three younger sons. "My older brothers Mike and Tom were working on the boats with Dad, and our sisters—Marie, Mae, Nelly, and Frances—were helping our mother and going to school," wrote Dominic in one of the autobiographical passages of *Real Grass, Real Heroes* (1990), a memoir he wrote with Bill Gilbert about the 1941 American League season.

That they were in America now didn't mean that the DiMaggios didn't follow traditions. The girls would be groomed for marriage, not careers, and whatever formal education they received was a luxury, maybe even a frivolous distraction, not a right. Still, most likely it was Rosalie, the former schoolteacher, who made sure that her children went to school. To Giuseppe, the boys being in school was time not spent helping him on and with the boat. In his version of the American Dream, a man got ahead through hard work and success was measured by his ability to feed, clothe, and shelter his family. Sons helped their father do that.

But this was not Isola delle Femmine, where little changed for decades. In America, you had to read and write English to get ahead. All the DiMaggio children spoke Sicilian at home and with their immediate neighbors, while learning English and studying American history at school.

Tom and Mike, the two oldest boys, were closest to sharing their father's outlook. Tom was a bright kid with a good head for numbers and sound common sense, but neither he nor Mike went past the seventh grade. They worked with Giuseppe on the boat. Both would eventually take up the occupation of fisherman, to Giuseppe's approval. In contented moments as he sipped wine (some of which he made himself) on Sundays, Giuseppe must have envisioned the day when he and all five of his sons would come home with their catches and the DiMaggios would be prosperous indeed.

Giuseppe did not approve when every so often Tom and the stockier Mike made time to play the strange American game called baseball. There was no gain in that. He would have to make sure that such a silly, unprofitable exercise was not passed along to his three youngest sons.

"My father always said that Tom was the best ballplayer of all the brothers," says Joanne DiMaggio Webber. "But my grandfather was not going to allow him to play a game when there were responsibilities to the family and there was money to be made. He got his way with Tom and Mike. Then my father came along."

THREE

ALTHOUGH ITS HISTORY is relatively unknown, baseball on the West Coast contributed mightily to the growth of the sport as the national pastime. More specifically, it had a profound impact on the DiMaggio brothers when they were exposed to it. But there would have been no DiMaggios at all in professional baseball if it hadn't been for Vince.

He was the rebel of the family. Not that he was a rude or obstinate child, but he had an upbeat disposition and loved to talk, the opposite of his father. Vince also had no interest in fishing and didn't hide that from his parents. There were two things Vince wanted very much to do: sing and play baseball, in that order. His chief ambition was to be on the opera stage.

From early on, Vince displayed a fine tenor voice and a good ear. He only had to hear an aria by Puccini or Verdi once to be able to sing it. Giuseppe didn't necessarily object to this. The idea that Vince might become a professional opera singer probably seemed as fanciful as his becoming the mayor of San Francisco someday, but the boy could entertain. He was an outgoing, happy-go-lucky kid who would set up on a street corner and burst into song. Passersby impressed by selections from *Rigoletto* or *La Bohème* dropped coins in the precocious boy's hat, and he was good about bringing this unanticipated income home. As long as he kept doing this and didn't shirk his fishing duties, Giuseppe was fine with his middle son's singing.

Giuseppe Jr., or Joe, as everyone called him, looked up to all his older brothers, but was closest to Vince. They were just two years apart in age. Joe admired and envied Vince's personality, the way he could make people laugh or swoon with a song. Joe was very quiet and rarely spoke. English hadn't come easily for him. At school some kids made fun of him when he mispronounced words or helplessly slipped back into Sicilian. (They also made fun of his large, protruding ears.) Joe figured it was best, then, to say nothing, because no one could laugh at that. He couldn't sing like Vince, and he had no interest in opera, but Joe did tag along when Vince snuck off to watch their older brothers play that strange but exciting game at the local sandlots.

By the end of the first two decades of the 20th century, baseball was big in the Bay Area. The sport had been brought west before the Civil War by gold seekers and others who emigrated from the East Coast. (Baseball teams had sprouted by the dozens every spring in New York City and New Jersey in the 1850s, with the borough of Brooklyn alone boasting 70 clubs.) Two years before the Civil War began, in 1859, the Eagle Base Ball Club was formed in San Francisco. Teams founded during the war in the Bay Area included the California Theater Baseball Club and the Pacific Base Ball Club. Many young men first played baseball between battles during the Civil War, and when they came home the sport expanded greatly. The Pacific Base Ball Convention was held in San Francisco in 1866 to coordinate the activities of the two dozen clubs existing by then in the Bay Area.

The Recreation Grounds at the intersection of Folsom Street and 25th Street was the city's first ballpark. One indication that the sport was rapidly catching on was the fact that 3,000 fans showed up on Thanksgiving Day 1868 to watch the Eagle Club thrash the Wide Awakes, an Oakland team, 37–23. The following year the Cincinnati Red Stockings came to town, traveling west on the just-completed transcontinental railroad. The five exhibition games weren't pretty for the local teams that took the visitors on: the Red Stockings racked up a combined score of 289–22. But the contests against the Ohio professionals earned headlines in all the newspapers.

More teams formed in Oakland, Stockton, Sacramento, and other surrounding communities as well as in San Francisco. These were amateur clubs, consisting of men with occupations, often middle-class ones, who played baseball strictly for recreation. But this was about to change. In 1871 the National Association of Professional Base Ball Players was founded; as its name implies, this organization promoted the hiring and paying of men whose occupation it would be to play the game. In the Bay Area, an increasing number of clubs began paying promising players and wooing talented amateurs.

It was a milestone for local baseball in 1876 when the Pacific Base Ball Convention dispatched the Centennials (commemorating the 100th anniversary of San Francisco's founding), a squad of 15 players, to Philadelphia to participate in a national tournament. The team returned in triumph, with a 6-1 record. Two years later, the Pacific Base Ball League was formed. Though it consisted of only four San Francisco teams, it was significant as the first organized baseball league on the West Coast. The subsequent California League teams played 30 games in 1886, and 170 only six years later. Ernest Thayer's "Casey at the Bat," which would become a staple in ballparks around the country, was first published in the *San Francisco Examiner* in June 1888.

With national economic ebbs and flows, leagues in the Bay Area came and went, expanding or contracting. But soon after Giuseppe

DiMaggio arrived, a revived and reestablished California League featured six teams consisting of all professional players. Ten years after Giuseppe's arrival, in 1908, Mike Fisher, a native of San Francisco, created the Reach All-Americans, the first team to go on a barnstorming tour to introduce baseball to Japan.

As his sons were growing up, the last thing Giuseppe wanted them to be doing was playing baseball. What little he knew of the local games was that there were "too many shoes, too many pants." Though he himself played bocce during the little free time that fishing afforded him, he didn't want his sons involved in any sports. Part of this attitude can be attributed to the bias of a man from Italy trying to retain the culture and attitudes of the old country, and baseball was so brazenly American. But it was at least equally important that, as Tom and Mike grew up, Giuseppe needed them on the boat fishing with him. If for whatever reason one of them didn't go out on the water on any given day, the result was more work for Giuseppe and less catch to show for it. Baseball, like school, was an unwelcome distraction that didn't put food on the table.

Recalled Dominic: "Baseball violated Dad's code of life, which emphasized the work ethic. But Mom would stick up for us and calm him down eventually. Later she'd even cover for us if we weren't around. But we had to be careful about coming home with torn pants or a cut or a sprain that would be a dead giveaway as to where we had been. When those happened, we tried to slip into the house and touch up the evidence, or get rid of it altogether, before running into Dad."

In an interview with the former baseball commissioner Fay Vincent for Vincent's book *The Only Game in Town* (2006), Dominic further explained: "Dad thought [baseball] was a waste of time but Mother took it from the point of view that we were all young men and we liked to play games and this was a good game, nice and clean. Dad would find Vince's spikes and glove; he'd take them and throw them in the trash bin. And as fast as he did it, Mother would go out, take them out, and hide them until the next time Vince was to use them. He was the first one that this happened to."

Tom and Mike continued to comply. When not in school, they went down with their father to Fisherman's Wharf, where the *feluccas*— Italian boats with lantern sails—were congregated. Each, though, still managed from time to time to play in pickup games in the nearby lots and drift in and out of informal leagues, just for the fun and competition. In this they had Rosalie's subtle encouragement— she wanted them to grow up as Americans and to be active, healthy boys. They were burdened enough with trying to learn at school, coming from a Sicilian-speaking household. Despite their skills, neither Tom nor Mike would ever pursue a professional career. Tom became the family businessman, and Mike would be the only one of the five brothers to spend the rest of his life as a fisherman.

Of the DiMaggio brothers, only Joe, in *Lucky to Be a Yankee*, wrote a first-person account in any detail of his childhood in San Francisco. The book must be taken with some grains of salt: Joe often either remembered some events incorrectly or was being deliberately vague. Published in 1946, when Joe was a returning war veteran and resuming his career as arguably the most famous athlete in America, it was a sanitized autobiography. The philosophy of Grantland Rice, the dean of American sportswriters (who wrote the book's foreword), still held sway: great athletes were heroes and examples to the children of America, so only the positive was presented. Today we may laugh to read the squeaky clean biographies and autobiographies of Babe Ruth, Ty Cobb, and others of dubious character, but in the 1940s it was routine treatment for famous players, as well as what the public expected.

But there is no compelling reason to doubt Joe's recollections of his childhood. The few he offered throughout his life did at least remain consistent. In Joe's memories, Giuseppe was an old-country man who could be stern and stubborn in his views about his children, especially his sons, but who provided for his family. He expected to be obeyed at home, and his sons probably feared him a bit—typical in those pre–Dr. Spock days—yet there is nothing to indicate that Giuseppe was not loved and respected too.

Rosalie was the more educated and possibly more intelligent of the two parents. All three brothers who made it to the major leagues would credit her support. As the parent who spent all of her waking hours with her children, Rosalie was more likely to have been the one who impressed upon them that the new country and its culture, including sports, were to be embraced.

Joe's recollection was that he began to play baseball at age ten, mostly when he trotted after Vince to the North Beach playground. He was attending the Hancock Grammar School and "played well enough to be on the usual teams with the kids from around the block." Instead of a diamond, Joe and his classmates played on a cleared space of ground that was known as the Horse Lot—a nearby dairy supplier used it as a parking area for its milk wagons. The bases were large rocks, the ball was a relic held together with bicycle tape, an oar handle served as a bat, and not being able to afford gloves, they caught with bare hands, which was made somewhat easier by the stickiness of the tape.

One might think that the fourth DiMaggio brother, given the examples of the first three, would be eager to continue to play baseball whenever and wherever he could. Not so. "Baseball to me in those days was merely an excuse to get away from the house," Joe recalled.

As was pretty much any sport. A classmate at Francisco Junior High School, Dario Lodigiani, is quoted in David Cataneo's collection of recollections, *I Remember Joe DiMaggio* (2001): "I lived on Telegraph Hill in North Beach, the Italian district. On the bottom of the hill is where Joe lived. And in between us was the playground. We were in that playground every day. And whatever sport was going on, we'd play it. He was a quiet kid. Never said too much. But he was a good athlete, no matter what sport we played. We played baseball, we played touch football. Basketball. We even played tennis. He was a heckuva tennis player."

When he became old enough, Dominic tagged along with Vince and Joe to the North Beach playground. He remembered one particular touch football game that showed how athletic and graceful Joe already was:

"There was a fellow named Louis Daresta. He later became an all-American football player. During the early part of the game, Joe had done something to embarrass Louis somewhat. A little later in the game, Louis, who was a tough little football player, was running interference for the guy who had the ball. And the only one left between them was Joe. Louis felt he was going to take a shot at Joe. So he bent down low and started after Joe as if to knock his legs out from under him. And Joe held his ground and the runner was right behind Louis. When Louis got to Joe, Joe just gingerly bounced back a little and with both his hands hit Louis on the back. And because Louis was down so far, he lost balance. He fell and skinned both his knees. All torn up. Of course, this was on a tar field. And Joe reached over Louis and touched, with two hands, the ball carrier."

OF THE SEVERAL SPORTS he played in his adolescent and early teenage years, the one that Joe enjoyed most was tennis. His favorite players were Maurice McLoughlin and Bill Johnston, because they "came from San Francisco and I wanted to be like them." (Actually, McLoughlin hailed from Nevada; he was the first tennis champion from the western United States.)

Joe's most compelling reason to follow sports was to get "away from the chores of fishing." For Joe, avoiding fishing with his father was neither an act of rebellion nor an indication of laziness—though, truth be told, he hated to get up before the sun—but a physical necessity. The smell of the boat literally made him sick. To Giuseppe, having a son who couldn't fish—and who further embarrassed him by spending much of his time on the boat retching over the side—meant that the kid didn't have much future in anything. He called his fourth son *lagnuso* (lazy) and *meschino* (good for nothing), but the boy shrugged him off. Eventually, Giuseppe gave up on making Joe a fisherman and suggested other trades to him. Joe was fine with working and making money, as long as no product from the sea was involved and he didn't have to wake up early. "He liked to sleep," Lodigiani said. "When we played ball on Sundays, if you didn't go wake him up, he wouldn't show."

Joe joined Vince on street corners for hours every day hawking copies of the *San Francisco Call-Bulletin*. Vince was easily the more popular newsie of the two, because all Joe could do was shout headlines, but Vince could shout headlines and sing arias.

When he wasn't performing bits of *Don Giovanni* to sell newspapers, Vince continued to pursue his other passion. By the time he was a student at Galileo High School, he was a third baseman on the varsity team. His plan was to earn his letters on the school's diamond, and his hope was to be scouted by a major league team or two; then, after graduation, he could at least try out for the San Francisco Seals. If he made the team, he could play simply because he loved baseball, and who knew what could come of that. Maybe the money he made from the Seals could pay for formal training as a singer.

But then the stock market crashed and the Great Depression began. Vince never made it to graduation. Despite pleas from Rosalie to stay in school, he quit to find jobs that would make more of a contribution to the family than street-corner newsboy and classical crooner. Dominic took his brother's place on the street selling newspapers. Usually, he and Joe could be found on the corner of Sutter and Sansome Streets, only now, without Vince, there was no more singing.

FOUR

WOULD JOE DIMAGGIO have ever made it to the major leagues without the help of his brother Vince? The jury will always be out on that one. It can be argued that Vince's passion for baseball led Joe in that direction too. Without Vince and without much education and ambition, Joe might have drifted into some kind of physical job that allowed free time to hang around with his friends. One day he would have met a nice Italian-American girl from North Beach and settled down to start a family.

Then again, thanks primarily to the Pacific Coast League, many young men in the Bay Area in the early 1930s loved baseball. Though never recognized as one of the major leagues, it was the most prominent and popular regional league west of the Mississippi River, and a number of its best players went on to the majors. Joe might have given it a try at some point. If he had done that, he was so naturally gifted that he would have ended up on the San Francisco Seals, and from there he would have had a shot at the majors.

But Vince made it a sure thing. He provided a fast track for his brother to get on the Seals, and Joe's natural talent took over from there. For that to happen, though, Vince had to blaze a trail that Giuseppe had proclaimed was not to be traveled.

"My brother Vince started it all," remembered Dominic. "He was two years older than Joe and started sneaking out to play baseball when he was junior high school age. My parents were from the old country, born and raised in a village in the suburbs of Palermo. They didn't take too well to the American game of baseball, especially Dad."

The middle DiMaggio brother, who appeared never to face a day he didn't like, did bring in money to the family from other jobs. He even went out on the *Rosalie D.* with Tom and Mike from time to time to give their father a day off. Yet even as the economy tanked, Vince kept finding time to play baseball. He couldn't help himself, the same way he couldn't stop talking and singing. He and Giuseppe fought over the time he spent playing a game instead of bringing home more money. One day the arguments stopped, though, because Vince was gone—he had run away to play baseball.

A scout from the Lumber Leagues north of San Francisco had seen Vince play in one of the local games. The players were amateurs, but when Vince connected, the ball traveled a mile. He was a good fielder too, whatever the position. The leagues offered him a contract to play professionally. Still a minor, he brought the contract to Giuseppe for his signature. Nothing doing. In addition to his other objections to baseball, Giuseppe had to have realized that if he set Vince free, it would be harder to prevent Joe, the next boy, from playing games instead of getting a real job. He probably wasn't worried about Dominic, who, on the cusp of his teenage years, was too scrawny, actually liked going to school, and wore thick eyeglasses, unlike any ballplayer.

Vince filed an appeal with his mother. Rosalie may well have wanted to help him, but there was no way she could defy her husband. Case closed, according to Giuseppe. But the rebel Vince had another way out: he forged his father's signature on the contract and headed north. Joe had to be impressed, but as usual he said nothing.

"Just think, if my father hadn't made that decision, there wouldn't have been any Dom or Joe in the big leagues, maybe not in baseball at all," says Joanne.

Vince had a good season in 1931 with the Lumber Leagues, which served as a kind of minor league for the Pacific Coast League. At the end of the season, right after he turned 19, the Seals offered him a contract. In San Francisco in the 1930s, that was like a kid from the Bronx being signed by the Yankees.

A San Francisco team had been part of the Pacific Coast League since it began in 1903, along with franchises in Seattle, Portland, and Los Angeles. The team took its name from the creatures who enjoyed sunbathing on the rocks in the bay. Until 1958, when they were replaced by the major league franchise the San Francisco Giants, the Seals were one of the most successful franchises in the country, winning 12 PCL titles and four Governor's Cups (for winning the postseason playoffs). In 24 seasons, the Seals won 100 games or more.

The Seals played their first game before 5,500 fans who paid 25 cents each on March 26, 1903, at the Recreation Grounds. The home team downed the Portland Browns 7–3. There weren't quite enough wins that year, though, as the locals went 107-110 and wound up in fourth place, 29.5 games behind L.A.'s PCL entry. For fans, one of the attractions of the league was that the West Coast climate allowed the teams to play over 200 games per season. But the extended season led to a lot of wear and tear on the players, especially pitchers. Some were fine with that. In 1903 the apparently rubber-armed ace Jimmy Whalen compiled a record of 29-21.

The team's first winning season was 1905, when Whalen earned 30 victories. The following April the team's home park was destroyed when the earthquake struck. The team resumed play two weeks later in Idora Park in Oakland, its temporary home, and began construction on a new stadium in San Francisco, Recreation Park. It opened on April 6, 1907, with 10,000 fans (now paying 35 cents each) in attendance.

The Seals won their first PCL pennant in 1909 with a 132-80 record. A postcard commemorating the title win showed a group of seals frolicking on the rocks with the players' heads superimposed on them.

For years afterward, the Seals frustrated their fans by not winning another championship. This was actually good news for the PCL; with five teams winning championships from 1909 to 1918, the competitive balance increased the league's popularity among fans throughout the West Coast. In 1915, when the Salt Lake City Bees joined the PCL, the Seals captured the pennant with a 118-89 record, led by Spider Baum's 30 victories and 25 from Skeeter Fanning. They won another title in 1917. That season featured the debut of a left-handed pitcher named Francis Joseph O'Doul, who would later have a powerful impact on baseball in the Bay Area, as well as on the DiMaggio brothers.

During the 1920s, as the three brothers were coming of age and becoming fans of the team, the Seals continued to have a loyal following. The club made good money by selling players to major league franchises. Some of them, including Harry Heilmann, Paul "Big Poison" Waner and his younger brother, Lloyd "Little Poison" Waner, Earl Averill, Dolph Camilli, and Ernie Lombardi, became stars; a few are in the Baseball Hall of Fame. Third baseman Bob Pinelli, who played for the Seals from 1927 to 1931, went on to work for 22 years as a major league umpire. His last game behind the plate was Don Larsen's perfect game in the 1956 World Series.

There were players who did well on the Seals but couldn't find a career in the majors and were glad to go home to the welcoming fans, who were generous with their favorites. One was Ping Bodie, who evenly split 18 years between PCL teams and the majors. For four of those years, the genial, wisecracking Bodie—the model for the narrator in Ring Lardner's "You Know Me Al" stories—was Babe

Ruth's roommate on the New York Yankees. He later told reporters that when they were on the road, he saw a lot more of Ruth's suitcase than its owner. Bodie was a very good hitter, batting .348 in his final season in the PCL at age 41, but he was one of the slowest runners in baseball. This led to one of the best lines in baseball reporting, written by Arthur Baer after Bodie tried to steal a base: "He had larceny in his heart, but his feet were honest."

Fans streamed into "Old Rec," as the Seals' ballpark was affectionately known. It was certainly no marvel of design. It had been constructed with chicken wire and warped lumber, and it creaked when the west wind came off the Pacific Ocean. It was 311 feet to the left-field seats, and only 235 down the right-field line, though a 50-foot fence snared many balls that would otherwise have been home runs. The home and visitors' clubhouses were wooden cottages in back of center field, where there were no seats. The park could accommodate 16,500 people.

Women were admitted free on weekends, but could sit in the first four rows of the grandstands only if escorted by a man. Everyone wore hats, and most men wore coats and ties. Many people rented a seat cushion for a nickel to avoid bench splinters—and to use as a projectile when they objected to an umpire's call.

Eight rows of benches under the grandstand were nicknamed the "Booze Cage," because before Prohibition everyone who paid for a 75-cent ticket to sit there got a shot of whiskey or two bottles of beer. During Prohibition, Booze Cage spectators were given soft drinks and added their own alcohol to it from flasks. The section did not allow women; tipsy fans could be profane in their comments to the opposing teams, and sometimes fistfights broke out.

By the end of the 1920s, the PCL consisted of eight teams. For the many fans who could only read about the 16 major league teams in the papers (the nearest major league city was St. Louis), their PCL team was as important as any major league team, if not more so. The competition between the PCL teams was fierce. The players loved the game and loved to win—especially once the Great Depression took hold and they became anxious to be kept on the payroll. They earned a certain level of celebrity by playing well, yet they were very much part of their communities. In San Francisco in the 1920s, few people owned cars. That included Seals players, who could often be seen in uniform on ferries and trolleys, heading to the ballpark along with the spectators.

Lefty O'Doul was the star of the 1921 season, going 25-9 with a 2.39 ERA, but the Seals finished two games behind the Los Angeles Angels. O'Doul had been born in San Francisco on March 4, 1897, in a tough Irish neighborhood known as Butchertown. When he was in seventh grade, a female teacher introduced him to baseball and to pitching. Lefty led his school to a city championship. At 16, he quit school to go to work with his father at a slaughterhouse. He didn't give up baseball entirely, playing in Sunday sandlot leagues. In 1917, when he was 20, the Seals took notice of the 17 straight games he won for the sandlot team the Native Sons and signed him.

After his brief debut in 1917, O'Doul spent a year learning the ropes with a team in Des Moines, then won 13 games for the Seals. The New York Yankees reached across the country to purchase his contract in 1919. During that season, though, he developed a sore arm. He hoped to rebound in 1920, but instead of winning games, he put more of his energy into carousing with his new teammate, Babe Ruth. The next year the manager, Miller Huggins, banished O'Doul back to the Left Coast, just in time for his revived arm—and bat, as he hit .338 in 74 games—to produce a second-place finish for the Seals. Unfortunately for San Francisco fans, who were enthusiastic supporters of the handsome, generous, and flamboyant hometown hero, O'Doul was invited back to New York.

In the 1922 season, the Seals averaged five runs a game and won 127 games and the league championship. The following year the pitching staff notched 112 complete games in the 210-game season and the team repeated as league champion. After a close-but-no-cigar season in 1924, the Seals ran away with the pennant in '25, going 128-71 with Frank "Turkeyfoot" Brower's 36 homers and 163 RBI and Paul Waner's .401 average leading the way. (Paul Waner went to the Pittsburgh Pirates after the 1925 season; his brother Lloyd joined him there in 1927, and the two Hall of Famers were teammates for 14 years.)

Lefty O'Doul was back in the San Francisco spotlight in 1927, not as a pitcher but as a hitter. His 1922 season with the Yankees had been a washout, and he was sent to Boston. The following year wasn't any better, and the Red Sox let him go. The sore arm continued to plague him in 1924 with the Salt Lake City Bees. But there were two big upsides to that season—he was back in the PCL, where fans cheered him everywhere, and he made the conversion into a full-time player who hit much better than anyone expected, .392 in 140 games.

O'Doul was even more impressive in 1925, playing in 198 games and rapping 309 hits in a staggering 825 at-bats. His average was .375, and he drove in 191 runs. The following year, the Salt Lake team headed west to become the Hollywood Stars. Despite his hitting .338 with 116 RBI, the Stars looked to unload Lefty. The Seals were happy to pay just $7,500 for his services.

It turned out to be a steal. O'Doul hit .378 with 33 home runs and 158 RBI, scored 164 runs, and scampered for 40 stolen bases. His reward for being voted the PCL Most Valuable Player in 1927 was $1,000.

Another exciting event for baseball fans in the San Francisco area that year was the arrival of O'Doul's old pal Babe Ruth. The Bambino was coming off a season in which he broke his own record for home runs by clubbing 60 and combining with Lou Gehrig, Tony Lazzeri (a San Francisco native who had graduated from the PCL), and Bob Meusel to produce "Murderers' Row" for the world champion New York Yankees. After the season, Ruth put together an exhibition team of major leaguers looking to earn extra money, the Bustin' Babes. The team barnstormed up and down the West Coast, taking on sandlot squads, including a series at Recreation Park.

One indication of the popularity and success of the Pacific Coast League is that, when the Seals earned their next title, in 1928, each member of the winning team received a check for $9,000; by contrast, each player on the New York Yankees that year received only $5,813 for winning the World Series. Joining the Seals' staff and winning 18 games was 19-year-old Vernon "Lefty" Gomez. It is unlikely that 13-year-old Joe DiMaggio, seeing him pitch that season, could imagine how important Gomez would be to him in a few years. After that season, Gomez was sold to the Yankees.

By the time of the stock market crash in October 1929, the Seals had earned seven PCL championships, more than any other team in the league—especially, their fans liked to point out, the cross-bay Oakland Oaks. The following year saw the last game at Recreation Park, a 17–7 win by the Seals over a squad of major league all-stars. When Vince DiMaggio became a member of the Seals organization late in 1931, the team's home was Seals Stadium, at Bryant and 16th Streets. They would remain there for as long as the franchise continued to exist, through 1957.

The Seals were never a rich franchise, but they at least had been a profitable one through the 1920s. That changed in the years after the stock market crash, as happened with many businesses and families. During the four years following the crash, the national unemployment rate jumped from 3.2 percent of the labor force to almost 25 percent. San Francisco was hit as hard as anywhere. Giuseppe, being self-employed, couldn't lose his job, but the demand and thus the prices for his catches declined.

It had to grate on him in 1931 that one of his able-bodied sons had spent a long season playing baseball up north instead of helping to keep the family afloat financially. Vince showed no sign of mending his ways the following year. He played for a Seals farm club, the Tucson Lizards of the Arizona-Texas League. This must have seemed something like madness to Giuseppe, who may also have felt that he had lost a son.

Dominic later explained: "Dad was a fisherman, a man who worked hard because he had to and because he believed you're supposed to. . . . That's the way Giuseppe DiMaggio was—a determined and independent man who never let anything interfere with him as he worked to reach his goals." But, Dominic added, "that same attitude helped all of his baseball-playing sons more than he ever knew."

Vince found the best way to blaze that forbidden trail and make everything possible for his two younger brothers. First, he made the most of his months in Tucson by leading the league in home runs with 25 to go with a robust .347 average and 81 runs batted in. Second, he showed up suddenly at the Taylor Street house late that summer of '32. The baseball season wasn't over in San Francisco, but it was in Tucson: the bankrupt Lizards had disbanded, a victim of the Depression.

"When he got back from Tucson, Arizona, you could have sopped him up with a blotter," Dominic told Fay Vincent. "He was so thin and lost so much weight."

But Vince had saved almost every penny he had earned as a professional, and he had a presentation to make. This time, when he confronted his father, it was not to argue but to put $1,500 in cash on the kitchen table. Vince told a suspicious Giuseppe that he had earned it legitimately—from playing baseball. Giuseppe went from suspicious to astonished. Fifteen hundred cash from playing a silly game for boys?

"Well, that's a different story," he told Vince.

Giuseppe stroked his thin mustache and thought that maybe he had been wrong about Vince . . . and that maybe his next boy, Joe, could make money playing this not-so-silly game too. Plus, there was another son after that.

"Dad came to me, and I was just a little guy at the time," Dominic recalled, "and said one day—I'll never forget—he said, 'And when are you going to play baseball?'"

It was already happening. Giuseppe just hadn't expected it from "little Dommie."

FIVE

ALTHOUGH HIS OLDER BROTHER had returned home a sort of hero with all that cash, Joe didn't say anything about his own interest in baseball. He liked living in the family home, liked how his mother and sisters doted on him. He didn't want to have to go into exile, and he was not going to rebel against his father as Vince had. Instead, Joe did what he had to do to bring in a few bucks here and there. And with subtle support from Rosalie, he played baseball.

The turning point had come in 1931.

It wasn't the best time to open a new stadium anywhere in the United States—except, apparently, in San Francisco, where 18,000 people, including the specially invited Ty Cobb, squeezed into Seals Stadium on opening day, April 7. The 8–0 shutout of Portland by Sam Gibson was a harbinger of the season: the Seals would win another pennant behind Gibson's 28 victories, with a .314 team batting average. The new park's dimensions of 360 feet to left, 365 to right, and 400 to center took a toll on power hitters, but the Seal batters made the adjustment by becoming better contact hitters. Local boy Frank Crosetti drove in 143 runs with a .343 average. (When the season ended, the Yankees bought his contract and he began a 37-year career as a player and coach in New York.) Meanwhile, Henry "Prince" Oana, a native of Hawaii, had 161 RBI on just 23 home runs.

By that season, with Vince playing pro ball up north, Joe had become more serious about baseball. He'd lost interest in tennis, and he had just turned 17 as Christmas 1931 approached. Galileo High School was history. In his autobiography, Joe says he stuck it out in the school for two years, but according to Dario Lodigiani, "he was there a couple of months, and he dropped out. He never went to school anymore. I wouldn't say his studies came hard to Joe. He just didn't care about them. If Joe made a point to actually learn something, he would have been a good student. Joe, he was pretty sharp."

Unlike Vince, Joe dropped out of school not to help support the family, but because he simply didn't like school. He later reflected that "if I had to do it over again, I'd have stuck with schooling a lot longer than I did. My mother's judgment on the subject of education was correct, as it was in most all other matters." This smacks more of posturing for young readers than sincere regret.

Joe much preferred hanging around the neighborhood, finding jobs here and there for pocket money and playing baseball when it suited him. He would prepare by sitting alone at the North Beach playground, rolling Bull Durham cigarettes. "Because he was such a good player, he was the only one the director let smoke during games," reported Dante Benedetti, who grew up in the neighborhood, in *I Remember Joe DiMaggio*.

One day, in one of those chance occurrences that seem significant only later, Joe was looking to buy Christmas presents for his parents when Bat Minafo and Frank Venezia called him over. Venezia had once been one of Joe's regular pals, but they had been avoiding each other after a disagreement a year earlier. Both boys knew that Joe had displayed flashes of being a very good athlete and had socked the ball around on the local sandlots. Earlier, they had formed a club called the Jolly Knights, which Joe had refused to join, and now the club was starting up a baseball team. With real uniforms to wear. In spite of the tension between them, Bat and Frank asked Joe to be on the team. Not having much else going on, Joe gave a typically terse response: "Okay."

As he recalled, "I was a pretty cocky kid in those days, and I said to myself, 'If Vince can get dough for playing ball, I can too.'"

Joe did not make any money from baseball in the 1932 season, but he came to enjoy it, and he and others discovered that he was very good at it. He had grown to a full six feet, two inches tall, and though still slender, there were strong DiMaggio muscles in his shoulders and chest. Joe hit like Vince—when he connected, the ball took off. But Joe connected more often than Vince, who during the '32 season in Tucson was showing a propensity for striking out.

The Jolly Knights won a lot more games than they lost. Joe cost them runs with spotty play at short and third, but he gained them many more by sending the ball screaming between infielders or over the heads of outfielders in whatever park they played. When the team's success attracted a sponsor and a new name, Rossi Olive Oil, the players were able to upgrade their uniforms and equipment. Up north, Vince heard about his brother's team and issued a challenge to the Rossi boys to come play the Lumber Leagues. Vince was glad to see his brother when Joe made the trip up with his team, but not glad at all when the Rossi team beat up on the Lumber Leagues teams.

It can't be said that Joe played baseball purely for the love of it. After all, though he wanted nothing to do with fishing, he was a son of Giuseppe DiMaggio. Money talked. It talked to Joe that summer when a scout for the Class A Sunset Produce team—Rossi was in the B League—gave him two dollars after he hit a long home run.

So long, Bat and Frank and the rest of the Rossi bunch. Joe moved up to the next level of baseball in San Francisco, settling in at third base for the squad sponsored by Sunset Produce. Again he showed that he was a raw but natural hitter. In the 18 games he played for Sunset Produce, Joe batted .632 and was rewarded with a pair of featherweight baseball shoes.

After watching him play, Fred Hofmann, a former Yankees catcher, made Joe an offer. Hofmann managed the Mission Red A's, another Class A team underwritten by the San Francisco Missions, a PCL franchise that shared Seals Stadium with the more popular team. Hofmann offered Joe a contract for $150 a month, which was very good money for a teenager, and a lot better than being handed two bucks here and there.

But Joe refused it. Another opportunity had come along. After Vince returned to San Francisco from Tucson, the Seals put him on their roster. They needed help. The proud franchise had little to be proud of late in the 1932 season. They were mired in fourth place and would finish 13.5 games behind Portland. Still, Vince had finally made the PCL, the best level of play next to the major leagues, and he was ecstatic and eager to prove himself. He didn't have time to adjust to PCL-level pitching, though, and ended the season with a modest .270 average and six home runs.

According to the story told through the years by both Vince and Joe, Augie Galan, the Seals' regular shortstop who would later star for the Cubs and Dodgers, had been invited to accompany Prince Oana home to spend some time playing ball in Hawaii, making extra money on a barnstorming tour. The Seals manager, Ike Caveney, could replace Prince with Vince in the outfield, but complained that he'd be stuck without a shortstop.

Vince, never one to repress himself, blurted out, "What's the matter with my brother Joe? He's a shortstop."

And another DiMaggio joined the Seals roster.

Joe got into just three games before the '32 season ended for the Seals. His debut was on October 1 against the San Francisco Missions. He went 1-for-3, with his first hit a triple. Vince was more of a factor in the Seals' 4–3 victory that day, going 2-for-4 with a double. In six more at-bats that season, Joe managed only one hit, a double, and had two runs scored.

Both brothers were back for spring training with the Seals in 1933. Vince would fight for a starting job in the outfield. If Joe was going to stick with the Seals, it would have to be with his bat. His strong throwing arm was not suited for the infield. He had a hard enough time handling the grounders hit his way, and then it was even more of an adventure when he sidearmed the ball toward first base. During one exhibition game, Joe narrowly missed bouncing one off the noggin of Charlie Graham, the Seals' owner, who was sitting in the stands behind first.

Fortunately, he was able to hit anything a pitcher threw to him. As Joe reported, "I just stood up there and slashed away, and it was my hitting which kept me from being chased right out of the park."

When not dodging errant throws, Graham saw enough promise to take a chance—a pretty substantial one. He offered Joe a contract. Technically, Giuseppe was offered the contract, since at 18 Joe could not legally agree to anything. But what did Giuseppe know about baseball contracts? He hadn't even signed Vince's. A family tradition began: Tom had the best business head on his shoulders, so he negotiated on behalf of the family.

Tom DiMaggio and Graham went back and forth. Every time Joe hit a long homer or had a multihit game (forget the errors), Tom's position improved. Finally, Graham agreed to pay Joe an amount unprecedented for an untested rookie, $225 a month, at least 50 percent more than other rookies were being offered. Tom said yes, and Giuseppe signed immediately.

Suddenly, playing a game his father had once ridiculed, one he had never been as passionate about as Vince, had made the second-youngest DiMaggio sibling the family's highest-paid wage-earner. Giuseppe had no problem with one of his children making twice as much as he did. Wasn't this why he and Rosalie had come to

America from the other side of the world? It was just so unexpected that their eighth child would get ahead by playing a game.

At the 1933 training camp, Joe got extra instruction from Caveney, who had played shortstop with the Cincinnati Reds. However, it wasn't enough: Joe continued to bobble balls and endanger anyone sitting on the right side of the field. Because of his shyness, Joe wasn't impressive to others off the field either. One club report described him as "a gawky, awkward kid, all arms and legs like a colt, and inclined to be surly." When the 1933 season opened, Joe was on the bench.

Surprisingly, Vince rode the pine next to him. He had injured his arm and could not make throws from the outfield, and there was no room for him in the infield. Since Vince could not make a good case for getting out on the field himself, he spent time advocating for his brother. Vince, Joe later recounted, "kept telling me that I had the ability, and couldn't miss."

Vince's generosity early in the 1933 season—and its eventual impact on baseball—cannot be understated. As the older brother, he could have expected Joe to promote him to the manager, not the other way around. Vince had played professionally the previous year in the Pacific Coast League; Joe had three games under his belt. Also, with Vince waiting for a starting spot to open up, pushing for Joe to get the job risked more bench time and lower earnings for himself. But for the happy-go-lucky brother, Joe's potential and simmering desire to prove himself were the priorities.

During an early game, Caveney sent a nervous Joe up to pinch-hit for the right fielder, Ed Stewart. He was so shaky that he couldn't lift the bat off his shoulder, but it turned out okay—the pitcher couldn't get the ball over the plate and Joe walked. When the inning was over, instead of sending Vince or Prince Oana out to take Stewart's place, Caveney told Joe to play right field. He never played the infield again.

The transition to the outfield did not go flawlessly. "Joe was very sensitive," reported Louis Almada, an outfielder on the San

Francisco Missions in 1933, in *I Remember Joe DiMaggio*. "One time he was coming in on a fly. A lazy fly. He was coming in and he had his hands up. I don't know what happened. Maybe he stumbled or something. He had his hands up, and the ball hit him on top of his head. It bounced up in the air and of course he caught it. All the guys laughed. All the players laughed, and he resented that. He had rabbit ears. He heard the players laughing and yelling, 'Get a basket out there!' and 'You'd better put on a catcher's helmet!' Just popping off. He resented that. He was very proud."

In what might appear to be a cruel irony, early in the '33 season, with Joe showing signs that he could hit PCL pitching, and with Stewart as backup, the Seals decided that there was no room on the roster for Vince. The club released him.

"Just when I was glorying in success, Vince was cut loose," Joe lamented more than a few times over the decades to combat the accusation occasionally dredged up that he had pushed Vince out of San Francisco baseball. But the 18-year-old rookie had no say in the Seals' personnel decisions. And Vince always insisted, "Don't ever say that I was in any way jealous of Joe and his success in baseball. He was my brother, and I was proud of him."

But being unemployed was a big blow for Vince, as he had a wife to support. He had met Madeline while playing in the Lumber Leagues. Her parents had emigrated to America from northern Italy, but Vince, still pursuing his own path, didn't care that Madeline was not Sicilian. Her father had died when she was very young, in the 1917 flu epidemic that swept the United States, leaving Madeline's mother a widow who did not speak English, with four children. When she went to a store, she would put money on the counter and the shopkeeper would count out what he was owed, pushing the rest back to her. Eventually, she married a man who had worked with her late husband, and they had a child together.

In 1931, Madeline had been dating a man she expected to marry. That changed when he took her to a baseball game and she and

Vince spotted each other. Soon, the future husband became an ex-boyfriend. Never one to agonize over a decision, Vince determined that he and Madeline should walk down the aisle. In his self-imposed exile, he did not inform his parents until he came home and surprised Giuseppe with the $1,500 cash. Madeline was the second surprise. Now he had to figure out how to support her.

The problem seemed to be solved when the Seals, under pressure financially with attendance down, re-signed Vince. Joe, who had struggled at the plate after his brother's departure, responded by batting over .300. Then, in May, Vince was axed again by the penny-pinching club, and he wondered if his hard-earned PCL career was over. But soon the Hollywood Stars signed him. Injuries had taken their toll on the Stars, including one to outfielder June Taitt, and the team—in the red because of the Depression and still suffering from the indignity of seeing the crosstown rival Los Angeles Angels capture the PCL championship—were stocking up with new players as best they could. The team signed Vince to replace Taitt.

If Joe was unhappy about the Seals finally letting his brother go for good, he didn't show it. In fact, in his first full season with the Seals he displayed the demeanor that would mark his entire career on the field. In *I Remember Joe DiMaggio,* Bill Raimondi, a catcher with the Oakland Oaks during the 1930s, recalled that Joe "was a very quiet guy on the field. Didn't bother anybody. He'd hardly say hello to you. Nothing fooled him. He ripped everything. In the Coast League, they'd knock you down. He'd just move out of the way. Never said a word. Go back up there and take his cuts. He had trouble with one of our pitchers. I think it was Roy Joiner. He came close and Joe took exception. They had a little skirmish. No blows were struck. They just started talking to each other. That was the first time I ever saw Joe get riled up. That was probably the only time."

Happy to be roaming right field, where his strong arm was an asset, Joe had a breakout year at the plate, one of the most remarkable ever seen in the Pacific Coast League. That he hit .340 at only 18 was special enough, even in a league that featured plenty of offense. But offering a preview of what he would do with the Yankees eight years later, in the 1933 season with the Seals he collected at least one base hit in 61 consecutive games. The previous PCL record was 49 games; the major league record was 44. The 61-game streak had nothing to do with the quality of the pitching. The PCL was loaded with good players at most positions, including on the mound, and competitively it was only one level lower than the major leagues—plenty high enough for a teenager facing PCL pitching for the first time.

The club owners couldn't have been happier. As relatively inexpensive as tickets to the ballpark were, many people in the midst of the Depression were thinking twice about spending that money. It can't be said that Joe DiMaggio single-handedly saved the Pacific Coast League, but his thrilling quest for a new record did bring in the fans.

"When my streak passed its thirtieth game, attendance increased at every park I played," Joe recalled. "A few writers went so far as to claim my streak stimulated interested in the league at a time when it was facing financial collapse. I was too much of a kid at the time to pay much attention to that."

The streak had begun May 28. Because of a bruise, Joe had tape around his right thumb in that game. Even after the thumb healed, he superstitiously had it taped every day after that; otherwise, for the first half or so of the streak, Joe took it all in stride. He later admitted, however, that "by the time I was approaching forty games, the pressure was really on me."

There were, of course, close calls. After hitting in 42 straight games, Joe batted against Tom Sheehan of Vince's team, the Hollywood Stars. Sheehan was a veteran, having been a teammate of Babe Ruth on the Yankees. He was coasting 12–1 and had two outs in the ninth inning when Joe, who was 0-for-3, dug in. On a 3-2 count, he lined one into the outfield to preserve the streak. When the ninth inning began in the 49th game, Joe was again hitless and the Seals were again losing. If he batted at all that inning, he would be the seventh batter. All six players reached base ahead of him (one was hit by a pitch), and Joe doubled in the winning runs.

Then there were games when Joe took care of business right away. "DeMaggio [Joe's name was frequently misspelled early on], 18-year-old batting sensation of the Coast League, either has nerves of steel or he has no nerves at all, for the kid slammed out a single in the first inning of the game last night," reported the *San Francisco Chronicle*. "That hit drove in two runs and smashed the record of forty-nine games made by Jack Ness eighteen years ago."

"There were people who would go to the ballpark, and when Joe got a hit, they'd leave," remembered Dario Lodigiani, who had not yet made it to the PCL. "They just wanted to see Joe get a hit. I went out there a few times as a kid to watch him. There was a fellow named Buck [later Bobo] Newsom, who had played in the big leagues. He was pitching for Los Angeles. He came out and made a statement: 'If when we play the Seals he's still got the streak going, I'll stop him.' The first pitch he threw to Joe, Joe hit it against the wall for a double."

According to future major leaguer Eddie Joost, "I was playing for the Mission Reds in '33. I was only sixteen years old. I was playing third base one day in San Francisco. [Joe] hit a ball right between my legs before I could get my glove down. That's how hard he could hit the ball."

The streak came to an end on July 26 against the Oakland Oaks. Ed Walsh Jr. held Joe hitless. "I caught the last out he made in the game that ended the streak," said Emil Mailho, an Oaks outfielder. "People said to me, 'Why the hell didn't you drop it?' I said, 'They never drop them when I hit them.'" It's a good line, but Mailho was wrong. It was Harlin Pool who caught Joe's ninth-inning shot.

During the streak, Joe batted .405—104 hits in 61 games. With his typical reserve, Joe had not bothered to correct the sportswriters who often reported his name as "DeMaggio" in their stories (including his first appearance in *The Sporting News*, a national publication), but he finally did after the July 26 game so that it would be engraved the right way on the watch he was to be awarded by the PCL.

There was a reward for the hitting streak that Joe valued even more—his father's approval. Giuseppe had begun to think well of baseball when Vince returned home with real money in his pockets, but now his fourth son was making him proud. His namesake was so good at baseball that the whole city was talking about him, and misspelled or not, his name was in the newspapers. Thousands of people every day were cramming into Seals Stadium to watch Joe DiMaggio.

"Bocce ball?" Giuseppe, who looked at the box score in the *San Francisco Chronicle* every morning to check how Joe did, said dismissively. "No money in bocce ball. Baseball, that's the game!"

Joe played in 187 games in 1933, more than he would play in any future baseball season. He had an incredible 762 at-bats and 259 hits—28 of them home runs—and 169 runs batted in. Still shy of his 19th birthday, Joe DiMaggio had become the Bay Area's brightest baseball star. But there may have been some resentment among the Seals about his rapid rise. They would choose Augie Galan, who batted .356, as the team's MVP. Despite Joe's performance, the Seals ended the season in sixth place with an 81-106 record.

In L.A., Vince embraced the opportunity given him by the Hollywood Stars, who put him in the outfield where he belonged full-time. It looked like a lost season for the Stars by the middle of August, with the club mired in fourth place. But with winning series against Portland and Oakland, a pennant drive was under way. Two weeks later, when the Stars went into a series against the Sacramento Solons, they were just a game behind the Angels. Though nothing he did would remind fans of his brother's hitting streak, Vince was in the thick of the drive with timely hits and superb fielding. The Stars beat up on Sacramento, and when they faced the Angels on September 6, they were in first with a one-game lead.

They squared off in a doubleheader on a foggy night in Los Angeles before a PCL-record crowd of 24,695. The first game was a pitchers' battle between Frank Shellenback and the home team's Buck Newsom that the Angels won, 2–0. The second game was postponed. The Stars broke the first-place tie by beating the Angels, 11–8, the following day, but the home team took four out of the next five contests to move ahead by three games. (To save on travel costs, it was not unusual for a PCL series to be seven games.) The deflated Hollywood squad stumbled toward the finish line, winding up in third, seven games behind the Angels. Still, their 107-80 record was impressive, and Vince couldn't help but feel some satisfaction that he had contributed to that; the Seals, without him, wound up 25 games under .500.

Vince's power numbers weren't great—11 homers and 65 RBI— but his .333 average in 74 games with the Seals and Stars (only seven points lower than Joe's season average) showed that when given the chance, he could hit in this league. When the L.A.-based club traveled north to play in San Francisco, Vince happily watched the fans at Seals Stadium cheer Joe on. He was even glad when his own fans cheered Joe during the hitting streak. In the middle of the Depression, what was good for the game was good for every player able to keep collecting a paycheck.

ON THE VARSITY SQUAD at Galileo High School, Dominic was nicknamed "Bunky," after a kid character in a popular comic strip. Even though it wasn't his preferred position, he played second base because, unlike Vince and Joe, he didn't have a strong arm and playing second required shorter throws. But he worked at it. "By the time I was a senior in 1934, my arm had grown so much stronger that I was a pitcher and a shortstop," he reported in *Real Grass, Real Heroes*. He hit .400 that year, yet batted ninth because the coach wanted to spread the offense throughout the lineup.

"Hitting at the bottom of the order wasn't my biggest disappointment in high school, though. That came when we lost the championship in the final game of the season. I came in as a relief pitcher in the eighth inning with the bases loaded. We lost the championship on a sacrifice fly. That kind of crushing disappointment can make a baseball player grow up in a hurry."

At 17, though only five-foot-seven and 135 pounds, Dom was hooked on baseball, following in his brothers' base paths. However, he would become the first of the five DiMaggio brothers to receive a high school diploma, and he entertained the thought of becoming a chemical engineer. He even had a plan for a while of making it to the professional level for just one year, then quitting to pursue a more regular career. But over time that plan faded.

When given an opportunity in the outfield at Galileo High, Dominic invented a style of playing center that he would employ throughout his career and that would make him arguably the best center fielder in the major leagues. He stood at a right angle to the plate, with his left foot facing the plate and his right foot parallel to the center-field fence. Dominic found that he got a better jump on the ball by facing the left-field foul line as the pitch was thrown. It didn't matter to him if the batter was a lefty or righty (though that would affect where he stood in center). With this unprecedented style, Dominic got a quicker start on fly balls over his head, he could come in faster on line drives, and he charged ground balls better. A few coaches and managers tried to change his stance, but for the next 18 years no one could dispute the results.

WHAT COULD JOE do in the 1934 season to top a 61-game hitting streak? To begin with, he could make more money—despite the club's precarious finances, Tom negotiated a raise for his brother—and then he could be sold to a major league club. After enjoying success with two other Bay Area Italian-American prospects in Tony Lazzeri and Frank Crosetti, the New York Yankees had been scouting the Seals, and it was rumored that they would offer as much as

$75,000 to buy DiMaggio's contract. The Seals certainly could have used the money, but Joe was still under 20, and he and his parents didn't want him going anywhere, especially to the other side of the country. The idea was to let him have another good year, let him get a little older, and then maybe the Seals would make even more money off him.

"If Dead Pan has a good year in 1934 he's certain of a big-league tryout next Spring," wrote the syndicated columnist Jack Kofoed, using the nickname the San Francisco press had given the stoic and silent Joe the previous season. "He simply can't miss if all the stories I've heard from the Coast are true. He'll leave the boys at North Beach and the smelly seamen at Fisherman's Wharf and come East to see what it's all about. I wonder who will get him? Will he some day be trying to fill the shoes of Babe Ruth, or of Al Simmons or Big Poison Waner. Giuseppe DiMaggio! What a name for a baseball hero! It doesn't sound right."

Then, to the shock and dismay of fans—and certainly the DiMaggio family—his career almost ended during the season of '34.

There are two versions of what happened. Joe's version was that after a doubleheader in June, he went to the apartment of one of his married sisters for dinner. On the way back home to Taylor Street, Joe sat in a cramped position in a taxi, and when he got out and put weight on his left leg, it collapsed on him. "There was no twisting, just four sharp cracks at the knee, and I couldn't straighten out the leg. The pain was terrific, like a whole set of aching teeth in my knee, and I don't know yet why I didn't pass out." He claimed that he was able to stagger to a movie house nearby, and the manager drove him to the nearest emergency room.

The other version can be found in Richard Ben Cramer's detailed biography, *Joe DiMaggio: The Hero's Life,* based on reports in the *San Francisco Examiner.* A Sunday in May was Family Day at Seals Stadium, featuring the Stars playing the home team in a doubleheader—which meant DiMaggio versus DiMaggio. Each team notched a win, and Vince and Joe each had two hits. The *Examiner,* citing police sources, had Joe getting into his car at Fourth and Market Streets after midnight. He didn't own a car then, but anyway, the implication was that he had been out drinking and fell. The identity of his companion was never ascertained, and Joe stuck to his own version. Vince may have been with him, and Joe's version of events may have been an attempt to protect his brother. Imagine what trouble Vince would have been in if he had been out carousing with his younger brother and Joe wound up in the hospital.

In any case, Joe missed weeks of action with tendon problems. Even when he returned, the left knee was gimpy. Because of all the games he missed, he managed only 375 at-bats, but he collected 128 hits, good enough for a .341 average, one point higher than the 1933 season. His total of 69 RBI, though, was 100 below the previous year's total. The Seals, who had gotten rid of a few veterans in cost-cutting moves, missed Joe's production. They ended the season in fourth place.

Vince had turned 22 that September and put in a full season with the Hollywood Stars. He had grown into a strong man at five-eleven and 183 pounds, and though his average fell to .288, he had power that he had not displayed before in the PCL. He smacked 17 home runs and drove in 91 runs. He had a better year than his younger brother.

The Stars, though, had a disappointing season. They had acquired 32-year-old Smead Jolley. PCL fans remembered him as a sturdy left-handed hitter who in 1927 and '28 had posted averages of .397 and .404 for the Seals before going on to spend several seasons in the majors. With Jolley in the outfield next to Vince, along with a couple of other fresh faces, the Hollywood club expected finally to dethrone the Angels. But owner Bill Lane's heart attack on opening day augured that the year wouldn't go as planned.

The Stars enjoyed visiting San Francisco because they knew they were going to be entertained when Vince took them to the DiMaggio home on Taylor Street. "It was great fun going there," recalled Bobby Doerr, a Jefferson High School prospect who joined the Stars in mid-season that year. "The food was wonderful, and Mama DiMaggio was so generous—there was always a lot to eat. I loved watching the veteran ballplayers try to drink Papa DiMaggio under the table. He made his own wine in the cellar, as people did in those days, and these old-line ballplayers would come in, and they would drink the wine hard and fast the way they drank whiskey. Mr. DiMaggio—he always had this little cigar in one hand—would just hold his glass and sip it slowly and watch them, and pretty soon they would go under the table instead."

By season's end, pitcher Joe Sullivan had done his part, compiling a 25-11 record. Jolley, Johnny Bassler, and future baseball executive Fred Haney all hit over .300. Vince and Jolley had been solid run producers. But a 97-88 record wasn't nearly good enough, and the Angels sailed to another championship.

Joe had come back after the injury, but he certainly didn't appear to be as good as new. The Yankees were hesitant about adding him to the club. Joe later wrote that hitting .341 "was good enough, but the 'wonder' tag was off me. I was labeled 'crippled' now."

In November, the Yankees sent him to a specialist in Los Angeles, who determined that with a combination of treatments and rest, the knee would be fine. That was good enough for Yankees' owner Jacob Ruppert (of Ruppert Brewing Company, addressed as Colonel Ruppert for the rank he'd achieved in the National Guard), general manager Ed Barrow, and manager Joe McCarthy. The club paid $25,000 for an "option" on Joe, meaning that he would be shipped off to New York after the 1935 season.

Strapped for cash, Charlie Graham, the Seals owner, had to grit his teeth and take the offer. (In *Lucky to Be a Yankee*, Joe contends that Joe Cronin, manager of the Red Sox and also from San Francisco, told him afterward that if the Yankees had passed, the Boston club had intended to offer $60,000 to the Seals for his contract. If this was true, beginning in 1939 the Red Sox would have had Joe DiMaggio in center and Ted Williams in left and conceivably would have been the most successful major league team of the mid-20th century, instead of the Yankees.) When the time came, New York would also send five players west to fill out the Seals lineup.

Joe made that '35 season a memorable one for San Francisco fans. After a slow start, his knee regained full strength. He flirted with .400 for much of the season and finished at .398—which was not good enough, however, to earn the PCL batting title. Oscar "Ox" Eckhardt of the Mission Reds finished one point ahead. Eckhardt went on to play for the Brooklyn Dodgers in 1936, but was never again mentioned in the same sentence as Joe DiMaggio. The Seals won the PCL title that year, and Joe picked up the MVP plaque. To go with his stratospheric average, he had slugged 34 home runs and led the league in both RBIs and runs scored.

More than just the healed knee helped Joe produce such a scintillating season. Lefty O'Doul was back in town. There was no baseball figure in San Francisco more popular than O'Doul, including Joe. The city had been in mourning after he left the Seals at the end of his great 1927 season. Many remembered that a Kids Day he sponsored that September drew an overflow crowd of 20,000 into Recreation Park, which would remain the all-time record. He was not a particularly good fielder. "He could run like a deer," commented a *Chronicle* columnist. "Unfortunately, he threw like one too." But he could hit. Playing for the Philadelphia Athletics in 1929, he knocked out 254 hits and had a .398 average, which has been exceeded only twice in 84 years. No hitter in major league history who hit 32 or more home runs in a season has ever struck out fewer times—19. And his combined average of 330 hits and walks that year is still a National League record as well.

From the A's, O'Doul went to the Brooklyn Dodgers. In 1930 he joined a group of All-Stars that included Lou Gehrig and Lefty Grove to play a series of 17 games in Japan. Total attendance was 450,000.

The tour was the beginning of a mutual infatuation between O'Doul and Japanese baseball fans. He returned in 1934 with Ruth, Gehrig, Gomez, Jimmie Foxx, and other American luminaries in tow. At the end of the 1934 season, he retired and returned to San Francisco. His lifetime average of .349 remains the fourth highest in major league history, behind Ty Cobb, Rogers Hornsby, and "Shoeless" Joe Jackson. He is not in the Hall of Fame, however, because his career game total of 970 is below the required 1,000.

Lefty took over as manager of the Seals in 1935 and had a strong influence on Joe DiMaggio. "I never taught him anything about hitting," O'Doul said about Joe. But he was being too modest. Louis Almada of the Mission Reds had numerous opportunities during the '35 season to watch Joe emerge as a great hitter: "Lefty O'Doul told Joe to spread his feet out. Hit off his back foot. He said, 'Don't move until you see the ball. Just wait until the ball gets on top of you. Hold your bat back. Hold your bat up high.' O'Doul had to correct a few things. Joe didn't just fall into it right away. But you could see that tremendous change that came over him."

The most significant change was that Joe became more of a pull hitter. O'Doul had played in cavernous Yankee Stadium, and he knew, especially as the season progressed, that Joe was bound for New York. O'Doul had seen many fly balls to left-center, center, and right-center that would have been round-trippers in the PCL fall into gloves. By urging Joe to pull, O'Doul was helping him to develop the skill to hit homers down the left-field line, only 300 feet long in Yankee Stadium.

O'Doul gave Joe more than technical instruction. No matter what he did on the field, Joe was still an awkward, socially stunted young man. In *I Remember Joe DiMaggio*, Steve Barath, the Seals third baseman who was his roommate on the road in the 1934–35 seasons, said, "Joe was never friendly. I mean, he was friendly with me, but he didn't want to go out. He was just scared of the world. Shy. That's the word for him."

"The biggest thing Joe learned from O'Doul was how to live like a hero," wrote Richard Ben Cramer in *Joe DiMaggio: The Hero's Life*. "Everybody knew Lefty, everybody watched him, said hello to him, loved him. And in the middle of it all, Lefty did just what he wanted. He was handsome, at home anywhere he went, always the best-dressed man in the room. The admiration of males he accepted with offhand grace, and to the adoration of females he extended a courtly and catholic welcome. For Joe, this brush with the hero's life wasn't quite like hitting—he couldn't just do it himself the next day. But if he was going to be a big-leaguer, a *New York* big-leaguer . . . this was his chance to learn at the master's knee."

Lodigiani remembered that "O'Doul was New York–smart from all the years that he played in the major leagues. He played with New York, especially. He kind of smartened Joe up, told him what to do, what to wear, how to dress. First thing you know, when he comes back, when you see him, Joe looked like a department store. He looked great."

The Yankees' interest in Joe was hotter than ever when the '35 season ended. It certainly helped that in an article in *Collier's* magazine late in the season O'Doul declared that Joe would be a national star within two years. What a bargain he looked like now, a phenom from San Francisco in exchange for just $25,000 and five players who were not much more than castoffs. Joe's .361 three-year average in the PCL had Ruppert & Company in New York believing that he was more than ready for the major leagues and could probably step into the starting lineup.

And the Yankees needed the help. Babe Ruth, who had gone from slugger to sluggish, had been banished. On May 30, he had played his last game, back in Boston where he began, this time for the Braves. For the third year in a row the Yankees finished in second place. This trend could continue, or worsen, if the club didn't find a young player to plug into the middle of the lineup next to Lou

Gehrig, who would turn 33 in June and whose offensive stats were down significantly from his season in 1934.

So the Yankees mailed Joe a contract with an offer of $5,625 in salary. Joe showed the contract to O'Doul as well as to Tom. O'Doul turned to his pal Ty Cobb, who had Joe write a letter to Ed Barrow asking for more money. Barrow offered $6,500. Cobb dictated another letter to Joe. Barrow wrote back saying that $8,500 was his final offer and that Joe should "tell Cobb to stop writing me letters." Joe signed the contract in November and celebrated his 21st birthday.

There was rejoicing in the DiMaggio household. Giuseppe and Rosalie were about to see a son of theirs earn what to them was a fortune, and on the world's biggest stage. Maybe Tom and Mike had some regret that they hadn't been given the chance to try baseball, but there was nothing to be done about it; that door had closed for them a good ten years earlier.

Another older brother might have been jealous that Joe was going to the major leagues ahead of him. But Vince believed that his time would come, maybe after just one more season with the Hollywood Stars. His increasing power showed that he was close—he had finished the season with 24 home runs (fifth in the PCL, though 10 behind Joe) and 112 RBI to go with a .278 average. He had been a star on the Stars, who otherwise had a bad season. A 73-99 record indicated a franchise in trouble, as did drawing only 90,000 fans total. And anyway, Vince wasn't the grumbling kind. He wanted Joe to do well and make the whole family proud.

For Dominic, meanwhile, Joe's promotion was like a beachhead. If Joe did well, maybe Dommie would get a chance too. Dominic was still undersized and slim, still wearing the thick eyeglasses that gave him more of a scholarly than athletic look, but the desire to play pro baseball was burning inside him, and he was going to take his shot.

Though he would always call San Francisco home, there was to be no looking back for Joe. He recalled: "When I packed my baseball togs in the dressing room of Seal Park [after his last game], I was sorry to leave the fellows I'd been with for three years; sorry to leave Lefty O'Doul. . . . I was sorry, yes, but I was glad too, for the Yankees had picked up my option and I was headed for the big leagues, headed for the team I wanted to be with most of all."

SIX

Joe had never been east of the Rocky Mountains. In fact, the farthest east he had ever been was his birthplace, Martinez. Now here he was, in February 1936, leaving the shelter of his large family and familiar San Francisco surroundings to travel 3,000 miles across the country. It helped that he traveled every one of those miles in a car with two other Italian-American hometown players, Tony Lazzeri and Frank Crosetti. The established stars would chaperone Joe to the Yankees' spring training camp in Florida.

At 21, Joe was by far the youngest of the three, and the least prepared for the trip. After saying good-bye to his parents, brothers, and sisters—displaying to Marie the signet ring she had given him—he climbed into the backseat of the Ford that Lazzeri, well established in the Yankees lineup, had recently purchased. And there he remained for the entire weeklong journey. The veteran players were chagrined to learn that Joe didn't know how to drive a car, so they chauffeured as well as chaperoned him.

He had no idea what was waiting for him in St. Petersburg, and Crosetti and Lazzeri thought it best not to tell him. They knew that the New York reporters were already hailing Joe as the next Babe Ruth who would immediately restore the Yankees to glory. (The irony of one headline, "Rookie May Don Ruth Mantle," would only become clear 15 years later.) In fact, there was already a backlash to all the press Joe had been receiving before he even took his first swing as a Yankee. According to one New York newspaper headline, "DiMaggio Comes Up with Two Strikes on Him as Innocent Victim of Lavish Newspaper Ballyhoo." The caption to an accompanying cartoon read, "The old ballyhoo will be DiMaggio's toughest foe. Fans who have been reading the nice things said about him will expect Ruth, [Shoeless Joe] Jackson and Cobb all rolled into one."

The veteran teammates knew that was too big a burden for any ballplayer to bear, especially a 21-year-old who had lived with his parents in the cocoon of San Francisco. No matter how well he had played in the Pacific Coast League, Joe could easily crash and burn in the New York spotlight. And with Joe rarely one to initiate a conversation, "we went two or three hundred miles at a clip without any of us saying a word," recalled Crosetti, who would room with Joe.

That he had been far away from the major leagues was actually an advantage for Joe. Most of his experience in baseball was knocking the cover off the ball against any kind of pitching. His relative ignorance of pitchers in the American League allowed him to remain confident that he could hit anyone, anywhere.

In the evening of the last Sunday in February, the San Francisco trio pulled into St. Petersburg. The next day, wearing Yankees jersey number 18, Joe stepped out onto Miller Huggins Field. There he encountered George Selkirk, Johnny Murphy, and Harry and Dixie Walker. For a week the workouts were informal. Then came the first official full-squad workout, presided over by Joe McCarthy. The strong and intimidating Lou Gehrig slapped Joe on the back and said, "Nice to have you with us, Joe."

The pitcher Red Ruffing came up to him and said, "So you're the great DiMaggio. I've heard all about you. You hit .400 on the Coast, and you'll probably hit .800 here because we don't play night games and throw in a nice, shiny white ball anytime one gets the least bit soiled."

Joe would learn that Ruffing liked to tease his teammates. And he learned the prevailing Yankees attitude toward newcomers: if you help us win, that puts more money in my pocket and you're okay with me. Cost me money and you're gone. The expectation in St. Petersburg was that Joe would help the Yankees be champions again.

Joe McCarthy insisted on "the Yankee Way." "It is impressed on you right off the bat that you're a professional now, you're in the majors and it's up to you to act like a major leaguer, not only on the ball field but away from it," Joe wrote a decade later, when he was the personification of the Way. McCarthy "stresses dignity, which may sound out of place among ball players, but which is definitely a morale lifter. When Horseplay gets too rough, or laughter too loud, among a group, McCarthy is likely to walk over and say quietly, 'You fellows are Yankees. Act like Yankees!' He doesn't have to say any more."

The quiet dignity of the team—represented daily by Gehrig—and a winning tradition combined to create the perfect environment for Joe. Though 3,000 miles from home, he immediately felt that this was where he belonged.

The backlash did not amount to much, and the normally tough New York press gave him a pass. Reporters tossed him softball questions, and Joe answered them briefly and modestly. "I don't think anything I said made good copy, because I haven't the knack of saying things that can be blown up into headline quotes. . . . All I was thinking about was getting a regular job with the Yankees."

He had a piece of good luck with that. The starting center fielder, Ben Chapman, was holding out for more money, and Dixie Walker had a sore arm, so there was room in the outfield. When spring training games began, McCarthy put the rookie in the starting lineup—in the three-spot, where Ruth had been entrenched all those years. In his first at-bat, against the St. Louis Cardinals, Joe tripled—just as he had done in his first Seals at-bat. That, he thought, was a good sign.

The way the lithe but muscular newcomer batted—combining inherited strength with Lefty O'Doul's instructions—impressed observers. "DiMaggio is a peculiar batsman," wrote Dan Daniel of the *New York World-Telegram*. "He is not a long swinger, but a wrist swinger, with a terrific pull on the ball. In stance, one foot from the plate, DiMaggio reminds you of Joe Jackson. But in his application of power at the very last fraction of a second Joe is more reminiscent of Tris Speaker. How DiMaggio gets so much power on the ball when it is right on top of him is amazing. The Italian lad has big strong arms, with tremendous wrists. His back muscles ripple in their sheaths."

After five exhibition games, the transition to major leaguer was going smoothly enough. But then, in a game against the Boston Braves, as Joe slid into third base, Joe Coscarart, a third baseman who had played for Seattle in the PCL, fell and landed on Joe's ankle. That injury wasn't severe, but the treatment was. An inattentive trainer put Joe under a diathermy lamp for too long, resulting in a foot burned badly enough that a doctor told him he couldn't play for three weeks. After McCarthy sent him north to New York to recuperate, Joe missed playing in the opening day game against the Senators, with President Franklin Roosevelt throwing out the first ball. Worse, he had no chance to crack the starting lineup now that Chapman had ended his holdout.

As consolation, Joe got his first look at New York. "I was the typical, gawking country kid when I stepped off the train at Penn Station. It's a good thing Paul Krichell, Yankee scout, was there to meet me or I might still be wandering around the station." When Joe was able to go on a guided tour of the city, it included a very important stop. "One of the first things I did in New York was to hobble to Yankee Stadium. I had never seen anything like it and it was a little frightening to know that this was to be my stamping grounds for as long as I could make it."

In April, Colonel Ruppert's personal physician examined Joe's "barking puppy." The burn was healing, but the wound kept reopening. Joe was out of action the entire month. In calls home to Giuseppe and Rosalie, he worried that his career with the Yankees was over before it began.

Finally, at the end of April, the doctors cleared Joe to play. McCarthy had him ride the bench until May 3, when he started in left field against the St. Louis Browns at Yankee Stadium. Chapman was in center, with Selkirk in right. In the infield were Red Rolfe, Crosetti, Lazzeri, and Gehrig. Bill Dickey was the catcher, and pitching was the former San Francisco Seal Lefty Gomez. Joe, wearing number 9, showed right away that he belonged—after a groundout in his first at-bat, he singled, tripled, and singled, and the Yankees cruised to a 14–5 win. In the game he collected his first run scored and first run batted in. The effect on a revived Gehrig was obvious— the cleanup hitter had five runs scored and two RBI on a 4-for-5 day.

Joe's first home run a few days later, smacked against the Philadelphia Athletics, propelled the Yankees past the Red Sox into first place. By the end of the month, his average was .411. There really had been no need to worry about American League pitching. Forget Gehrig, Dickey, Gomez, and the rest of them—the newspapers spilled all their ink on the rookie. Joe was on his way to becoming an even bigger star in New York than he had been on the West Coast. Writers in other cities joined the chorus.

"I got an eyeful of DiMaggio this afternoon in those two games against Washington, and, brother, methinks they haven't overrated him much," praised Shirley Povich, a *Washington Post* columnist. "If there's anything that DiMaggio can't do on a baseball field, I dunno what it is. That .380 batting average he's sporting around is no myth (as three consecutive doubles off Buck Newsom's pitching in the second game attest) and the only thing that will stop that guy from dragging down every ball hit into his field is the fences."

WHILE JOE WAS establishing himself in the starting lineup of the Yankees, Vince and Dominic were trying to navigate their way toward the major leagues. For Vince, 1936 would be his fourth season with the Hollywood Stars, and he had to wonder if this was as far as he was going to get. Sure, hundreds of men over the years had played their entire careers in the Pacific Coast League and had few if any regrets. The fans were great up and down the West Coast, the money wasn't bad (especially with so many other people not having jobs at all), and he could still spend plenty of time in San Francisco with his family and all the DiMaggios except Joe. But Vince was 23 when the season began, and that was getting to be a bit grizzled for a hopeful. By now he had given up the dream of being an opera singer, but he wasn't ready to give up the dream of being a major league ballplayer.

Vince was now a San Diego Padre. The Hollywood Stars had lost 99 games the previous season and more than a few of their fans. Owner Bill Lane decided it was time for a move, and the growing city of San Diego had long sought a team. In early 1936, Lane moved the team there, where they were renamed the Padres. They made their debut on March 1 as winners against the Seattle Rainiers at Lane Field.

Dominic turned 19 in February 1936 and was a full year out of high school. He became the first of the DiMaggio children to attend college, still thinking about chemical engineering. But like his brothers, he had the baseball bug bad by this time. He was young enough and smart enough that if he couldn't advance in the game, he could go back to college and a career. He had a job at the Simmons Bed Factory in San Francisco, and there were many guys his age envying the steady paycheck. He was a good, reliable worker and well liked by the people at Simmons.

That season, fitting baseball in around his schedule at the factory, Dominic played for the local sandlot team, the North Beach Merchants. Though he played mostly shortstop instead of the outfield, as he would have preferred, he was making an impression as a good contact hitter and an aggressive base runner, as well as making the plays he had to make in the infield. The Seals took notice and began to scout him. The modest Dominic thought that "by that time any baseball player in San Francisco named DiMaggio was going to get a good long look from the scouts." Still, "I wanted to make sure of it," he said later.

If there were any doubts about Dominic's baseball ambitions, they were dispelled when he quit his job. Or tried to. The Seals and the Cincinnati Reds were about to hold a combination baseball camp and tryouts, and the players who did the best would be offered a chance to make one club or the other. Dominic intended to give it a full shot. His boss, however, wouldn't allow him to quit; instead, he told Dominic to do his best and the job would be waiting for him if the tryout was unsuccessful.

There were 143 men at the camp. Dominic would always be known as a gritty player, and grit was what he needed now to overcome his nervousness and inexperience. That his brother Joe was already a legend wouldn't help—he had to be better than the other players.

And he was—or close enough. Dominic played hard, hitting solidly and showing what he could do in both the infield and outfield. He made enough of an impression that his days in a mattress factory were over. "I was called into the Seals' offices from the field, where I had been trying out, to sign my contract, along with my brother Tom who had been Joe's business adviser and was about to become mine."

Dominic's career would prove that he was a genuinely talented player, but on that day in the spring of 1936, was it also the case that the Seals signed him because he was Joe DiMaggio's kid brother?

Money was still tight for the Seals, and they had lost their biggest star. A DiMaggio in the lineup had to help attendance. The Seals didn't hold a press conference every time they signed a player, but Walter Mails, the club's PR man, arranged one for Dominic. Wearing a new Seals uniform and with Tom DiMaggio standing behind him, Dominic signed his contract in front of a group of reporters. With that ceremony over, Mails invited everyone in attendance to "have a beer." Dominic followed the reporters into the ballpark's dining room to be part of the celebration, but Mails told him, "You can go down and chase some more fly balls now. We're all through with you."

It didn't matter. What was most important was that in 1936 the three DiMaggio brothers were all what they had aspired to be: professional baseball players.

IN LESS THAN three months, Joe had made enough of an impression on American League fans that he was on the All-Star team. By the end of May, when he was hitting over .400, he had become so popular among the New York fans that he needed a police escort when he left Yankee Stadium. His teammates didn't seem to resent all the attention the 21-year-old was receiving from the press and the fans. When Billy Knickerbocker of the Cleveland Indians tried to hit Joe in the head with a throw, Lazzeri led the charge of Yankees out of the dugout to teach the shortstop a lesson.

The week of the All-Star Game, Joe was on the cover of *Time*. If anyone should have been jealous it was Gehrig, as the "Iron Horse" was having a resurgent season. But the big first baseman was happy that the Yankees were once again the powerful team from the days when he and Ruth anchored the lineup, and a trip to the World Series seemed certain.

When the American League and National League squads took the field on July 7 at Braves Field in Boston, Joe was the first rookie to have made an All-Star roster. It would have been impossible to keep him off it—he was batting .358. Recalling his swift ascent, he offered in his autobiography, "Freshmen aren't ordinarily picked for this game, but here I was in the starting lineup with the cream of the crop, certainly a far cry from the pick-up games I'd been playing not too many years before on the old Horse Lot in San Francisco." He was "confident I was going to have my biggest day in baseball. It turned out to be my poorest public exhibition."

The first All-Star Game had been played in 1933, and the American League had won all three contests since. Lefty Grove of the Red Sox started, but the National League countered with a powerful one-two punch, Dizzy Dean of the Cardinals and Carl Hubbell of the Giants. Still, many believed that adding the sensational Yankee rookie to the lineup virtually locked up a fourth victory.

Instead, Joe took much of the blame for the AL's first defeat. In the first inning, against Dean, he hit into a double play. In the next inning, he charged a line drive off the bat of Gabby Hartnett, but instead of dropping into his glove for a shoestring catch, the ball bounced under and past him. Hartnett wound up with an RBI triple.

In the fourth inning, with lefty screwballer Carl Hubbell pitching, Joe popped up to Leo "The Lip" Durocher at short. In the fifth, his former Seals teammate Augie Galan homered to right, upping the score to 2–0. Billy Herman singled to right, and when Joe couldn't find the handle on the ball, Herman cruised into second on the error. He ended up in the dugout a minute later when Joe "Ducky" Medwick singled him home. Joe had a second chance against Hubbell in the sixth—but instead of redeeming himself, he dribbled one back to the mound.

He was embarrassing himself not only in front of the 25,556 people in the seats but—via the Mutual, CBS, and NBC radio networks—the fans in New York and family and friends in San Francisco. If this was how he stacked up against the better players in baseball, maybe he'd be returning to pickup games at the old Horse Lot. The American League rallied in the seventh, with the National

League up 4–0, but Joe wasn't part of it. Gehrig smashed a homer, and Luke Appling singled in two runs. With the tying run on base, Joe pounced on a Lon Warneke pitch, but the ball flew directly at Durocher.

He was given one more opportunity in the ninth, with two outs and Charlie Gehringer on second base. He popped out to Herman at second, and the game was over. In five times at bat, the balls he hit never left the infield. Joe lamented that he was "a young man who had learned something and learned it the hard way."

The next day's newspapers, especially in New York, were tough on the rookie. Dan Parker in the *Daily Mirror* compared him to a not-highly-regarded heavyweight boxer: "Poor Giuseppe DiMaggio found himself in the same predicament as Primo Carnera breaking in a new pair of shoes. At every run, Joe encountered a new pinch. In every pinch he fell down. McCarthy's prize rookie won the hand-gilded mountain goat antlers . . . by donating three runs to the National League cause and refraining from batting in a half-dozen or so that he might have driven home."

For a ballplayer who hadn't endured much criticism since he first picked up a bat, the caustic comments stung. Still, Joe thought that his dismal performance "may have been the most important event of my baseball career. It opened my eyes to many truths, to the fact that anything can happen in any one ball game, or series of games; that things are hardest just when they look easiest."

Teammates, reporters, fans, and friends who later marveled at Joe's stoicism on the field and his apparent lack of emotion could readily understand the self-reflecting he did after the 1936 All-Star Game. He vowed to "bear down in every inning of every game." The boy who had found playing baseball back in San Francisco an effortless exercise realized that to excel against the bigger boys in Boston, Chicago, Detroit, and elsewhere, talent wasn't enough—he had to work harder than anyone else.

Two weeks after the embarrassment of the All-Star Game,

McCarthy moved Joe into center field, out of necessity. Joe, playing right field, had chased down a ball off the bat of Goose Goslin that should have belonged to Myril Hoag, playing center. Hoag and Joe collided. Hoag was hit in the head so hard that a blood clot formed and he would require brain surgery. McCarthy saw Hoag's tragedy as Joe's opportunity. Except for an experiment at first base in 1950 suggested by Casey Stengel, Joe would be the center fielder for the Yankees for the rest of his career, his superiority in the league challenged only by his brother Dominic.

All the New York players had to do was keep breathing to win the pennant. When they clinched it on September 9, it was the earliest a team had done so in the major leagues. The season ended with the Tigers a speck in New York's rearview mirror, 19.5 games out. Though he still didn't get the headlines that Joe did, Gehrig was back to being the foundation of the Yankees. An average of .354, 49 homers, and 152 RBI earned him a second Most Valuable Player Award, his first since 1927. Joe had set the table nicely for Gehrig by batting .323 with 206 hits (his 15 triples led the American League), and with the Iron Horse in the order behind him, no one could pitch around the rookie (who had only 39 strikeouts). Joe logged 29 home runs and 125 RBI. Gehrig and four former PCL players—Joe, Lazzeri, Crosetti, and Gomez—were headed to the World Series.

MEANWHILE, VINCE HOPED the Padres would improve enough to get into the PCL playoffs. A promising youngster helped. On June 27, in a game against the Sacramento Solons, Ted Williams made his PCL debut. It was not an auspicious start: Henry "Cotton" Pippen struck out the beanpole 17-year-old with three pitches. Nevertheless, from this point on Ted Williams would figure in the lives of all three of baseball's DiMaggio brothers, his life and career interlacing with theirs as friend and teammate to Vince and Dom and as rival to Joe.

Teddy Samuel Williams was a San Diego native, born on August 30, 1918. Sam Williams, his father, a mixture of English and Welsh, met May Venzor, a woman of mostly Mexican descent, in Hawaii. He was in the U.S. Army, and she was training to be a Salvation Army officer. Ted was born eight years later, and his brother Daniel two years after that. Sam had an unhealthy relationship with alcohol, and May devoted most of her life to her obsession with the Salvation Army. Neither had much time left over for their sons.

Ted grew up wanting to play baseball all the time. In his autobiography, *My Turn at Bat,* he recalled, "We lived in a little $4,000 house on Utah Street my mother had gotten through the kindness of the Spreckles family, a prominent family in San Diego. My mother was going to pay them back, but I don't think she ever did. The North Park playground was a block and a half from my house. It had lights and we could play until nine o'clock at night." The park became his home because his mother "was gone all day and half the night," his father didn't come home until late at night, and "I remember being ashamed of how dirty the house was all the time."

Ted played on the baseball team at Horace Mann Junior High and then for the team sponsored by the American Legion Padre Serra "Fighting Bob" Post. In three years on the high school varsity, his batting average was .430. Though he had a picture of Babe Ruth on his bedroom wall, the boy's heroes were Charles Lindbergh, Bill Terry of the New York Giants, and Cotton Warburton, a star on the University of Southern California football team.

The youngster had unofficial tryouts with the Los Angeles Angels of the PCL and also with the St. Louis Cardinals. But he wasn't eager to be that far north or east, away from friends. Being away from his home, however, wouldn't have bothered Ted very much. In his autobiography, Williams defended his father—whom the kindest reporters would later describe as a "wanderer"—stating, "He stuck it out with my mother for twenty years, and finally he packed up, and I'd probably have done the same. My mother was a wonderful woman in many ways, but gee, I wouldn't have wanted to be married to a woman like that. Always gone. The house dirty all the time. She was

religious to the point of being domineering, and so narrow-minded.
. . . My mother had a lot of traits that made me cringe."

After graduation from Hoover High School, Ted joined the
Padres. His mother signed the contract that was to pay her son $150
a month. Lane could have afforded more—the Padres were a hit in
San Diego and would lead the PCL in attendance that year—but at
six-three and only 148 pounds, Ted did not evoke visions of a power
hitter, surely not one who would go on to club 521 home runs for
the Red Sox. Yankee scout Joe Devine came to San Diego to look
him over. If the youngster had performed well, Ted Williams and
Joe DiMaggio might have ended up on the same team. But Devine
concluded that the teenager "is a very slow lad, not a good outfielder
now and just an average arm. There is big doubt whether Williams
will ever be fast enough to get by in the majors as an outfielder."
The scout did allow that Williams "shows promise as a hitter, but
good pitching so far has stopped him cold." The Yankees passed.
(Williams contended in his book that the Yankees turned him down
when his mother asked for a $1,000 signing bonus.)

He had a solid season, and though it was not as eye-opening as
Joe's had been in his first year in the Pacific Coast League, Williams
impressed many of his teammates and rivals with his potential.
Before a game against the visiting Seals, Lefty O'Doul was observ-
ing batting practice. Suddenly, he ran out of the dugout to Williams.
To the somewhat startled rookie he said, "Don't let anybody ever,
ever fool with your batting stance and your hitting. You are perfect."
Then O'Doul returned to the dugout.

By the fall of 1936, the Pacific Coast League had a new system
to increase fan interest and attendance. The season was divided in
half, and each city that won each half would be celebrating a first-
place finish. When the regular season ended, the top two teams of
each half went into a playoff for the Governor's Cup. This year the
first-round contest was between the Padres and the Oakland Oaks.
During the season, San Diego had won 17 out of the 28 games the

two teams played. Alas, that didn't seem to matter. Williams homered, but the Padres lost the first game 6–3, then the second game 4–3, and the third game 5–4. They rallied for a 7–1 victory, but lost the fifth game, 7–6. Oakland went on to win the Cup, earning each team member $220.

BACK IN NEW YORK, Joe played in the first of his six Subway Series games, never losing one of them. In 1936 the opponent was the New York Giants, a team seeking to restore its glory after a few lean years following the reign of manager John McGraw, which had ended after the 1932 season. The new National League pennant winner had three future Hall of Famers: first baseman and manager Bill Terry, NL home run king Mel Ott, and Hubbell, the All-Star screwballer who was also the National League MVP. The front page of the October 1 edition of *The Sporting News* proclaimed, "11 Series' Vets Give Giants Edge in Experience." Perhaps a slight edge for Joe was that his mother, escorted by Tom, made the trip east to see the World Series and New York City.

Hubbell put on a show in the first game at the Polo Grounds, defeating the overmatched Yankees 6–1. Joe managed just one of the Yankees' seven hits. Unfortunately for the Giants, Hubbell couldn't pitch every day. In the second game, against Hal Schumacher, the new edition of Murderers' Row crushed the Giants, 18–4. In the bottom of the ninth, the Giants' Hank Leiber sent a Gomez pitch soaring to center. Joe, playing only his second game in the Polo Grounds, did an about-face and ran. He caught the ball over his shoulder and would have crashed into the fence had it not been opened to allow President Roosevelt's limousine to exit after the last out. Joe hurtled through the opening, his momentum carrying him up the steps to the bowels of the ballpark. When he turned around, there was Roosevelt saluting him out the limousine's window.

The Yankees took the third and fourth games, then the Giants rallied to win the fifth, a ten-inning nail-biter. With Hubbell ready to return for Game 7, the sixth game looked like a must-win for the Yankees. Lefty Gomez was on the mound against Fred Fitzsimmons. The Yankees scored three runs early, but there was no quit in Terry's team. The Giants pushed runs across in three different innings.

When Joe walked to the plate at the top of the ninth, the Yanks had only a 6–5 lead. He lined to left for a single. Gehrig followed with a single, and Joe slid safely into third. It was Bill Dickey's turn, and the veteran catcher smacked one to the right side of the infield. Terry fielded it cleanly. But Joe was already racing home. He stopped, feinted as though he was returning to third, and when Terry threw it there he bolted down the line again. Eddie Mayo at third fired the ball to Harry Danning, the catcher. Everyone in the stands held their breath, waiting for the collision. But Joe leaped, launching himself over Danning, and landed with his hand touching the plate—safe.

The Giants went into a funk, unable to stop the ensuing carnage. By the time the Yankees were finished, the score was 13–5. It was the first world championship for the Bronx Bombers since 1932, when Ruth had still been the main attraction. Joe had rapped out nine hits in the six games.

Joe returned to Taylor Street in triumph—a world champion, the son of an illiterate Sicilian immigrant fisherman who had been saluted by the American president. By North Beach standards, Joe was a pretty well-off guy. He had earned $14,900. From playing baseball! Giuseppe marveled.

The *San Francisco Chronicle* reported, "No first-year man ever got anything like the money that will start falling into his lap. It is estimated that the earnings of the 21-year-old . . . will amount to $40,000 or more this year. For service to the Yankees, Joe will collect $15,000. Radio appearances, advertising and ghost-written articles assure $10,000. A vaudeville tour is expected to net the rest. Joe is to tour with his brother Vince. At first it was thought the boys would merely bat fungoes into the balconies, but it develops that the

DiMaggios will offer songs, funny sayings and dances. Joe practiced his tap-dance routine between World Series games."

The vaudeville tour never happened, but even without it, the DiMaggios had become royalty in the neighborhood. With Vince and Dominic working as professional ballplayers and bringing in money too, the Depression seemed to be well over for the DiMaggio family. Out of habit, Giuseppe would still wake at 4:00 A.M., but he didn't go out to his Monterey Clipper boat to fish as much. He left more and more of it to Mike. With her children grown—the youngest was now 19—and with that baseball dough, Rosalie no longer had to work as hard either. Besides serving as the family business manager, Tom was looking into various business ventures in San Francisco, where there was much excitement about the construction of the Golden Gate Bridge.

In December of that year, Vince finally made it to the majors at 24. He signed with a Boston club—not the Red Sox, but the National League Boston Bees. He would have preferred an American League team—playing with Joe on the Yankees would be best of all—but the Bees would do.

The Seals had had a dismal year, finishing in seventh. Needing fresh blood and more fans, the team was eager to give another DiMaggio a shot. It was expected that Dominic would be in the starting lineup for the 1937 season.

As 1936 drew to a close, there was no bigger star in American sports than Joe DiMaggio. Not Olympic star Jesse Owens, not heavyweight champion Max Baer.

It was the best thing that could happen to the DiMaggio family. It would turn out to be the worst thing to happen to the DiMaggio brothers.

PART II

What does freedom mean to me? Oh my! Thank God I was born here. Thank God my folks migrated here. Look at what America has done for the DiMaggios!

—DOMINIC DIMAGGIO

SEVEN

Giuseppe and Rosalie DiMaggio could now tell their neighbors on Taylor Street that they were to have two sons playing major league baseball. And what a big deal it was when the word spread—*both* DiMaggio boys would be in the headlines in 1937.

Vince was going to a very different organization, however. The talented Yankees had needed only one important piece to fill the void left by the departure of Babe Ruth. The club that had signed Vince was pretty much all void.

When he first told his friends in San Francisco that he was going to be playing for the Boston Bees, most of them didn't know what the heck he was talking about. Whoever heard of a major league team named the Bees? Many people in Boston wished they hadn't.

Originally the Boston Braves, the team had some proud history. The Braves had swept the Philadelphia Athletics, managed by Connie Mack, in the 1914 World Series, the first time there had been a Series sweep. When Braves Field opened the following spring, it was the largest ballpark in the major leagues. But by the 1930s, the glory years seemed over. Before the 1935 season began, the Yankees looked to unload a spent Babe Ruth, and the owner of the Braves, Judge Emil Fuchs, saw an opportunity to entice fans to fill his 40,000-seat stadium. Ruth became a vice president of the club as well as "assistant manager"—in both roles, he was to be consulted on personnel moves.

The Babe, alas, had nothing left in the tank, and National League pitchers showed him no mercy. He was batting .187 when he had one last power surge in a game against the Pirates in Pittsburgh in late May. He clouted three home runs, the last three remaining in his arsenal. Then, on June 1, he retired, ending his career in the city where it had begun when he was a teenager on the Red Sox. In 1935 the Braves posted a .248 winning percentage, the third worst in major league history. Fuchs lost control of the team, and new owners, instead of changing the team, changed its colors, to blue and yellow, and its name, to the Bees. They posted another losing record in 1936.

Whatever the name of the team, it was a professional National League club, and Vince had a shot at cracking the starting lineup. A supportive Lefty O'Doul told reporters about the former Padre: "Vince is a marvelous outfielder, with a throwing arm second only to his brother's, and, although his hitting is a bit weak, the ball travels when he connects."

It was an opportune time for Vince to get away. "My mother later told me that she threw the sheets over everything and we headed east," says Joanne DiMaggio Webber. Vince was taking not only his wife but their baby daughter, whose birth the previous fall had prevented him from being at the World Series with his mother and brothers. Vince was in a bit of hot water again with Giuseppe. Joanne was named after Madeline's mother, which was not according to Sicilian tradition. Once again, Vince was the rebel. And once again, he found it best to go play baseball and prove himself if he wanted to return to his father's good graces.

That the Bees had sent a pitcher, Jim Chaplin, outfielder Rupert

Thompson, and $20,000 to the Padres in exchange for Vince meant they expected more than a benchwarmer. As O'Doul said, Vince was already an excellent center fielder—he had led all Pacific Coast League outfielders the previous year with 31 assists—and at the plate he could send the ball a mile, though even in exhibition games, opposing pitchers found they could make him miss more than he should.

"Vince doesn't hit as frequently as some but his bat speaks with plenty of extra-base authority," reported the *Brooklyn Eagle* in its spring training update from Florida. The comparisons to Joe began immediately: "Vincent DiMaggio follows the well-defined footprints of his famous kid brother. But neither his price tag nor his name assures him a regular job in the Boston outfield. He'll have a lot of opposition."

It was a happy circumstance in February 1937 that both the Yankees and the Bees trained in St. Petersburg, allowing Joe and his brother to grab dinner some days after practice and home preseason games. That Vince was the older brother and Joe already a big star in baseball made for some ribbing between the two. Both were still young enough and uncertain enough about their futures to avoid genuine rivalry. They hoped that Dominic would somehow do well enough that a big league team would purchase his contract from the Seals. Wouldn't it be great if all three brothers were eating steaks in Florida next spring?

The only time Vince and Joe would face off all year—unless the Bees got to the World Series, which was highly unlikely—was an exhibition game between Boston and New York. But Joe didn't play. He was benched with a sore arm. "I couldn't throw without pain but kept telling myself that the warmer weather would bring the arm around."

It didn't. When a physician examined him, he diagnosed enlarged tonsils and an infected tooth, neither directly connected to his right arm. For the second year in a row, Joe went north by himself. He had the tonsils and the tooth removed. When he made his season debut on May 1, he went 3-for-4 and his arm was fine. Now he wore number 5, which clubhouse manager Pete Sheehy had given him. No subtlety there: Ruth had worn number 3, Gehrig number 4, and now it was Joe's turn to join the pantheon of pinstripers.

The press didn't give Vince much of a grace period as he prepared to make his debut with the Bees. Writing while on a train heading north from spring training, Joe Williams began his column in the *New York World-Telegram:* "You get to talk with a lot of baseball people in the South—managers, scouts, old players, current stars. There were two things most of the baseball people I talked with agreed on unanimously. One was that Joe DiMaggio was going to be an enduring sensation in the majors. The other was his brother Vincent wouldn't last beyond mid-season. And the odd part of this is the baseball people concede Brother Vincent has almost as much mechanical ability as Joe. It seems to be a question of temperament. One brother's got it and the other hasn't."

Williams continued: "Nothing ever seems to disturb Joe. On the other hand, Vincent is addicted to nervous moods. Joe plays as if he knows he's good; Vincent as if he isn't sure. The two brothers are alike in mannerisms at the bat and in the field. In the unimportant practice maneuvers, it is difficult to tell them apart. But when the game starts and the pressure is on, Joe stands out and Vincent doesn't. The baseball people"—none of whom, apparently, covered the '36 All-Star Game—"say this is a mental condition. They say Joe has made himself a great player because he has confidence in himself, something Vincent lacks."

Denigrating Vince by comparing him to Joe was contagious. Jimmy Cannon, who would go on to become one of the more famous sports reporters and columnists in the country (and a confidant of Joe's), covered the May 16 game when the Brooklyn Dodgers visited Boston. After the Bees managed to tie the game against Van

Lingle Mungo and send it into extra innings, Vince came up with the pitcher Danny MacFayden on second.

Cannon reported: "By the way, it was Vincent, The Wrong DiMaggio, the Mussolini of the North Side, who chopped in the winning run in the eleventh with a well-hit single which rolled almost to the centerfield fence as MacFayden ran all the way home from second."

So much for Vince's not standing out when the pressure was on. It was the beginning of a turnaround for him after struggling at the plate in the first weeks of the season. That so little was expected of him or the Boston Bees may have helped him to relax.

Meanwhile, Dominic was on the opening day roster of the Seals, but unlike his brother Joe four years earlier, he wouldn't be in the starting lineup. He had a lot to learn. And, it was hoped, some more growing to do. A photograph of the team at the beginning of the season shows Dominic sitting second from left in the first row, looking more like a batboy than a professional baseball player. With his fragile appearance and eyeglasses, he already had the nickname "Little Professor." O'Doul, however, saw not only the talent in him but the fierce determination not to be left behind by his brothers.

Richard Leutzinger, in his biography of O'Doul, wrote about Dom: "Early in his career, many thought he was a mediocre talent, trying to cash in on big brother Joe's name and fame. The need to refute that accusation may have made him the most determined of the three brothers."

The Seals started Dominic at third base. That didn't last long. Dominic recalled that "in the process of throwing [the ball] to first base it landed right up in the bleachers." With an arm like that, the team moved him to the outfield. When he got the chance to play early in the season, he usually made the most of it, at bat and in the field. On April 23, his double drove in the winning run in a 3–2 game against the Seattle Indians. It was reported after the next game: "Like Joe, like Vince, like Dominic! The third of the DiMaggio brothers, who at 20 is playing in the outfield for the San Francisco Seals, threw out two members of the Seattle Indians when they tried to stretch singles into doubles."

Offensively, Dominic's secret weapon was O'Doul. It was obvious that, unlike his brothers, Dominic would not hit for power with his comparatively slight stature. He had to be a contact hitter—more like O'Doul had been. The manager worked hard with Dominic, teaching him various hitting techniques. "Always look for the fastball, and you can always hit the fastball or the curveball off the fastball," he emphasized to his willing pupil. O'Doul also worked on Dominic's stance, teaching him how to square up at the plate and be balanced. "Well, I could hit, but I would not have been able to hit in the professional ranks with my [previous] stance," Dominic realized. "I might have been a .200, .210, .215 hitter, and I would not have been hitting a lot of long balls. But the change that Lefty performed on me, that turned me completely from just a so-so hitter into a good hitter."

BACK IN ACTION and knocking the hide off the ball batting in front of Gehrig, Joe also impressed teammates and fans with the way he patrolled center field. If anything, he was even more graceful than in his rookie year—almost every play looked easy. He was like a maturing colt, his long legs eating up long distances as he loped after towering flies and liners alike; his keen sense of where the ball was every second was helped immeasurably by reflexes and a hypersensitive hearing that allowed him to be on the move an instant after the crack of the bat.

Joe had a slightly different outfield to learn the first few weeks of the season. In an acknowledgment that the Gehrig era was giving way to the DiMaggio era—and "Ruthlessly" so, one might say— the Yankees had made the Stadium more homer-friendly for right-handed batters. After they replaced the aging wooden structure in left-center and center with concrete bleachers closer to home plate, the "Death Valley" that had existed since Yankee Stadium opened in 1923 was not quite as imposing. The franchise was signaling that it would look after its new golden boy.

But Joe's maturing physical strength—he was now a lean but solid 200 pounds—and his year of experience with American League pitching were probably more responsible than changed Stadium dimensions for the 'taters flying off his bat. In one game against the Browns, he hit a Howard Mills pitch 450 feet into the left-field seats, the farthest a ball had ever been hit in that direction. On July 5, Joe hit his first major league grand slam.

Another way the Yankees organization looked after Joe was in assigning Lefty Gomez as his roommate. Six years older than DiMaggio, the pitcher was from the Bay Area and had been with the Yankees since 1930, so he really knew the ropes in New York and the other cities where the team played, on and off the field. In several ways he took up where another Lefty (O'Doul) had left off, giving Joe on-site advice and demonstrating how to be a big league ballplayer and celebrity.

It couldn't have been easy. Joe was not a talker and not much of a socializer. He was coming out of his shell a bit as he started hitting a few New York watering holes—in one, he was introduced to a head waiter named Bernard Shor whom everyone called "Toots"—but on road trips he stayed in his hotel room. Gomez later recalled that a highlight of the week for Joe was Wednesday, because that was when the next *Superman* comic hit the newsstands. To keep this obsession out of the newspapers, the much-less-recognized Gomez bought the comics for his roommate.

The presence of three Italian-American stars on the team—DiMaggio, Crosetti, and Lazzeri—led to the inevitable ethnic jokes from teammates. Reportedly, during a laugher against St. Louis (as most games were against the hapless Browns that season), a Browns runner headed for second. Lazzeri and Crosetti raced toward the base, and Joe ran in from center to back up the play. He was only halfway there when Gomez threw the ball to him, and the runner was safe.

At the end of the inning, McCarthy growled to Gomez, "What the hell was that about?"

The pitcher replied, "Someone called out, 'Throw it to the dago,' but nobody said which dago."

The incensed manager yelled to his team, "Whoever said that, from now on, specify *which* dago!"

Not everyone was a Joe DiMaggio fan. In a column he might later have wanted to retract, the *Washington Post*'s Shirley Povich wrote: "The Yankees' young Italian boy is seemingly too goldarned content to hit his home runs and those long triples and let it go at that. He has none of Ruth's flourish and gusto, none of Dizzy Dean's self-admiration. And because of that, he will set no salary records no matter how many slugging records fall before the power of his bat."

In 1937 Giuseppe and Rosalie could also claim they had a movie star son. It was not unusual for sports stars in the first full bloom of fame to be asked to appear in a Hollywood production. Jack Dempsey, Walter Hagen, and Babe Ruth all gave acting a shot, though the roles were usually little more than cameo appearances to boost attendance for pedestrian productions. Joe's turn came that August. He agreed to deliver three lines—a total of only six words, though still a lot for Joe—in the musical comedy *Manhattan Merry-Go-Round* filmed at the Biograph studios in the Bronx. The lighthearted romp starred Ann Dvorak, Gene Autry, James Gleason, Cab Calloway, and a hot new sensation from New Orleans—and also the product of a Sicilian family—Louis Prima.

It took 12 takes for Joe to get through the scene. No wonder he never made another movie. Relieved that it was over, he chatted up one of the chorus girls, a blonde from Minnesota named Dorothy Arnold. Then Joe left for Yankee Stadium, with no inkling that he had just met his future wife.

* * *

VINCE WAS HAVING a solid season, playing hard and helping a bad Bees ball club get better. In a June 10 game against the
Cincinnati Reds, Vince showed his power potential by homering in
the fourth inning and then doubling in Gene "Rowdy" Moore in the
eighth for the Boston victory. A reporter wryly asked him after the
game if there were any other ballplayers in the family. Keeping a
straight face, Vince replied, "Just a guy named Joe."

The reporters in Boston became more tactful and supportive
of Vince as the season went on. In the other National League cities, however, he was peppered with questions about Joe, each one a
veiled criticism of him for being "the wrong DiMaggio." But Vince
went out there every game and played hard. What else could he do?

The 1937 All-Star Game gave Joe a chance to redeem himself
after his dismal performance the previous year. It was the first All-
Star Game attended by a sitting president, with Franklin Roosevelt
making the trip from the White House to Griffith Stadium, home
of the Washington Senators. There were familiar faces in the lineup
for the American League: New Yorkers Gomez, Gehrig, Rolfe,
and Dickey, as well as Mel Harder and Earl Averill of the Indians,
Charlie Gehringer and Hank Greenberg of the Tigers, and Lefty
Grove, Joe Cronin, and Jimmie Foxx from the Red Sox. Dizzy Dean
again started for the National League, as did Gomez for the "Junior
Circuit." In the bottom of the third inning, Averill hit a liner that
struck Dean in the foot and broke his toe. (When Dean returned to
pitching for the St. Louis Cardinals later that season before the toe
had healed, his changed delivery injured his arm. Though only 26,
he was never a dominant pitcher again, and at 31 the former ace of
the Gashouse Gang retired.) The AL cruised to an easy 8–3 victory.
Joe returned to New York feeling a lot better than he had a year earlier, not only because of the win but because he had notched his first
All-Star Game hit.

As the season progressed, the Yankees saw only token opposition from the Detroit Tigers and Cleveland Indians. The pitching was strong, led by Gomez and Ruffing, who would both win more than 20 games, and Bump Hadley contributed with 11 victories. Dickey was a workhorse behind and at the plate—he caught 140 games and batted .332 with 29 home runs and 133 RBI.

The club was easing out George Selkirk, who had replaced Ruth in the outfield in '35, and easing in Tommy Henrich. The Ohioan who earned the nickname "Old Reliable" would roam the green grass next to Joe into the 1950 campaign. He had begun the '37 season playing for the farm team in Newark. After ten days there, Henrich was batting .444. When Yankee outfielder Roy Johnson made light of a tough loss to the Tigers, McCarthy told Ed Barrow to trade him. Johnson was soon gone, and Henrich was promoted. By the end of the season, he had made the talent-rich Yankees richer.

He and Joe worked out a system in the outfield. "If I wanted the ball, I called for it, and DiMaggio gave it to me," Henrich told Fay Vincent many years later. "If I didn't call for it, get out of the way, because DiMaggio is gonna catch it. And it was as simple as that."

Joe tried to keep up with how Vince and Dominic were doing. Playing on three different teams in three different leagues, the brothers didn't often cross paths, and they had little direct contact with each other. The two older brothers called home to try to catch Dominic, and if he wasn't there, they got updates from Giuseppe. Their father still checked the sports section every morning on rising at 4:00 A.M., and now he had the activities of three sons to stay on top of. The local papers accommodated him by running a "DiMaggio Digest" every day that kept track of their baseball exploits. Giuseppe would relay information to the boys back east in a mixture of English and Sicilian.

"The DiMaggios were playing well from one coast to the other," Dominic explained. "The 'Digest' had a picture of each of us, plus a report on what we did the day before and a table showing our batting averages, number of games, runs, hits, doubles, triples, home runs, runs batted in, putouts, assists, and errors." Giuseppe and Rosalie were bursting with pride. In the house on Taylor Street, "pictures of three baseball players now shared the wall space which previously had been reserved only for Christian saints."

Joe genuinely wished the best for his brothers, though he could be a tad patronizing. "From almost the start of the season, stories were coming in from the Pacific Coast about another DiMaggio. This time it was Dominic, the kid the rest of us never thought would make a ballplayer because he was short and skinny and wore glasses. Dominic didn't look like a ballplayer."

Dominic continued to show that size didn't matter in Pacific Coast League competition. Under the scholarly appearance and friendly demeanor was a tough player who wouldn't back down. Most likely, the toughness was a product of DiMaggio stock, enhanced by being the youngest of nine children, with four older brothers. Yes, Dominic was the baby of the family and at times had been treated as such. But in his view, being the baby also meant always having to prove he belonged at the grown-ups' table. That was doubly true in baseball for a player with the last name of DiMaggio.

Besides Dominic, there was not a lot of talent on the 1937 Seals. When the regular season ended, third baseman Frankie Hawkins had the highest batting average on the team. His .324 was modest compared to hometown hitters of the past. Dominic wasn't far behind, at .306. He could get on base, he ran aggressively, he made few mistakes, and nothing got by him in center field. O'Doul pulled a rabbit out of a hat and got the Seals to second place, at 98-80, missing first place by four games. Dominic looked forward to the next season when, with O'Doul in his corner, he could build on his progress and maybe be ready for the majors. He had thrust himself into the starting lineup and appeared in 140 games with almost 500 at-bats. He hit only five home runs, but he saved a lot of runs for the Seals with a .967 fielding percentage in center.

When the Seals played the Padres during the season, Dominic and Vince's former teammate, Ted Williams, greeted each other warmly. Ted had begun to fill out and was showing more promise as a player. According to Joanne DiMaggio Webber, "My father had taught Ted Williams how to eat. Ted had been just skin and bones when he came to the Padres in 1936. My father would get him to eat better for his strength, and of course he could feast when the Padres were in San Francisco and my Grandmother Rosalie was cooking."

Ted's best friend on the Padres in the '37 season was Bobby Doerr. He and the infielder were two of the youngest members of the team, both liked fishing, and to kill time on road trips they went to the movies to watch Westerns. There was a little friendly competition too—who was going to make it to the majors first?

On road trips to Portland, Williams and Doerr became friendly with the clubhouse boy there, a homegrown product named Johnny Pesky, who had not yet impressed anyone as a player. So did Dominic. "I certainly do remember John as the clubhouse boy," he told Bill Nowlin for his biography of Pesky. "We'd come up to Portland and John was there and he took care of the clubhouse."

Williams wound up the season with a .291 average, 23 home runs, and 98 RBI. The Padres had an easy time of it in the play-offs. Williams got his club off to a fast start in the first game, going 4-for-5. The Padres swept Sacramento in the first round, then did the same to Portland and were handed the Governor's Cup. Before the year was over, the Red Sox gave Bill Lane some cash and four minor leaguers to purchase Williams from the Padres. Ted was less than thrilled: "I read about that for the first time in the paper and I was sick. The Red Sox didn't mean a thing to me. A fifth-, sixth-place club, the farthest from San Diego I could go. I sure wasn't a Boston fan."

+ + +

JOE TOOK ADVANTAGE of the Yankees' gift of a shorter Death Valley. For once, "Larrupin' Lou" Gehrig was not leading the team in home runs. His end-of-season totals of 37 round-trippers and 159 RBI would have led many teams, but Joe had emerged as the man brandishing the heavy lumber for the Bronx Bombers and at one point was on pace with Ruth's 1927 season.

His stance at the plate had become one of the most distinctive and imitated in the game. When Joe stepped into the batter's box, he stubbed his right toe into the dirt in back of his left heel. Then he spaced his feet precisely four feet apart, with more of his weight on his left leg. He stood erect with the bat on his right shoulder (no choking up) as he waited for the pitch. He was deep in the batter's box and close to the plate. Joe, it appeared, could wait until the last moment before deciding to swing at the ball.

In the second half of the season Joe faded from Ruth's pace, but he still showed an uncanny ability to get the right hit with men on base. The 167 runs he would knock in, in 151 games, would be one of the highest totals ever in Yankee history and his personal best, at age 22. These totals also demonstrated that Joe was already a great hitter no matter what the dimensions of the ballpark.

The Yankees steamrolled down the stretch. They finished with 102 wins and a .662 winning percentage. The Tigers saluted from afar, finishing an unlucky 13 games out. (The St. Louis Browns finished a woeful 56 games out.) Joe's 46 home runs led both leagues, with Greenberg and Gehrig finishing second and third in the AL. His .346 average was 21 points higher than his strong rookie year.

In the World Series, familiar faces were waiting for Joe, Gehrig, Dickey, Crosetti, Lazzeri, Gomez, and the rest of the Yankees: the New York Giants had again won the National League pennant.

Watching from a box at Yankee Stadium, Vince had better seats than any of his teammates enjoyed. The Boston Bees had played well down the stretch. They had no chance for a National League title, but after their dismal records of recent years, finishing over .500 would be a triumph. On September 14, they swept a doubleheader from the Cubs, 9–0 and 4–2. Vince helped out with his bat in the first game; in the second, he "suffered a possible fracture of his left collarbone in making a sensational catch of Stan Hack's high, short fly to left center. . . . DiMaggio was taken to a hospital." He was back in the lineup a few days later.

As the season drew to a close, it seemed that Vince's toughness—mental as well as physical—had won over many in the press. A columnist who wrote as "The Old Scout" opined in September, "All things considered, this has been a fairly satisfactory year for Vince DiMaggio. Vince fooled a lot of people, including Owner Bob Quinn, who had given up on him before the season was a month old. His hitting is improving, and there never was anything wrong with his fielding. He has helped the Bees far more than was expected." Vince, he went on, "is gaining confidence and with more experience and less ballyhoo about the fact that he is the brother of the Yankee star, he is expected to fan less frequently and improve his average of .260 or thereabouts."

Vince came close, batting .256. It would be his lowest as a professional. The Bees finished fifth in the eight-team league.

As his wife had done the previous fall, Giuseppe DiMaggio made the long cross-country trip to be at the 1937 World Series when it began in New York. He was accompanied on the train by Tom and Dominic.

"Yesterday," Bob Considine wrote in his *New York Daily Mirror* column after the elder DiMaggio's arrival, "was a considerable day in the life of a red-faced, stocky retired crab-fisherman. He had come all the way across the country from his native San Francisco, where he raised a brood of children in a section called Cow Hollow, to see one of his progeny—Joseph—play ball."

When Joe went off to batting practice, "Poppa DiMaggio stayed behind awhile, to puff one of the cigars Jim Braddock gave him and look out the window of the Mayflower Hotel. He would go out to Yankee Stadium in a little while, sit in the box seat his son had bought for him, and watch his boy play for the first time since Joe became a Yank."

Considine also revealed to his New York audience a new DiMaggio venture in San Francisco, a seafood restaurant on Fisherman's Wharf named Joe DiMaggio's Grotto. "Tom DiMaggio looks after that too, and Mike, who keeps to the sea he has always known, supplies it with its seafood." Giuseppe was impressed when Angelo Rossi, the mayor of San Francisco, became a regular customer. It was a piece of the American Dream when the mayor came to shake your hand and eat your food.

The first game of the Series was tight, with the Giants clinging to a 1–0 lead into the sixth inning, Carl Hubbell and Gomez dueling. In the bottom of the inning, the Yankees broke through when Joe drove Gomez in. When the inning was over, the Yankees were up 7–1, and they would cruise to an 8–1 triumph. There was an identical outcome the next day, this time Red Ruffing gaining the win and Joe having his second straight 2-for-4 game. It was only slightly better for the Giants at the Polo Grounds—they lost 5–1.

They finally won in Game 4, 7–3, staving off elimination. (Gehrig hit his 10th World Series homer, and it would prove to be his last.) But they lost the next game, 4–2. According to one account, "Papa DiMaggio, who came all the way from San Francisco to 'see Joe hit some home runs,' finally was rewarded when his big son catapulted a drive a few feet inside the left field line in the third inning of yesterday's finale." Joe and his teammates would each receive $6,500 in winner's money.

During the off-season, Tom ran the restaurant on Fisherman's Wharf, Mike supplied the fish, and Vince, Joe, and Dominic were on hand to greet customers and talk baseball. Tom and Joe had an idea of what to do with some of the fourth son's money—buy their parents a house. If there was a silver lining to the Depression, it was that anyone with money to spare could get a lot for it.

The DiMaggios found a house on Beach Street in the Marina District. Among the "amenities" that Giuseppe and Rosalie hadn't enjoyed on Taylor Street were a garage and a living room. To the immigrant, middle-aged couple, their new home was a palace, and baseball had bought it for them.

EIGHT

THE NEW YORK YANKEES made a curious move for the 1938 season: they got rid of Tony Lazzeri, shipping him to the Chicago Cubs. They replaced him with a talented farmhand, Joe Gordon, but still, the team was tinkering with the core Italian-American group from San Francisco. That group included the man emerging as their best player, which he would presumably be for at least a decade. It was incredible, then, when general manager Ed Barrow sent the American League home run champion a contract with the salary set at the same $15,000 as the season before.

When Tom DiMaggio eyed the insulting contract in San Francisco, he told Barrow, no dice. Colonel Ruppert demanded that Joe appear in his office on January 21. Joe told Barrow and the Colonel that he wanted $40,000, almost giving them both heart attacks. They claimed that even Gehrig didn't make that much. Joe was unimpressed with the $25,000 counteroffer. Take it or leave it, Ruppert told him. Joe left, returning to San Francisco.

The Yankees were not accustomed to such insolence. This 23-year-old son of a Sicilian immigrant who grew up in a house that stank of fish and who could hardly put a sentence together was refusing to play ball with the marquee ball club of the major leagues? The Yankees leaked stories to the press about how greedy Joe was, a tactic they would use for decades with rebellious players. Joe looked worse in the public eye when the club announced that Gehrig had signed a contract worth $39,000.

The holdout gave Joe and Dominic their only opportunity to spend spring training together. The Seals were getting ready for the season at their facility in Hanford, southeast of San Francisco, near Fresno. Joe wanted to be ready for the season himself whenever his brother Tom approved a contract offer. He called Lefty O'Doul, who invited Joe to camp. This could have been an awkward situation for Dominic, who had earned the starting center fielder job, but Joe mostly took batting practice.

Players and reporters who said Joe never got angry on the ball field missed a scene in Hanford, which may have indicated the stress he was feeling from his ongoing feud with Ruppert and Barrow. One afternoon a left-hander trying to make the Seals, Jimmy Rego, was on the mound. Joe sent one ball after another over the fence, each one farther than the last one. Rego realized he'd better forget practice and pitch like it was a real game or O'Doul would send him home. He cut loose. Rego recalled to David Cataneo: "And, Jesus, I was throwing hard and shoving the bat right up his ass. [Joe] was so pissed off. He threw the bat halfway out to the mound. He said, 'You son of a bitch, what are you trying to do, pitch a ball game?' I said, 'No, but it sure looks like it, doesn't it?' And he walked off the diamond."

But he stayed in San Francisco. The Yankees continued spring training in St. Petersburg, and when that wrapped up they worked their way up to New York, playing a few exhibition games along the way. Seeing an opportunity to go from worst to first, the St. Louis Browns offered $185,000 for Joe, but Ruppert said he wasn't for sale. New York opened the season—the third consecutive year without

Joe in the lineup—with an 8–4 loss in Boston. After three games, with his team 1-2, Tom and Joe gave in and sent a telegram that Joe was getting on a train heading to New York.

When he got there, he signed for $25,000. But because it would be almost two weeks into the season before he could play, the Yankees docked him $1,800. Tom and Joe wouldn't forget this. Dominic made note of it too. When he got to the major leagues, he would be one of the pioneers of what became the players' union.

That winter, Vince's former teammate Ted Williams had headed east with hopes of cracking the roster of another Boston club, the Red Sox. The Sox had invited Williams to spring training in Sarasota. Ted made the trip with borrowed money. In his first appearance on the field, his player-manager, Joe Cronin, yelled at him and called him "kid." It stuck. (The "Splendid Splinter" nickname came later.) When spring training ended, the 19-year-old was farmed out to Minneapolis.

One of the more famous stories told about Williams's departure from Sarasota involves starting outfielders Ben Chapman, Doc Cramer, and Joe Vosmik. They were riding Ted hard for being cocky. He said to Johnny Orlando, the trainer, "Tell them I'll be back, and tell them I'm going to wind up making more money in this frigging game than all three of them put together."

For the time being, Ted had to borrow more money, this time from Orlando, to hop a bus. He came to like Minnesota. When he wasn't at the ballpark, he was off in the woods hunting or fishing. When he was at the ballpark, he was busy whacking the ball to all fields. By the end of the season, Ted had accumulated a .366 average with 46 home runs and 142 RBI. Bobby Doerr had beaten him to Boston, playing in 55 games that year for the Red Sox. There was no doubt, however, that they would be reunited in Beantown the next year.

While Dominic wore glasses unapologetically, Vince wasn't fond of them. Late in the 1937 season, he had worn them at bat (not in the field), and he claimed it was because he saw the ball better that his average rose. But he hoped that was only a temporary solution. A '38 spring training newspaper item offered that Vince "has been taking eye exercises this spring by moving a pencil back and forth from arm's length up to his nose and following it with his eyes. As a result, he is hoping he won't have to don the spectacles this season."

He should have. Vince already had the reputation of striking out too often and having special trouble with curveballs from righties. During the 1938 season, there were more strikeouts—a lot more.

As the season moved into summer, Joe was not slugging homers the way he had in 1937, nor was he knocking in as many runs. His batting average was down a bit too. Some reporters speculated that the holdout had affected his outlook, and that the booing he was receiving in many ballparks from embittered baseball fans was opening chinks in his confidence. To some extent, this was true. The season Gehrig was having didn't help either. Faltering at the plate, the Iron Horse was not the menacing force batting behind Joe that he had been the previous two seasons. Conceding the obvious, during the season McCarthy altered the lineup, moving Gehrig down to the fifth spot and making Joe the cleanup hitter. Gehrig didn't complain, and Joe took the move as his due. He would never say this in public, but it was clear to him that the Yankees were becoming his team.

And Dorothy Arnold was becoming his girl. It was not an easy courtship. She was in Hollywood a lot going on auditions and nabbing a bit part here and there, while Joe was in New York or on road trips. The girl from Duluth was nothing like the sort of Sicilian woman Giuseppe and Rosalie would have picked for Giuseppe Jr., but Joe was a huge star and things would never again be normal for the DiMaggios. And he had bought his parents a house, so they weren't going to give him grief about anything.

There was already a spirited rivalry between the supporters of the Yankees and Red Sox. On May 30, almost 82,000 fans poured into Yankee Stadium to see the two teams in a doubleheader. Six thousand more were turned away. Boston's Lefty Grove was riding an eight-game winning streak, but Red Ruffing twirled a shutout. Joe and the rest of the lineup put 10 runs up on the scoreboard. Then the Yankees edged Boston 5–4 in the nightcap, which featured the player-manager Joe Cronin slugging it out with Yankee outfielder Jake Powell on the field and, after they were ejected, continuing their fight beneath the stands.

Joe would later write, "The going wasn't easy for us in 1938." Only a star on the Yankees could think that way. Cleveland and Detroit were playing better that season, but the only tough part for Joe McCarthy's squad was that they didn't ease into first place and remain there until mid-July.

McCarthy again managed the American League team in the All-Star Game, in Cincinnati, and again Gomez was the starter. This time he was opposed by the Reds lefty Johnny Vander Meer, who already that season had hurled two consecutive no-hitters, against the Bees (striking out Vince, of course) and the Dodgers. Joe, Gehrig, and Dickey also represented the Yankees.

It was a tight game until the seventh, when the National League surged ahead on a "bunt home run," a play not likely ever to be duplicated in the majors. Frank McCormick singled, and the next batter, Leo Durocher, was told to lay down a bunt. He did. Jimmie Foxx charged in from third, grabbed the ball, and threw it into right field, where Joe was playing. He fired the ball home to nab McCormick, but it flew over Dickey's head. McCormick scored, and before Dickey could come up with the ball, so too did the hustling Leo the Lip. The final score was 4–1.

What Joe should have written was that the season wasn't easy for *him*. It was another very good one with a .342 average (seven points behind league leader Foxx), 32 home runs (way behind Hank Greenberg's 58), and 140 RBI. However, "It wasn't a year I cared to look back upon for many reasons. First of all, I was booed around the league by the fans for having held out so long, which wasn't exactly pleasant." The other reason was a concern he shared with his teammates and front office—the approaching end of Gehrig's career.

The Yankee captain was only 35 when the '38 season ended, and he had played in 2,122 consecutive games. Conceivably, with his strength, stability, and modest habits, Gehrig could play at a high level for several more years, especially with Joe batting in front of him and Dickey behind him. But there was no hiding the weaker numbers: 29 home runs, 114 RBI, and, at .295, batting under .300 for the first time since 1925, his first full year on the Yankees. The Iron Horse was losing steam and giving way to the next great star in New York. No one, though, anticipated how swift and tragic the transition would be.

OUT IN SAN FRANCISCO, the Seals record had declined, but not by much, to 93-85. The ageless Sam Gibson won 23 games—throughout the 1930s he had been the perfect example of a really good (with flashes of brilliance) Pacific Coast League player who just could not cross the Rubicon to the major leagues. Gibson had Hall of Fame credentials—he had well over 200 wins in his PCL career and over 30 in the majors—but only on the West Coast.

Dominic was devoted to avoiding that fate. A good showing by him and the Seals in the Governor's Cup playoffs could earn him that coveted invitation to a big league club. He had finished the season having upped his average to .307, with 202 hits. He still hadn't displayed power—over 70 percent of his hits were singles—but he was hitting the ball harder. O'Doul had impressed upon him the value of strong wrists, and Dominic had worked hard to develop them. His value to the team was in getting on base and scoring runs. And as Vince had done in 1936, Dom led all PCL outfielders in assists. (He would repeat this feat the next season too.) The Seals eked out a berth in the playoffs by just a half-game over the Padres.

In the first round, San Francisco faced the Seattle Rainiers, who were led by 18-year-old rookie pitcher Fred Hutchinson and his 25-7 record. (He would go on to have a very good career as a coach and manager, helming the Cincinnati Reds, who won the 1961 National League pennant.) Dominic scored after greeting Hutchinson with a double in the first. The Seals went on to take two of three games in Seattle, and then they eliminated the Rainiers by taking a double-header in San Francisco. Dominic led the way, rapping out nine hits in the leadoff spot and going 2-for-2 with two walks and two runs scored in the clincher.

In the second and final round, they went up against the defending champion Sacramento Solons. The Seals dropped the first game, but Dominic's two hits helped his team to a 9–4 victory in the second one. The third game was a disaster for the Seals, a 22–3 thrashing. Three hits by Dominic couldn't prevent a 3–1 loss the next day. A 4–1 win in the next game gave the Solons the Governor's Cup. It had still been a good season for the Seals, and especially for Dominic.

The Yankees sailed into another Series, their victims this time the Cubs, with Lazzeri looking strange in the Chicago uniform. On hand again was Giuseppe, or "Papa," as many of the sportswriters referred to him. As the father of one of the most famous athletes in New York, he was viewed as something of a wise old sage who was as restrained verbally as young Giuseppe, yet he seemed to enjoy the attention. New York swept the underwhelming Cubs for their third consecutive world championship. Joe batted only .267 with a homer and two runs batted in, and Gehrig hit only .286 with no RBIs. But Dickey and Joe Gordon picked up the slack, and Ruffing and Gomez easily handled the Cubs lineup.

Giuseppe had a happy train ride back to San Francisco. It had been a satisfying year for his two youngest boys, Dominic and Joe. But signs pointed the other way for Vince. It looked like he might not stick around long enough to be in the big leagues with his two brothers. A new manager had greeted him at spring training: Casey Stengel. Then 48, Stengel was from Kansas City. He was nicknamed "the Old Perfessor" because he had coached the baseball team at the University of Mississippi before his major league playing career got on track. He began on the Brooklyn Dodgers in 1912, then played for the Pittsburgh Pirates, Philadelphia Phillies, New York Giants, and Boston Braves. His first stint as a manager was with the Dodgers in 1934. When the Bees had hired him the previous November, one of the first newspaper headlines he was associated with read: "Stengel Sees V. DiMaggio as a Great Asset." The subhead was, "Joe's Elder Brother Elegant Outfielder and Fine Hitter in a Pinch." The Old Scout's article began: "The astute Casey Stengel, new manager of the Boston Bees, was quoted as saying the other day: 'Watch Vince DiMaggio next year. He's going to be an outstanding asset of the team.'" The writer concluded, "Casey went out on the limb for Vince and the chances are he won't be far wrong."

Unfortunately, he was. It was a disappointing year for Vince, and an especially tough one to take given the year Joe had in the majors. More members of the press were pointing out the contrast in talents between the two brothers. As Joe collected more hits, Vince collected more whiffs at the plate. The manager never gave up on him, letting Vince play in 150 games with 540 at-bats, but the harder he tried the more pitches he missed. Pittsburgh columnist Bill Dooly wrote, "Vicious Vincent is noteworthy in that he's in the midst of creating slugging history that methinks will send his name roaring down the ages. A hitter remindful of his brother Joe only in that both use a bat, Vincent is specializing in striking out. Perhaps the greatest 'misser' to ever swing a bat at a ball without touching it, the Boston Bees' member of the DiMag family has already eclipsed the all-time National League record for whipping the ozone and is now going heavily for top honors to both leagues."

Vince attained that dubious honor. He led the National League in strikeouts. In fact, his 134 strikeouts were a new major league record. He broke the one set by Gus Williams of the St. Louis Browns back in 1914, and Vince's record would not be surpassed for almost three decades. Vince remained one of the best fielders in the National League, but fans didn't pay to watch a DiMaggio merely roam center.

It didn't help Vince's cause that his club's own fans were paying increasing attention to the other Beantown team. Tom Yawkey had bought the Red Sox in 1933, and his willingness to spend money on talent and the farm system in the intervening years was showing results. First baseman Jimmie Foxx, nicknamed "Beast," had a monster year, with a .349 batting average, 50 home runs, and 175 RBI. The Sox finished in second place. Though they were 9.5 games behind the Yankees, it was their highest finish in two decades. The Red Sox could be just one or two players away from dethroning New York.

Vince's days in Boston were numbered. The team hoped that his homers and his last name would be of value to other clubs and was trying to get something for him in a trade. Vince hoped to stay, thinking the club had good potential under a manager he liked. For several months, nothing happened. Then, the following February, as he prepared to head east for spring training, Vince received word that he had indeed been traded—to the Yankees. That he might share the outfield at Yankee Stadium with Joe—and, who knows, maybe Dominic someday—was exciting indeed.

NINE

VINCE WOULD BE GONE from the Yankees organization before he could even put pinstripes on. In February 1939, he was told to report to the Kansas City Blues, a Yankees minor league team in the American Association.

That stung. In addition to not being on the same roster as Joe, Vince would not be collecting a major league salary to support his family. And it was frustrating to be going backward to the minors. His first reaction was to try to buy his contract from the Blues and become a free agent. The club said no. Vince regrouped and decided that he was not going to sit around and mope about it. He'd had a rough 1938 season and obviously had work to do. Kansas City offered that opportunity. His new plan was to do well there and be called up by the Yankees.

For Dominic, the season couldn't begin fast enough. After two years of tutoring from Lefty O'Doul, he felt like a true hitter. All he had to do was lay it out there on the field. He was already one of the best outfielders in the Pacific Coast League, maybe the best center fielder of them all, as Vince and Joe once had been. At the plate he would drive the ball with more power now because he had put on weight, most of it muscle—when the Seals convened for spring training, he was at 171 pounds.

In Boston, owner Tom Yawkey and general manager Eddie Collins thought Ted Williams could be the final piece to fit into a pennant puzzle. Tall and lean and bursting with confidence after his excellent season in Minnesota (where he had met his future wife), Ted knew that this year he wasn't going anywhere but to Massachusetts after spring training. Like his future Red Sox teammate still in San Francisco, he couldn't wait for the season to begin.

On April 20, the Yankees and Red Sox squared off in the Bronx for opening day. It was the first time Joe DiMaggio and Ted Williams could look across a major league diamond and size each other up. It was also the first and last time Ted would play against a man he admired very much, Lou Gehrig. Red Ruffing struck Ted out twice. But on the third try, Ted lined the ball off the 407-foot sign in right-center for his first big league hit, a double. Even Joe wasn't fast enough to catch up to it. Announcing himself to Boston fans on opening day at Fenway Park against the Athletics, Ted went 4-for-5, including his first homer, which landed in the right-center bleachers. His first two hits on the day were off Cotton Pippen, who had struck him out in his first at-bat with the San Diego Padres in 1936. Only four games into the season, the *Boston Globe* cheered, "Ted Williams Revives Feats of Babe Ruth." He had yet to turn 21.

Of the young ballplayers in the American League, Ted appeared very soon to the press to be the one to challenge Joe DiMaggio. As the season went on, reporters noted their very different personalities at the plate, which to some extent mirrored their personalities off the field. Joe continued to stand rigid, disciplined, focused, gazing intently at the pitcher. Ted, from the left side, liked to wiggle his bat as his eyes danced around the field, processing where each player was positioned, and then almost as an afterthought he zeroed in on the pitcher, challenging the pitcher to get him out. The strike zone was branded on his brain, and he never had to guess—Ted *knew* if the pitch was a ball or strike. If it was called otherwise, the umpire was wrong. Joe rarely acknowledged the umpire, but Ted would glare when an umpire called a pitch wrong.

The Yankees were thankful that Joe could step up to the plate at all. For the first time in four years, he had survived spring training and opened the season with his teammates, among whom was a visibly fragile Gehrig. Though Colonel Ruppert had not exactly been a beloved figure, his death the previous January had been the first blow to the organization in 1939. (For Joe, the Colonel's death meant that when the club sent him a contract for the same $25,000 as in '38, he felt he had no choice but to sign it.) Now the foundation of the franchise on the field was showing cracks. Still, having Joe ready to play from the first day on made the Yankees even more confident of another championship.

Then came two more blows in a single week. On April 29, in a game against the Senators at Yankee Stadium, Joe ran to his right to chase down a single off the bat of Roberto Estalella. When his right shoe spikes got tangled in the wet grass, he went down hard and had to be helped off the field. The doctors' verdict was torn muscles in his lower right leg, quite possibly worse than anything that had kept Joe out before. He was to stay in Lenox Hill Hospital for further tests and treatment.

Three days later, Lou Gehrig removed himself from the lineup and was replaced by Babe Dahlgren at first base. Joe McCarthy was relieved that the captain did it before he had to, after watching Gehrig's sluggish movements and four measly singles in the first few games of the season. But the manager had lost his two superstars in one week.

While lying in bed, Joe had the opportunity to read through the May 1 issue of *Life* magazine. His photo took up most of the cover, and inside was a lengthy article by Noel F. Busch, "Joe DiMaggio: Baseball's Most Sensational Big-League Star Starts What Should

Be His Best Year So Far." In his book *Beyond DiMaggio: Italian Americans in Baseball,* Lawrence Baldassaro correctly chastises Busch for the ethnic stereotypes in the article, which includes a description of Joe as a "tall, thin Italian youth equipped with black hair" and "squirrel teeth" and the observation: "Instead of olive oil or smelly bear grease he keeps his hair slick with water. He never reeks of garlic." Otherwise, the article was a straightforward recounting of the DiMaggio story beginning with Giuseppe's arrival from Sicily. It noted that when Rosalie attended the 1936 World Series, she traveled across the continent "in a drawing room on a stream-lined train, carrying an armful of Italian sausages for Joe," and that the Fisherman's Wharf restaurant bearing Joe's name "makes a specialty of DiMaggio *cioppini,* a delicacy made out of crabs, tomatoes, sherry wine and garlic."

Joe soon got the good news that his injury was not as severe as first feared. He was moved to St. Elizabeth's Hospital for further treatment. It took a month before Joe was back in action, and he expressed to writers the hope that Gehrig would be right behind him. The Iron Horse, though, would soon get the death-sentence diagnosis of amyotrophic lateral sclerosis (ALS). He would never rejoin the Yankees in regular play. In 1939 the Bronx Bombers truly were Joe DiMaggio's team.

On May 11, nine days after Gehrig left the lineup, the Yankees jumped into first place. There they would stay for the rest of the season, earning the reputation of being one of the greatest teams in baseball history.

This was not great news for Vince. He had devoted himself to becoming a star in Kansas City, and his efforts were paying off. He was hitting with power, hitting in clutch situations to drive in runs, and he may well have been the best center fielder the fans there had seen. On May 17, the Blues moved into first place in the American Association thanks to a homer by Vince. That it was measured at 480 feet is suspect, but it was an impressive clout that drove in three runs.

By mid-June, his average was at .335. On June 9, the Blues hosted a "Ladies Night" crowd of over 21,000. According to the *Kansas City Times*: "Such a crowd, which squeezed from the stands into the field enclosure and from the stands upon the right field embankment, was the largest here in years. Its size and its enthusiasm gave full proof that these young Blues are baseball idols. And, for such a roaring crowd, the Blues performed in heroic cloth. Vince DiMaggio bulleted his twenty-fifth home run of the year over the scoreboard in the first inning; he later smashed out a long triple to right center."

Three days later, a crowd of almost 24,000 flowed into the ballpark. However, many of them came not to see their new star, Vince DiMaggio, but his brother Joe—the Yankees were in town for an exhibition game. Harold Burr's coverage began: "This is the story of the brother of a hero. Vince DiMaggio, first brother-in-waiting to the Yankees' Joltin' Joe, hopes one day to play in the outfield at the Stadium and even dreams of an all-star DiMaggio outfield in the big leagues." The crowd also came out to see Gehrig, who hadn't played in six weeks. His last appearance as a player was in this game against the Blues, and his last at-bat was a grounder to second baseman Jerry Priddy. An item in the next day's *Kansas City Times* reported that Gehrig "remained here and leaves this morning for the Mayo clinic in Rochester, Minn., where the veteran intends to undergo a physical examination."

The Blues lost 4–1. Vince had a single and a walk in four at-bats. Joe played five innings, then told McCarthy his wrist hurt and he was done for the day. Interviewed after the game, before he and Joe grabbed a quick dinner (the Bombers had to leave town that night), Vince didn't talk about himself but about how Dominic was coming along with the Seals. "Gee, it would be great if we all ended up with the Yanks," Vince told reporters.

Dominic was indeed thriving on the field in San Francisco, having the year he had hoped for. The Seals contended through the 1939 season, led by the old and the young. Achieving almost legendary status for his durability, hurler Sam Gibson was having another fine year. Dominic was hitting everything in sight—not over fences so much, but lining the ball to all fields. In the middle of the season he flirted with .400.

He noticed more scouts showing up at Seals Park as well as in Los Angeles, San Diego, and other cities where his team played. In June the Cubs sent Clarence "Pants" Rowland, their top scout, to the West Coast "to look over Joe's little brother," it was reported. "The fact that the Cubs sent Rowland indicates special interest." The Associated Press reported that the Yankees had sent Joe Devine to watch Dominic play and speculated, "The Yankees may not appear to need Dominic, 21 years old [sic], a righthanded batter and thrower, but two DiMaggios in that New York outfield wouldn't do any harm at the box office, and Dom can handle the chores satisfactorily. . . . In a recent series against Hollywood not a single Hollywood runner advanced a base after Dom nabbed a fly. They all respect his precise throw."

Dominic felt that this was the season that would catapult him into the major leagues. Then he was sidelined by a wrist injury. As he recuperated, he hoped the wrist injury wouldn't affect his status in the market the same way the leg injury had done for Joe five years earlier.

In May, Ted Williams was the first player to hit a ball out of Briggs Stadium in Detroit, a feat that wouldn't be duplicated until Mickey Mantle did it 18 years later. He would turn only 21 in August, and as many in the press anticipated, he was already giving notice to Joe that this other kid from California was ready to share the spotlight.

Williams ate, slept, and dreamed baseball. His roommate that season was the pitcher Charlie Wagner, called "Broadway" for the stylish way he dressed. At night Wagner was more apt to be found in a bar than asleep in their room. Williams had asked to room with him because he'd been told that Wagner didn't drink and went to bed early. Ted didn't realize that report was a joke. One night when

Wagner actually was asleep, he was rudely awakened when his bed fell apart under him. Ted had been practicing his swing, and his bat hit the bedpost.

"I never saw a fellow that had baseball on his mind twenty-four hours a day," Elden Auker, another Boston pitcher, told Fay Vincent. "We had a mirror in the clubhouse and you'd see Williams up there about every single day taking dry swings and studying his swing."

THE YANKEE OFFENSE didn't skip a beat with Gehrig's departure. The day he took himself out of the lineup, the Yanks beat Detroit 22–2. Charlie Keller had been promoted from the Newark farm club, and he fit right into the hit parade, which became a full charge against American League competition when Joe returned. Joe immediately reestablished himself as one of the best hitters in baseball, with his average soaring toward .400. He tripled in his very first at-bat after returning from the leg injury. The Yankees were almost sadistic against second-division clubs. In a doubleheader against the Philadelphia Athletics, a once-proud franchise still owned and managed by Connie Mack, they clubbed 13 home runs.

There was another reason the Yankees were glad to have Joe back—he had become their biggest draw since Ruth's peak years. "Joe DiMaggio, greatest of the current crop of major league ball players and unquestionably destined for a niche at Cooperstown, today goes on display again in the Stadium," gushed Dan Daniel. "Once more the Yankees present an alluring player with box office magnetism as well as all the technical superlatives."

Even one of the saddest events in the history of sports didn't distract the Yankees. On July 4, the organization honored Gehrig. "Boy, that was a solemn deal," Tommy Henrich recalled decades later. "Especially when he says, 'I consider myself the luckiest man in the world.' What in the world, everybody knew by that July."

Gehrig had gotten the diagnosis two weeks earlier, from physicians at the Mayo Clinic. Ed Barrow and Joe McCarthy had to spread the word that the Iron Horse was not only done as a player, but that the rest of his life could be measured in months. Joe and the rest of his shocked teammates, as well as members of the Washington Senators, stood on the field as the main event of Lou Gehrig Day—an event unlike anything baseball had seen before—got under way after the first game of a doubleheader.

Shirley Povich's coverage in the *Washington Post* began: "I saw strong men weep this afternoon, expressionless umpires swallow hard, and emotion pump the hearts and glaze the eyes of 60,000 baseball fans in Yankee Stadium. Yes, and hard-boiled news photographers clicked their shutters with fingers that trembled a bit."

Gehrig began his brief address to the crowd by saying, "Fans, for the past two weeks you have been reading about the bad break I got. Yet today I consider myself the luckiest man on the face of this earth. I have been in ballparks for seventeen years and have never received anything but kindness and encouragement from you fans." After thanking the late Miller Huggins and Colonel Ruppert, McCarthy, Barrow, his mother-in-law, his parents, and his wife, he concluded, "I may have had a tough break, but I have an awful lot to live for."

It was very odd not to see Gehrig in the starting lineup at the All-Star Game, especially since it was played at Yankee Stadium. But New York had even more players on the American League roster than the year before: Red Rolfe, Bill Dickey, Joe Gordon, a revived George Selkirk, Ruffing, and Joe. Gehrig was on hand as the team's captain. Joe hit his first "Summer Classic" homer, and the American League won 3–1. Ted Williams did not make the team, as Joe had done as a rookie.

BY THIS STAGE, Joe DiMaggio was the toast of New York City's nightclubs, a role that, in his quiet way, he clearly enjoyed. Plenty of women were available, and he was such a celebrity that it didn't matter if he fed them any good lines or not. So his teammates and night-life friends must have wondered if it was a good idea when it became obvious that summer that he and Dorothy Arnold were heading for the altar. But he liked Dorothy. She was lovely, she adored him, and he was intrigued by her upper Midwest background, which was very different from his own. Maybe he even loved her.

Dorothy had left high school and her home in Duluth at 15 to join a traveling musical show. For the next three years, she racked up a lot of miles singing and dancing and acting in summer stock theater in New England. She decided to stay put in New York City and audition for bit parts. One of them turned out to be in *Manhattan Merry-Go-Round*. Two years later, in the spring of 1939, Dorothy was telling friends and reporters that Joe had asked her to marry him and the ceremony would take place that summer. Joe denied it, or at least said there was no wedding date set. Before the summer ended, and with a pennant race in full swing, Joe gave in. He and Dorothy would be married after the season, in San Francisco.

Wedding plans weren't going to distract him from being the best in baseball. A play against the Detroit Tigers demonstrated how good a center fielder Joe was—and also that he could still make a mistake, surprising his teammates. With one out, former Pacific Coast League player Earl Averill was on first, and at the plate was the powerful Hank Greenberg, who launched one deep to left-center at Yankee Stadium. Joe had taken off as soon as he heard the crack of the bat. As his outfield teammate Henrich later described it, Joe "ran as fast as he could to the center-field fence and when he got within one full stride—that would be about seven or eight feet—over his left shoulder, he turned his head to the left, and there is the ball. And he got his glove up and caught the ball. And that is the first time he looked for that ball since the crack of the bat. I call that the best one I ever saw. I'm telling you, DiMaggio was impressed by that too."

What Henrich knew—Joe, of course, would answer reporters' postgame questions with the fewest words possible—was that with his head down Joe began loping toward the infield. He thought there were three outs, but the ball he caught was only the second out.

Averill, who had rounded second on the sure double or triple, scampered back to first and was standing there by the time Joe looked up.

Only the Red Sox could make the Yankees sweat as they pursued their fourth consecutive American League title. The second week of July, Ted Williams & Co. arrived at Yankee Stadium with a seven-game win streak. They beat the Yankees in three straight games. The home team suddenly appeared rudderless without their ailing captain. They looked for leadership from the 24-year-old Joe.

But even after that nightmare series, the Yankees were still in first place. They snapped out of their funk, returned to their winning ways, and opened up a lot of space between themselves and the rest of the AL teams. There was no need for a stretch drive, they just needed to show up to play. When the season ended, New York had 106 wins and had been out of first place only 10 days all year. The Yankees were the only team in history to have earned 11 league pennants.

As late as September 8, when he was batting .408, it looked like Joe would be the first major leaguer since 1930 to bat over .400. Then his left eye became infected and inflamed. He went up to bat practically one-eyed. He wouldn't ask out of the lineup, and McCarthy, even though he saw his center fielder struggling, wouldn't pull him. It was amazing that Joe still collected hits at all, but he was at nothing like his previous pace. When the season ended, his average was a still-remarkable .381, first in the American League, yet disappointing too.

Many years later, at a banquet in Toronto, Joe and Bobby Doerr got to talking about the 1939 season. Joe said he thought it was the best of his career. But in a rare admission, he said, "We had the pennant clinched. I should have hit .400 that year. But Joe McCarthy insisted that I play. I just couldn't see the ball. I never could understand why he made me stay in the lineup." By then, Joe knew that Ted Williams, not him, had been the last man in baseball to bat over .400.

In 1939 Williams did everything he could to thwart the Yankees and bring a pennant to Fenway Park. He batted .327, hitting at least one home run in every American League park, the one at Yankee Stadium coming during the last game of the season. He became the first rookie to lead the American League in runs batted in, with 145.

"I can't imagine anyone having a better, happier first year in the big leagues," he later wrote. "Babe Ruth declared me 'rookie of the year.' They didn't have an official rookie-of-the-year award then, so that was good enough for me. Later the Boston writers made the same designation. The fans in right field were yelling with me and for me all the time, really crowding in there to see what I would do next, and that year nobody tipped or waved his hat more than I did."

But it wasn't enough. The Red Sox finished in second place, 17 games back. Clearly they were still a couple of players away from the AL crown. The first of those players would soon be on his way.

When the season ended for the Seals, Dominic's .360 batting average—53 points higher than in 1938—was second in the PCL. Dominic was first in the league in hits and runs scored, and second in stolen bases. He excelled again in the field too, leading the PCL with 27 assists. The Seals fell 4.5 games short of capturing first place, with Seattle taking the title. But their 97-78 record was a hit with the fans, and O'Doul—who at age 42 had batted .400 in 25 games—was more popular than ever in San Francisco.

He had become close to Dominic and was his biggest booster. O'Doul said he "had a quality a lot of otherwise great ballplayers lack: baseball instinct. He did the kind of things they don't put in the record books or box scores. When Dom was batting, his opponents didn't dare fall asleep. Dom would be at the next base before they woke up. When he got a single, his thought was 'second is the next base, then third.' Dom wasn't the kind of ballplayer who thinks, 'Well, I got my single for the day.' He kept his eye on the ball and was gone like a rabbit. He took perfect care of himself and he gave his utmost. He never had the natural talent of a great star, but he did things for me that his brother Joe never did."

There was no reason for a major league club *not* to sign Dominic. O'Doul approached his friend Bill Terry, still managing the New York Giants, but Terry said he didn't think Dominic could hit big league pitching. Worse, Prescott Sullivan, a columnist for the hometown *San Francisco Examiner,* wrote, "You can have him, dirt cheap, glove and all, for $25,000," the same amount Joe had signed for after a serious leg injury.

This time, however, Cronin wasn't going to miss out on a DiMaggio. The Red Sox offered the Seals $75,000 for Dominic's contract. It was an "I told you so" moment for O'Doul when he predicted to San Francisco reporters, including one from the *Examiner,* "He'll be a sensation up there—a positive sensation. He can't miss. I'm glad he's going to Boston because Boston is one town where the fans know and appreciate all-around good ball players. Boston is going to idolize Dom."

ALL THROUGH THE '39 season, Vince had done everything he could to be called up by the Yankees—driving in runs, crushing homers, covering the outfield. He had become a fan favorite. It had been the best season of his career. And Vince made a few lifelong friendships on the Blues. One was with another Italian-American player. "Phil Rizzuto was my babysitter," Joanne DiMaggio Webber recalls. "He was like a kid himself and lots of fun, and a very sweet man. And yes, he was scared to death of the lightning in Kansas City, he would always dislike going back there. Phil played all those years with Joe once he got to the Yankees, but he was more friendly with my father then than I think he ever was with Joe."

But the cruising Yankees had no need for an outfielder—especially not a center fielder, with Joe remaining healthy. And with Joe now as popular as he could possibly be in New York, there was no PR value in adding Vince to the roster. There was value in trading him, though, for prospects. On August 4, when Vince slammed his 37th and 38th homers, he was called into the Kansas City office to talk to Roy Hamey. He was sure this was it. He was going to New York. Instead, Hamey told him that when the season ended he was being shipped to the Cincinnati Reds for two minor leaguers and $20,000.

It hit him hard. The Reds already had a good team and were in a fight for the National League pennant. There was no open position for Vince to step into. At first, he kept trying while still with the Blues—he hit eight more home runs to finish the season with 46 and 136 RBI, leading the American Association. The Blues took first place in the league. Then they lost in the first round of the playoffs, and Vince packed his bags for Cincinnati. There, he just couldn't shake his disappointment. Appearing in only eight games at the end of the Reds' season, Vince hit an embarrassing .071.

The Reds won the pennant. It would have been wonderful for the DiMaggio family if Vince and Joe had faced off in the Series, but because he didn't join the Reds until after September 1, Vince was not eligible to play in the Series. If he went at all, it would have to be with tickets from Joe. In a way the Reds did Vince a favor, because they never stood a chance. The closest they came was in the first game, at Yankee Stadium, when they held New York to two runs, but the Yanks' Ruffing gave up only one. The Yankees went on to sweep the Series in four games.

The New York juggernaut had won 16 of the 19 World Series games played since Joe joined the team, including the last nine straight. If the Yankees could be this strong without Lou Gehrig and with Joe being only in his midtwenties, it seemed they could be world champions indefinitely. As Joe wrote: "I had come to the Yankees a naive kid of 21 and now I was an established regular on a club which was a champion among champions. With my forthcoming marriage, and all that had happened, I looked eagerly forward to 1940."

And why not? He had played four seasons in the major leagues and had four world championships to show for it.

The DiMaggios had two Most Valuable Players in the family that year. Joe was voted MVP of the American League. Dominic was named the MVP of the Pacific Coast League.

THE WHOLE CLAN gathered in San Francisco for Joe's wedding. They'd set the date for November 19, two days shy of Dorothy's 22nd birthday, six days before Joe turned 25. She had converted to Catholicism, pleasing Giuseppe and Rosalie. The ceremony took place at St. Peter and St. Paul, the church the DiMaggio brothers had attended as kids. Giuseppe and Rosalie were a bit bewildered by all the attention the event received. When the decade began, they were an immigrant couple still working tirelessly to raise their family. As the decade drew to a close, they were still a couple from the old country with limited English, but their sons were baseball stars. One was the most famous athlete in America (though a few might argue for heavyweight champion Joe Louis), he was about to marry a Hollywood actress from the hinterlands of Minnesota, and Mayor Rossi himself was a prominent guest.

A crowd estimated at 10,000 lined up to catch a glimpse of Joe and Dorothy going to and from the church. She managed to slip into the church without much notice, but Joe had to be escorted by police through the throng of mostly North Beach well-wishers. To these onlookers—some of whom, like Giuseppe and Rosalie, could remember the old country—this was a royal wedding.

Tom and Mike and their sisters (with their spouses and children, as all were married by this time) were already inside the church. Nelly, Marie, Frances, and Mamie were part of Dorothy's wedding party, while her sister, Irene Morris, was the maid of honor. Their parents from Duluth were also there. Dominic arrived in a cutaway tux like Joe's. "Isn't this silly?" he joked. "Someone just handed it to me and I had to put it on."

Tom, as the oldest brother—described by press accounts as the one "who always speaks for the family"—was Joe's best man. Dom and Vince were to serve as ushers, but Vince and Madeline arrived at the last minute and got caught up in the crowd outside. United Press reported that "San Francisco's North Beach Italian population turned out in a carnival spirit that jammed streets and broke police lines. Standing room was at a premium in the edifice and the crowd overflowed into Washington Square. Even the wedding party had to battle the crowd to get inside the church. One woman fainted in the crush at the doorway." Vince had to pound on a side door and prove that he was Joe's brother to get in.

According to newspaper accounts carried across the country, the most emotional of the DiMaggios was Marie, who through tears exclaimed, "I used to hold Joe in my arms—why, I raised him!" Cops escorted the newlyweds out of the church. After having photos taken at a studio, they arrived to cheers at the wedding reception at Joe DiMaggio's Grotto on Fisherman's Wharf, where Mike still tied up his boat. Lefty O'Doul was there, along with many friends, now men, who had run with the DiMaggio boys in their North Beach days. While the reception was still in progress, Joe and Dorothy slipped off to begin their honeymoon.

Vince and Madeline had lived on their own from the day they were married seven years earlier, but Joe had a different idea about his new domestic life: why not just live in the Beach Street house bought with his money?

In *Joe & Marilyn*, Roger Kahn writes, "Joe may have expected Dorothy to become simply one more of the admiring and supportive DiMaggio women. She would decorate, pack suitcases for his trips, perform in bed, cook, and root. All that he excluded from his expectations were Dorothy's own needs. He wanted to live in San Francisco. She preferred Los Angeles or New York. He wanted a hausfrau, but picked a woman who had rejected domestic life for show business. He wanted a pliant pinup. Instead, he found someone with strong ideas of her own. The marriage never had a chance."

TEN

IT WAS A Pacific Coast League reunion when Dominic arrived at Boston's spring training facility in Sarasota and met teammates Ted Williams and Bobby Doerr. They had been born within 18 months of one another. Tom Yawkey was so pleased with Ted's 1939 season that he had doubled the rookie's salary to $10,000. In his third season with the Red Sox, the then-20-year-old Doerr had batted .318 with 73 RBI. A core group of hungry young players was forming. The Yankees just couldn't win five pennants in a row—no team ever had. Surely 1940 was Boston's turn.

"As a member of the Yankees in 1940, I had no idea what it was like to end the baseball year without a trip to the World Series," Joe recalled later. "I was about to be brought back to the reality that the Yankees were, in truth, mortal." He still made a heavenly salary, though, signing a contract for $32,500 before heading to St. Petersburg.

There was a high level of uncertainty in the spring training camps of all 16 major league teams. The 1939 season had been in full swing when Germany invaded Poland. No one knew at the time what would come of that, but in February 1940, with France, Great Britain, Italy, and other countries involved in fighting in Europe and Japan expanding its empire in Asia, there was no doubt that the world was at war and it wouldn't end soon. Would the Americans get involved? If they did—and most people thought they would—what would be the impact on the national pastime?

To make room for Dominic on the Red Sox roster, Joe Cronin had to cut a player. He had already sold the contract of 21-year-old Pee Wee Reese to the Brooklyn ball club for $75,000. Reese would go on to anchor the infield of the Dodgers for 18 years and be inducted into the Hall of Fame. Outfielder Joe Vosmik had a much less bright future in baseball, but he also attracted money from the Dodgers. The deal opened a spot for Dominic.

Joe's opinion of his youngest brother was improving. "Dominic came up with the best of recommendations. There was no longer any doubt that Dom was getting by on the family name. He was a ball player in his own right . . . indeed, I had no doubt that Dom would make the grade."

Boston's veteran catcher Moe Berg took one look at Dominic at early practices and declared to reporters, "You know me, I've seen a lot of rookies in my time. I don't go overboard with a splash. I don't say this boy will be better than his brother Joe. I wouldn't know about that. But this boy is a ball player; he has everything, all the ingredients—like cioppino." Reporters respected Berg's opinions. The Princeton graduate knew a dozen languages, including Japanese and Sanskrit.

With Vince in Tampa with the Cincinnati Reds, for the first time all three DiMaggio brothers were in major league spring training camps. Joe maintained that he was "happy over the fact that my brothers were in the major leagues with me," and there is no reason to doubt him.

In his syndicated column, Joe Williams wrote, "The old-time baseball writers used to refer affectionately to Henry Chadwick as the Father of Baseball. It would seem fitting to bestow this distinction today upon Pere DiMaggio. There is something unusual about a major league team that doesn't have one of his sons on it these days. We know of no other father who has contributed that many sons to the uplift and perpetuity of what is called the great national pastime."

It was not a fun rookie spring training camp for Dominic, however. During the very first exhibition game, Boston versus the Reds, he sprained an ankle sliding into home—and in a way it was Vince's fault. Williams came up with the bases loaded, Dominic on second and Johnny Peacock on third. The sophomore outfielder singled. Because he thought there was some chance it would be caught, Peacock hesitated. Dominic, with a better angle, saw that Vince wasn't going to get to the ball and took off. Vince grabbed the ball right after it bounced and fired a strike to the plate. Peacock slid safely into home. Right behind him, Dominic slid awkwardly to avoid spiking his teammate in the back. The ankle injury was the result. As John Kiernan reported in the *New York Times,* "The throw knew no brother, and Dominic was lifted from the ground and helped to the hospital ward for treatment."

Dominic recovered in time to be in the lineup at Griffith Park, against the Senators, on opening day of the season. "The first time I walked into Fenway Park was a day in April 1940," he recalled about the subsequent home opener. "There was ice on the field. Coming from California, it was a bit of a shock to me. I was wondering how we were going to start on time." Another day when Dominic reported to the ballpark, there was snow lingering on the field. When reporters asked what he thought about that, Dominic—who at 23 was seeing snow for the first time—replied, "I know when I was a kid even before I went to Galileo High School—named after a great Italian scientist, by the way—I used to get a big kick out of reading [a poem] by Whittier who, I understand, was a local boy, about 'Snow, snow, beautiful snow.' Then there was another by James Russell Lowell, another local boy who made good, which started 'The snow had begun in the gloaming and busily all the night.' That was a sad one that used to make me feel like weeping." The "Little Professor" had begun to intrigue Boston fans before he even played.

Because of Dominic's injury, Boston had slotted veteran Doc Cramer in center field. Williams was in left field, and a gimpy Dominic had to play right. If he wanted center field back, he'd have to take it from Cramer—not easy considering that Cramer had batted .311 in 1939.

With Dominic now in the majors, articles like "The Amazing DiMaggios" appeared in magazines and newspapers in the spring of 1940. Tom Laird, a San Francisco writer, opined in *Collier's* magazine that Dominic was "the greatest twenty-two-year-old [sic] player in the game today." Even Ty Cobb, Joe's onetime contract negotiator, claimed, "Dom's a throwback to the kind of ball players we used to have."

While Dominic was being hailed this way, Vince was facing what could be his last chance to stay in the majors. Always being compared unfavorably to Joe, he had never really had the press behind him, and he wasn't exactly lighting up the National League in Cincinnati.

He got a vote of confidence from Cincinnati executive Gabe Paul, who issued a press release championing the Reds' acquisition of Vince and stating, "It is doubtful whether the most famous of the DiMaggio boys, Joe, can field as well as Vince. This fellow is one of the best defensive men ever to don a spiked shoe, and his throwing arm is strong and accurate." He also referred to Vince's offensive outburst in Kansas City the year before: "That record was the cause of the Reds shelling out a fancy price for his services."

From the beginning of camp in Tampa, however, it was obvious to Vince that he was not in Cincinnati's plans as a starting outfielder. And in fact, once the season got under way, he only managed to get into two games before the Reds traded him to the Pittsburgh Pirates for Johnny Rizzo. Vince wasn't sure if this was good news or bad. In

Pittsburgh he might be a starter. But the Pirates hadn't won a pennant since 1927.

In New York, Joe missed the start of the season yet again. He had injured his right knee sliding into second in a tune-up at Ebbets Field against the Brooklyn Dodgers. He watched the opening day game from the bench for the fourth time in five years.

The Yankees missed him. Without him, they were an under-.500 ball club. Boston was in first place, in the unaccustomed position of looking down at a struggling New York squad. Even more than in his rookie year, the pressure was on Ted Williams to lead them to the pennant. As the Yankees had once done for Joe, the Red Sox altered the dimensions of their ballpark to help him do that. They built a new bullpen area and put box seats in right field that brought the home run zone for left-handed batters like Ted significantly closer. Sportswriters dubbed the new area "Williamsburg."

But at first it didn't seem to help. Ted was off his pace, hitting just over .300 in the first half of the season. Given the high expectations after his stellar rookie season, it was no surprise that he now heard his first booing fans, and the sportswriters attacked him. His teammate Dominic fretted for him. He'd watched how Joe handled the press in San Francisco. Joe didn't antagonize reporters, didn't take the bait, but Ted wasn't built that way. He'd grown up essentially parentless and fighting for himself. He could turn loud and confrontational when he felt that his manhood or abilities were challenged. It didn't help when manager Cronin discussed with a Boston reporter the possibility of benching him.

Ted lashed out. After one game in which he was booed, he told reporters, "Boston is a shitty town. Fans are lousy." When someone questioned his high salary, he responded, "I'd rather be traded to New York." He told another reporter that he was going to quit baseball and become a fireman. The next time the Red Sox were in New York, the Yankees' Lefty Gomez stared into the Boston dugout wearing a fireman's hat. As the coverage got nastier and more personal, Ted repeatedly told reporters to "go fuck yourselves."

Meanwhile, Dominic had been spending more time on the bench than on the field. Cronin, not completely sold on his ability to be a major league player, was playing Lou Finney instead. Then Finney and Ted Williams collided chasing a fly ball. Ted was carted off, and Cronin put Dominic in his spot. Now he showed his stuff. As one sportswriter put it, "The bespectacled speedster has been showing a brand of outfielding that makes the average major league patrolman look slower than your horse in the home stretch." When Ted returned to the lineup, Cronin shifted Dominic to center field.

The comparisons to his brother soon came. A typical comment: "He hasn't Joe's power at bat, which isn't surprising in view of the fact that he is three inches shorter and 40 pounds lighter. But he has an eye like a house dick and enough punch to hit any fence in the park and plant an occasional onion in the left field nets."

He developed a standard reply to the question "How do you compare yourself to Joe?"

"I can do two things better than he can," he'd say. "Play pinochle and speak Italian." When pressed for more detail, he'd say how proud he was of Joe, then stress, "Yes, he's my brother—and I'm *his* brother."

Boston readers loved it. It showed a new spunk from a Sox club that no longer felt inferior to the almighty Yankees. With a DiMaggio on each team, their rivalry grew hotter that season.

The brothers faced off for the first time in a five-game series at Fenway Park. For some of the reporters, it was like the other players didn't exist—this was a Joe versus Dominic series. The press and fans watched intently after the top of the first inning as Dominic ran in from center field and Joe headed there. What would their confrontation be like?

"Hello, Joe," Dominic said. Joe responded, "Hello, Dom." And they continued trotting their separate ways.

As Dominic remembered it: "The writers thought it was a case of two brothers being so reserved, so shy, that they hardly said anything to each other, but it wasn't that at all. We had a game to play, an important game. We couldn't very well stand out there and exchange news from home."

Dominic still managed to send a message, though—that he was another DiMaggio who belonged in the majors. In the five games, he rapped out eleven hits to Joe's nine.

The two teams were back at it again a week later, this time in New York. It was Dominic's introduction to cavernous Yankee Stadium, and his inexperience showed. After the first game, Dominic went to Joe and Dorothy's Manhattan apartment for dinner. (She had persuaded her husband that it wasn't good for their marriage to have her staying in San Francisco, waiting for him to come home in October.) Joe told his brother that he was playing too shallow. "That's a big field," Joe advised, "and the ball carries well in that part of the ballpark."

In the next day's game, Dominic positioned himself ten steps deeper. Sure enough, during one at-bat Joe sent the ball screaming to center. His brother outran it, and the ball fell into his glove. When a disgusted Joe returned to the dugout, teammates heard him muttering, "I should never have mentioned it to him."

"It was the biggest thrill of my rookie year," Dominic recalled, "and I was sure Mom would approve of the way I was listening to my big brother."

He didn't mention what had to be another big thrill, even if he was smart enough to realize the event was just another way to sell tickets. Though he was only a rookie, July 14 was Dominic DiMaggio Day at Fenway Park. "Nineteen hundred boys of Italian descent, members of the junior division of the order of the Sons of Italy, presented Dom with a military set and the Red Sox with a floral horseshoe. The bugle band of the Lynn, Mass. Sons of Italy helped to serenade the youthful DiMaggio." And in the second game of the doubleheader against the crosstown Braves, Dominic hit the first home run of his major league career.

Apparently, he was already viewed as an elite outfielder, at least in one teammate's eyes. Sam Mele was an outfielder on the New York University baseball team in 1940 who had been scouted by the Red Sox. One afternoon his coach drove him from New York to Fenway Park to participate in batting practice. He recalled the experience 72 years later:

"One guy behind the cage, he said, 'Take five swings.' I take four, and the last pitch, I didn't swing at. Behind the cage the guy said, 'Why didn't you swing the bat?' I said, 'Well, it was low.' He said, 'It wasn't outside, though. Come over here when you're done.' I did, and the guy was Ted Williams. We walked out to left field and we were talking baseball. When I asked him about fielding, Ted said, 'Oh no, no, no. Don't ask me. See that little guy in center field? You go ask him.' And he yelled over, 'Dom, Dommie! I'm sending this kid over, and teach him all you know about the outfield.' That was when I first met Dominic. Right away he started teaching me about getting in position, and how to be ready to charge with one foot in front of the other because you'll throw off your strong leg."

After a season in the Northern League, four years in the Marine Corps during the war, and a season in the Eastern League (where he would earn MVP honors), Mele would join Dominic in Boston's outfield.

In a late-season game at Yankee Stadium, Dominic was in center field twice when Joe came up to bat with the bases loaded. Both times Joe launched what looked to be triples, and both times Dominic raced them down. As Joe passed his brother on the field after the second one, he hissed, "You little heel."

That evening Dominic visited Joe and Dorothy for dinner again. When Joe opened the door, he said, "You have some nerve coming here for dinner after what you did to me." Suppressing a grin, Dominic said, "Joe, I couldn't go another inch for those balls."

That September, Joe and Dominic found themselves at the same hotel in St. Louis. The Red Sox, on an off day, had arrived, and the Yankees, having finished up a series against the Browns, hadn't yet left. Joe was sitting in the lobby smoking when his brother walked in. "Hello, Dom," he said. "Hello, Joe." After a pause, Dominic added, "I am tired, Joe. I'm going to bed." Joe said, "Good night, Dom."

The battle for first that month was between Detroit and Cleveland. The Red Sox had faded, and though the Yankees had had a late-season surge, it was too late. Detroit won the pennant. The Yankees, with an 88-66 record, finished only two games out, but after the success of the last four years, it had to feel like a dozen games. Boston came in behind them with an 82-72 season.

It was a very odd trip home to San Francisco for Joe. He hadn't wanted to linger in New York, to hang out at his favorite haunts—like the saloon Toots Shor had opened on West 51st Street—and face questions about what was wrong with the Yankees. He and Dorothy packed up their car and headed west. "It was a strange feeling to be driving back to San Francisco in my car and listening to World Series games on the radio," he would recall.

THE 1940 SEASON proved to be the turning point for Vince. For once, he was in the right place at the right time. The manager, Frankie Frisch, had decided to scrap his starting outfield of Rizzo and the aging brothers Paul and Lloyd Waner. When Vince arrived, he was installed in center field, with Maurice Van Robays and Bob Elliott on either side of him. The fans in Pittsburgh soon embraced him as the best center fielder in the National League.

Finally too his bat was showing the same pop in the majors that it had in the minors. With regular playing time and reemerging confidence, Vince's average approached .300.

"Pittsburgh was where my father could finally show that he was a talented player too," says his daughter Joanne. "He was far from home on the West Coast and not near Joe and Dominic on the East Coast—maybe that is why. They didn't even see each other during the season, being in different leagues."

They weren't seeing each other much in the off-season either. Vince had bought a house in Hermosa Beach, in Southern California, while Joe and Dominic remained in San Francisco. The DiMaggio brothers did get together between seasons, but as Dominic told a reporter in 1940, "When Joe, Vince and I get together in the winter time, it just so happens that we talk, when we do talk, about everything but baseball."

Vince played hard, while the Pirates generally played poorly. In one game in May the Giants scored 17 runs thanks in large part to seven Pirates errors. Frisch used three pitchers just to get out of the first inning. Small wonder that only a little more than 5,000 spectators were at Forbes Field that day. In another game against the Giants that June, the Pirates racked up another five "misplays," as they were charitably termed. Both of Pittsburgh's runs in that 4–2 loss came on a Vince homer. They finished the season in fourth place, a very distant 22.5 games behind the Reds.

Vince may have been disappointed to not be playing for a contender, but otherwise he had his best season in the big leagues. He hit .289 with 19 homers (fifth in the league) and 54 RBI. His goal was to have an even better season in 1941. As he headed home to California, he hoped that he would stay with the Pirates. He had given up the thought of playing with either of his brothers. After being on four different clubs in four years, he just wanted to stay in one place.

It had been a more satisfying season for Dominic than for either of his brothers. After a game at the end of August, when he was tied for the team batting lead with Jimmie Foxx at .313 (he finished at .301), owner Tom Yawkey gathered reporters together and declared,

"You can say for me that I'm quite satisfied with the Little Professor's work in the classroom. I only wish there were a couple more out on the Coast like him. I think I'd be tempted to offer them enough money to make them forget about fishing."

Though the pennant eluded the Red Sox again, they showed more potential than they had in decades. Ted Williams, Dominic, Bobby Doerr, and third baseman Jim Tabor were the young nucleus of a team that would definitely challenge the now-vulnerable Bronx Bombers. And vet Foxx had somehow alternated between catcher and first base, slugged 36 home runs, and driven in 119 runs. He and Dominic shared an apartment in Boston. Dominic remembered that "no future Hall of Famer was ever nicer to a rookie than Jimmie was to me. We ate together, and when Jimmie wanted to make the night a little longer, which was his tendency, we'd say good night and he'd go on his way."

As 1940 drew to a close with all three brothers back on the West Coast, the news was gloomier than ever about events in Europe. President Franklin Roosevelt had signed the Selective Training and Service Act of 1940, initiating the first peacetime draft in the nation's history. Vince was high on the list for his district, but it was possible that having a wife and daughter would lessen his chances of being called up. The 23-year-old Dominic seemed the most likely of the brothers to be called on if war came, but even Joe was vulnerable, having no children (though Dorothy was plotting to change that). It had to have crossed their minds that they needed to have especially good seasons in 1941, because it could be their last one for a while.

ELEVEN

THAT VINCE AND DOMINIC played in Joe's shadow was never more obvious than in 1941. The previous year Vince had had his breakthrough season with the Pirates and become arguably the best center fielder in the National League. Dominic had an excellent season too. But today Joe is the only DiMaggio whose 1941 season is remembered. This would be the defining season of the brothers' relationship as ballplayers. No matter what Vince and Dom did, they would not come close to equaling the Great DiMaggio.

But first Joe (with Tom again acting as his business agent) had to come to an agreement with the Yankees on his salary. Because the team hadn't done so well in 1940, the organization went on a cost-cutting spree. General manager Ed Barrow sent Joe and several other key players contracts with salary reductions—Joe's from a reported $32,500 in 1940 to $30,000. Joe and Tom sent it back unsigned, and the two sides settled into sniping at each other in the press. Dan Daniel of the *New York World-Telegram* reported that Barrow "insists that DiMaggio does not run enough, that his legs are not in first-class condition, and these reasons explain the injuries which

Giuseppe suffers each season." Play a full season, Barrow challenged Joe via the press, and more money will be on the table. Spring training began in St. Petersburg without baseball's best young player, but Barrow blinked first. On March 6, Joe signed a contract for $35,000, which was said to make him the second-highest-paid player in baseball behind Hank Greenberg at $42,000.

Barrow may have been blowing smoke about Joe's conditioning, but in truth, when he arrived at the Yankees camp, his throwing arm was sore. In exhibition games, he couldn't launch the ball from the outfield in his usual way. He was sluggish at the plate too. Joe may have been partly distracted by the plight of his pal Lefty Gomez, who was clearly on the downside of his career and having a rough time. Joe McCarthy was quoted as saying, "This man did wonders for the Yankees. It would be rank ingratitude to cast him off like an old pair of shoes, or a broken bat." But reporters noted that "Lefty thinks every appearance means the difference between 'stay' and 'go' and under his gay exterior he is the most harassed man on the New York club."

But all was well when the season got under way. The trainers treated Joe's arm. For only the second time in his career, he was in New York's lineup on opening day, and after eight games he was hitting .528. When he then went into a 12-game batting slump, Dominic helped him out of it. The Yankees and Red Sox met, and Dominic tripled, beat out a bunt, and doubled off the left-field wall in Fenway Park. His performance apparently woke Joe up; he began hitting again, including a 430-foot homer against the Athletics. The Yankee attack also featured Joanne DiMaggio's former babysitter: "Phil Rizzuto, the little Flea who has taken over at short for New York, made his first hits in the American League and tried resolutely to steal the headline from Big Wop," a sportswriter noted. Joe's mind was eased about Gomez too. The pitcher credited with saying "I'd rather be lucky than good" would be both lucky *and* good enough to go 15-5 that year, his last effective season with the Yankees.

In Boston, Ted Williams watched most of the opening day game from the bench. He had chipped a bone in his ankle in spring training. But the first regular-season game was a tight contest against the Senators at Fenway Park, and Joe Cronin, still Boston's player-manager, called on Ted to pinch-hit during what proved to be the winning rally. In a harbinger of the season he was to have, Ted delivered a single.

With Ted, Bobby Doerr, Dominic, and a still-contributing Jimmie Foxx, the Red Sox began the season scoring runs in bunches, collecting 14 against the hapless Senators, thrashing the Tigers 15–9, and beating the Yankees 13–5. Williams batted over .400, where he would stay into July. Dominic's play improved for a simple reason: he could see the ball better. An ophthalmologist had diagnosed him with "myopic astigmatism with exophoria" and prescribed special corrective lenses.

But he admitted that he still needed to toughen up his hands: "They became tender during the off-season because I spent the winter playing cards in Joe's new restaurant in San Francisco instead of deep-sea fishing with my father and my other brothers." Apparently, not much baseball was discussed during the card games. "Joe never volunteered any tips to me about my hitting, and I never asked him," Dominic told Shirley Povich of the *Washington Post*. "It's better that way, and we both know it. Joe's big and rangy and I'm on the stumpy side. We have different strokes. Anyway, we don't talk about baseball much."

The Boston fans were fully behind their team in the first half of the season, when it looked like the Red Sox would battle the Yankees and the Indians for the pennant. On Memorial Day, Fenway Park was packed with 34,500 people as the home team took on the Yankees. They split the doubleheader, the Sox losing 4–3, then pounding New York 13–0. Joe, who had two hits on the day, was not booed in Boston, but Dominic was the clear favorite, especially when he delivered two singles and a double. The *Boston Globe* ran a cartoon suggesting that with Dom hitting .382 to Joe's .315, fans were having difficulty remembering the older brother's name.

Still, by June 25 the Yankees were at the top of the American League. They had homered in 20 consecutive games, but that wasn't the streak people were talking about. Joe had hit in 37 straight games, only four games behind the American League record set by George Sisler in 1922. (In baseball prehistory, Wee Willie Keeler had hit in 44 straight games in 1897.) Joe's performance lifted the spirits of the whole team, who had been saddened by Lou Gehrig's death on June 2, a couple of weeks short of his 38th birthday. At the funeral in Christ Episcopal Church in the Bronx, Joe sat in a pew with Babe Ruth, Bill Dickey, Joe McCarthy, and others who had been Gehrig's teammates over the years.

On June 28, the Yankees were in Philadelphia for a doubleheader. In the first game, A's pitcher Johnny Babich tried to kill Joe's streak by throwing only balls, but with the count at 3-0, Joe reached way across the plate for a hit. He had another hit in the second game. His streak was now at 40, just one shy of Sisler. That day he went to visit a young fan in a Philadelphia hospital: 10-year-old Tony Norella, who was near death with an inoperable spleen illness. DiMaggio told Tony to stay tuned to his radio and he'd break Sisler's record for him.

The next day the Yankees were in Washington for a double-header against the Senators. "Fans Come from Miles Around to See DiMaggio Make History" was typical of that day's headlines. The *Washington Post* reported, "Spectators were lined up outside the park when Joe arrived before the game. When he stepped onto the field, they swarmed from the stands, pulling and tugging at him, pleading for autographs." Joe singled off Dutch Leonard in the first game and off Walt Masterson in the second, for a 42-game streak. Sadly, word came that little Tony Norella had died that morning before the games were played.

Even before the streak began, Joe had been as celebrated as any athlete in the United States. Now he crossed over to becoming a legend. Though he told reporters that every pitcher in the American League would be "trying double" to stop the streak, he declared with confidence that he would keep it going indefinitely. Against the Red Sox and in front of a regular-season-record 52,832 spectators at Yankee Stadium, Joe had hits in both ends of a doubleheader to tie Keeler at 44 consecutive games. When play halted for the All-Star Game, the streak was at 48.

Joe was no doubt glad for the All-Star break. For the first time, he would not be the only DiMaggio on the American League roster. Dominic, along with Ted Williams (batting .405), Bobby Doerr, Joe Cronin, and Jimmie Foxx, would represent the Red Sox. At the top of the seventh inning, Dominic was in right field, joining Joe in the outfield in a major league game for the first time, and Williams was in left. In the bottom of the eighth inning, Joe doubled (unofficially, his 49th consecutive game with a hit) and his younger brother drove him in with a single. In the ninth, Joe went to the plate with the bases loaded. He could manage only a grounder that scored one run. Williams followed him and smacked a soaring homer that struck the roof of the double-decked stands in right field.

"It was the kind of thing a kid dreams about and imagines himself doing when he's playing those little playground games we used to play in San Diego," Ted wrote in his autobiography. "Halfway down to first, seeing that ball going out, I stopped running and started leaping and jumping and clapping my hands, and I was just so happy I laughed out loud. I've never been so happy, and I've never seen so many happy guys."

When Giuseppe looked at the next day's newspaper, he slowly read: "From the San Francisco angle, we are unable to judge which was the mightier hit—Ted Williams's home run that won for the American Leaguers yesterday in the ninth inning, or Dominic DiMaggio's single in the eighth, driving in brother Joe."

With Joe's and Dominic's money helping to support the household, as well as revenue from Joe's restaurant, which Tom ran, Giuseppe was no longer rising at 4:00 A.M. to fish. Mike continued to fish, but his income supported his own family of five. One of the San Francisco newspapers visited Giuseppe and reported on "the jolly, rotund man of 68": "Now that he is a man of leisure, the elder DiMaggio gets up at 7 A.M., putters around the house, then goes down to Joe's restaurant. At noon, he goes home again where Mama cooks his lunch, then he returns to the Grotto for an afternoon session [or] stays home to pick up the reports of the games over the radio presented to him by his friends in North Beach's Italian colony. The big moment of the day comes at 5 o'clock, when Pop gets the late editions of the afternoon papers and checks up on the hits made by Vince, Joe and Dom."

The reporter asked Giuseppe—also described as "rosy-faced, with white hair, white mustache and twinkling eyes"—who was the best player among his sons. With Tom translating from Sicilian, he replied emphatically, "Joe! He makes three times as much money as the other two."

Joe's streak continued after the All-Star Game—a single on July 10, three singles and a homer on the 11th, a single and a double on the 12th, four singles during a July 13 doubleheader, a single on the 14th, and a single and a double on the 15th. Newspapers around the country avidly followed his exploits.

"Joe was handling all the attention from the press and fans well," Dominic remembered. "That 61-game streak with the Seals might have been good preparation for what he was going through. He was the only thing people in baseball were talking about at that point in the 1941 season."

In Boston, Dominic didn't have to wait until the next newspaper to find out how Joe did during that day's game. Ted Williams had made an arrangement with Bill Daley, who operated the scoreboard in left field at Fenway Park. Daly would call out to Ted when he received a report from wherever the Yankees were playing, and then Ted would yell "Dommie!" to get his attention and inform him of what Joe had just done.

"I didn't notice any change in Joe during the streak," Dominic recalled. "We had dinner a couple of times when the Yankees and Red Sox played each other, and we visited on the field. I was glad to see him holding up so well."

Not that Dominic made it easy for his older brother. In a game against the Red Sox, Joe made outs his first two times up. The third time up, the bases were loaded with two outs. He tagged one to left-center. When Dominic caught the long drive, half the ball was sticking out of his glove. "As soon as I caught it, I got a sick feeling in my stomach. You know, this is his third time at bat. On the way in, [Joe] was coming out to his place in center field, and I've got to pass this guy, and, gee, I'm feeling so sorry. And then I turn to give him an apologetic look, and he just turned at the same time and looked at me—believe me, if looks could kill, I would've dropped right there, and I said, 'Oh my God, I've made an enemy.'" Joe put the ball in the seats on his fourth time up, letting Dom off the hook.

When the Yankees arrived in Cleveland on July 16, in 55 consecutive games Joe had collected 51 singles, 16 doubles, 4 triples, and 11 home runs. That night he made it 56 straight when he had two singles, a double, and three runs scored. Incredibly, during the streak he had struck out only five times.

It ended the next day, thanks to Cleveland pitchers Al Smith and Jim Bagby and the stalwart fielding of Ken Keltner, who converted two smashes down the third-base line into outs. In the top of the eighth, Joe, with even many of the 67,468 Indians fans at Cleveland Stadium cheering for a hit, faced Bagby with the bases loaded and grounded to shortstop Lou Boudreau, who turned it into a double play. Typically, the Yankees won the game anyway, 4–3.

Joe was stoic about the streak ending (even though he missed out on an offer from Heinz "57 Varieties" Ketchup to award him

$10,000 if he hit in his 57th consecutive game). "I can't say that I'm glad it's over," he told reporters in the locker room. "Of course, I wanted to go on as long as I could. Now that the streak is over, I just want to get out there and keep helping win ball games."

In the more than seven decades since Joe's streak, only two other ballplayers have vaguely threatened the record—Pete Rose and Paul Molitor. Years later, Shirley Povich wrote in the *Washington Post* that "man would never walk on the moon, an actor would never get elected president, and nobody would ever break Joe's streak." Only one of those predictions remains true.

IN PITTSBURGH, THE Pirates under Frankie Frisch had started the season looking to do some damage in 1941. On paper they looked better than the Cubs, Braves, and Phillies. It seemed unlikely that they were ready to compete with the Cardinals or a reviving Dodgers squad for first place, but when Vince had mailed his signed contract to club president Bill Benswanger, he enclosed a note that read, "Best wishes for a pennant, and nothing less."

Vince had a solid spring training and was the starting center fielder. In March the Pirates issued a release about him that offered a glimpse of how his stock had risen in the organization: "When Frankie Frisch, on May 8, of last year, induced Bill McKechnie, the Cincinnati skipper, to give up Vince DiMaggio in exchange for Johnny Rizzo, the Pirate manager made one of the most profitable deals engineered by the Pittsburgh club in years. Vince is one of the greatest center fielders in the game, a natural ballhawk who turns many a seeming extra-base drive into a putout, plays ground balls like an infielder, and owns a throwing arm that is second to none in power or accuracy."

As the season progressed the Pirates played pretty good ball, and Vince emerged as the offensive leader as well as continuing to play excellent center field. Soon to turn 29, he had finally hit his stride in the majors. In July the Bucs were battling the Dodgers for first place.

On the 22nd, they drew to within a game when they beat Brooklyn, 8–3, at Ebbets Field, spurred by Vince going 2-for-3 with a home run. Vince was comfortable and confident at the plate. Fans in Pittsburgh had not had a lot to cheer about in recent years, so when Vince hustled and displayed the only real power on the team, the crowds at Forbes Field applauded enthusiastically.

As expected, the strongest contenders for the pennant were the Dodgers and Cardinals. But Vince was undeterred. When he saw a pitch he liked, he swung. He was well behind his brothers in making contact, but when Vince did connect, the ball went places. During one stretch in August, he hit three homers in three games that led Pittsburgh to a sweep of the Boston Braves. With power numbers down throughout the major leagues because of a less-lively baseball, Vince's performance was all the more impressive—21 home runs and 100 runs batted in. And he displayed impressive durability too by playing in all but three of Pittsburgh's games. Pitching would hurt the Pirates, but they had a respectable season. They finished 19 games back, but they were 81-73, one of the better records in the history of a franchise that had been established in 1887.

A FEW DAYS after Joe's streak ended, *Newsweek* noted, "Joe DiMaggio's perpetual-motion hitting streak . . . had put another up-and-coming young man in the shade." It was a reference to Ted Williams, who was hitting .412 during Joe's streak—four points higher than Joe. Earlier in the season he'd been hitting as high as .489. The fans weren't booing him anymore, and the press wasn't carping at him.

"I always sympathized with him when he had those problems with the media," Dominic recalled. "I was quiet, and Ted would get to talking about hitting in our little corner of the clubhouse—he never talked about fielding—and he would draw a crowd, and after a while he'd turn to me and say, 'Dommie, you think I'm full of shit, don't you?'" As the New York sports columnist Joe Williams informed his readers, "I invited him to dinner and spent three hours with him and couldn't develop any sort of story about Dominic. That same day I rode down the elevator with Ted Williams and between the eighth and the fourth floors I picked up my column for the day."

With the year Joe and Ted were having, and with Dominic now entrenched in the Boston lineup in his sophomore season, the rivalry between the Yankees and Red Sox again entertained fans. Well-known brothers like Dizzy and Daffy Dean or Lloyd and Paul Waner had played on the same teams, not on competing teams like Joe and Dom. It was exciting to watch the two center fielders and their teams going head to head.

"When I got to Yankee Stadium, the adrenaline flowed," Dominic told Fay Vincent. "I just loved playing in Yankee Stadium. I had all that room out there in center field and I was a line drive hitter. I loved playing against New York, and when they came to Boston, you could cut the atmosphere with a knife. It was just so full of tension. I mean just great."

When they won, the Red Sox—who would finish first in the league in batting average, on-base percentage, and runs scored—won big. They established a formula they'd follow for much of the decade: Dominic would get on base (and, beginning the next season, Johnny Pesky), and Doerr or Williams would knock him in.

But their pitching hurt them. Lefty Grove's career was in its final stage. On July 25, on his third attempt to win his 300th game, he defeated the Indians at Fenway Park, with Dominic catching the last out. That was it for the lefty. Winless in six more starts, he retired after the season with a 300-141 record. His .680 winning percentage remains the best of the 24 pitchers who have earned 300 victories or more.

In August, Ted Williams was hotter than the weather. It was something of a surprise that he was playing at all. In July, in a rainy game against the Tigers, Ted walked three times. Trotting down to first base after the third walk, the spikes of his left shoe caught in the soft, damp dirt and he reinjured his ankle. But he returned to the lineup with a vengeance. In a doubleheader against the Browns, he smacked three home runs. He slugged two more the next day. Nothing seemed to work against him. The White Sox tried a shift against him by swinging infielders and outfielders to center and right, but Ted just poked a double to left. On September 1, in a doubleheader sweep of the Senators, he hit three more homers.

Dominic was smacking his own. Against the Tigers in Boston, he hit a grand slam in the second inning, then followed up with a triple and double. On the 17th, Dominic's two-run single in the ninth inning joined his RBI in the third to give the Red Sox a come-from-behind win over Cleveland. On the 24th, he slugged his second grand slam, off Dutch Leonard, in a 7–2 win over the Senators.

All three DiMaggios were having stellar seasons, and the press couldn't get enough of them. Gossip columnist Louella Parsons wrote that a Hollywood producer was floating the idea of a film titled *The Great DiMaggio* that would focus on Giuseppe and feature Joe, Vince, and Dominic.

The dean of American sportswriters, Grantland Rice, was inspired to poetry in one of his daily newspaper columns:

Out the olive trail they go—
Vincent, Dominic, and Joe,
Lashing, flashing, steaming hot
In the fabled land of swat.
Where the big ash sings its song
For the glory of the throng,
Or the big mace through the fray
Sends the apple on its way—
Watch them as they whirl, careen,
Over the fields of verdant green.
Rulers of the batting eye,
Where their gaudy triples fly,

In the sunset's shining glow
Who is it that steals the show?
Vincent, Dominic, and Joe.

And one of the more popular acts of the time, Les Brown and His Band of Renown, came up with a tune titled "Joltin' Joe DiMaggio." Of course, it became the number-one song in America.

Joe twisted his ankle in a game in August. Before he was back in the lineup, his teammates threw him a surprise party. After a loud rendition of "For He's a Jolly Good Fellow," they gave him a silver humidor with the number 56 etched on it, with the inscription, "Presented to Joe DiMaggio by his fellow players on the New York Yankees to express their admiration for his consecutive game hitting streak. 1941." Also inscribed were the signatures of every player, and Joe McCarthy's.

There was every reason to throw a party. When they clinched the pennant on September 4, it was the earliest in the major leagues—another record that still stands. When Joe did return to the field, the Philadelphia Athletics paid the price as he slugged his 29th and 30th homers. The Yankees sailed through September and concluded the season with 101 wins, 17 games ahead of the Red Sox and 24 ahead of the White Sox.

Again, the Boston ball club had shown improvement but was bested by a machine with all its cylinders working. Dominic couldn't rival his brother's remarkable accomplishment in the 1941 season, but Ted was aiming to give it a good shot. As the games dwindled down to a precious few, Ted's average was consistently 40 or more points higher than Joe's. With a week left in the season, it stood at .406. Manager Joe Cronin suggested that Ted sit on it. The irascible left fielder responded, "If I'm a .400 hitter, I'm a .400 hitter for the entire season. Not a part of one. I'll play out the year."

But he hit under .400 that week, and his average was .39955—technically .400—going into the final weekend series against the

Philadelphia Athletics at Shibe Park. Saturday's game was rained out. That night Cronin again went to Ted and asked him to sit out the next day's makeup doubleheader. Ted refused.

According to Dominic, "It was a decision that I've always admired him for, one that all of us were proud of. . . . The books of baseball history show that Ted responded the way champions do."

In the first game, Ted faced right-hander Dick Fowler. The weather was damp and dreary, but because that Sunday was the last day of the season, both games had to be played. When Ted stepped up to the plate the first time, the A's catcher told him, "If we let up on you, Mr. Mack said he would run us out of baseball. I wish you all the luck in the world, but we're not going to give you a damn thing."

Williams singled. Next time up, off left-hander Porter Vaughan, he homered. He singled his next two times up, then reached base on an error. He was 4-for-5 in the game and easily could have finished over .400. But he still wouldn't sit. In the second game, he went 2-for-3. With Dominic and his other teammates silently urging him on, Ted had elevated his average back to .406. Such a day deserved a party, but Ted was not much of a drinker: "I don't remember celebrating that night, but I probably went out and had a chocolate milk shake."

As with Joe's streak that year, no player has bested Ted Williams's 1941 batting average. Of the thousands of men who have worn baseball uniforms since then, only George Brett, with .390 in 1980, and Tony Gwynn, with .394 in the strike-shortened 1994 season, came within hailing distance. (And if sacrifice flies had not been counted as outs in 1941, Ted would have hit .419.)

Joe couldn't touch several of Ted's other achievements that year. He was tops in the American League in home runs (37), walks, and runs scored (135). An even more remarkable statistic is that with his 145 walks and 185 hits, Ted had an on-base average of .574, meaning that he wound up on base (or with a home run) more than half the times he stepped up to the plate. His longest hitless streak the entire season was seven at-bats.

Dominic's batting faded as the season wore on, to .283, but his value to Boston was in scoring 117 runs. He could be counted on to set the table for Williams and Doerr, as well as the aging Cronin and Foxx. Dominic was third in the American League in runs scored—bettered by only his brother and Ted.

THE BROOKLYN DODGERS were finally back in the World Series in 1941, their first visit since 1920. Perhaps the biggest distinctions for the franchise since 1920 had been playing the first night baseball game in New York City—on June 15, 1938, at Ebbets Field—and the first game ever televised—against the Reds on August 26, 1939. They were led by Pete Reiser (a league-leading .343 average), Dixie Walker, Ducky Medwick, Dolph Camilli (National League MVP), Pee Wee Reese in his first full season and leading the league in put-outs, 22-game winners Whit Wyatt and Kirby Higbe, "Fat Freddie" Fitzsimmons (2.07 ERA at age 40), and manager Leo Durocher. They apparently posed the best challenge to the Bronx Bombers in the "Fall Classic" in a decade.

In the first game, at Yankee Stadium, Red Ruffing reminded everyone why he was considered such a money pitcher when his neat six-hitter resulted in a 3–2 win. But Wyatt got revenge with his own 3–2 victory the next day. At Ebbets Field, the Yankees' Marius Russo pitched a complete-game four-hitter, for a 2–1 win. Joe drove in one of the runs and had two hits.

He had two more hits on October 5 as the Yankees beat Brooklyn 7–4. This was the game with a play that would have Dodgers fans saying, "Wait till next year," for 13 more seasons. Brooklyn clung desperately to a 4–3 lead going into the top of the ninth. Tying the Series with another game to go at Ebbets Field would be a huge boost. Hugh Casey had already pitched three and a third innings, but Durocher left him in. This seemed the right decision when Johnny Sturm grounded to second and Red Rolfe grounded to the mound. Two outs. The dangerous Tommy Henrich came to the plate, but Casey struck him out—so everyone thought. But the catcher, Mickey Owen, let the ball get through. The alert Henrich raced to first base and was safe. That brought up Joe, who singled to left. He and Henrich then scored on Charlie Keller's double to right. Dickey walked. Joe Gordon doubled in two more runs. Rizzuto walked. Finally, a battered Casey got pitcher Johnny Murphy to ground to short for the final out.

In the bottom of the inning, the Dodgers' play reflected the total deflation of their 33,813 fans. With Murphy on the mound, Reese fouled out to Bill Dickey, Walker grounded to Rizzuto, and Reiser grounded to Sturm. The ball never left the infield, and the game was over. One headline in the next day's newspapers called the out that wasn't "Flatbush's Darkest Hour." Another said, "The Yanks Slip the Dodgers a Mickey." The demoralized Dodgers lost again the next day, and the Yankees had yet another World Series to their name.

THROUGHOUT THE SUMMER of 1941, most major league ball-players kept their eyes and ears on the ever-worsening news from Europe. By that time, Germany had overrun most of Europe and the Battle of Britain was on. On June 22, the Nazis invaded the Soviet Union, expanding the war. There were ominous rumblings from Japan in the Pacific too, but most ballplayers were more focused on Europe because they had ethnic ties there. With Italy the third party in the Axis, the DiMaggio boys had to wonder if they might have ended up in Fascist uniforms had Giuseppe and Rosalie never left Sicily. As it was, they could still wind up in uniforms should the United States enter the war. When the Selective Service announced that it was lifting the limit of 900,000 men who would be drafted, all professional athletes in their twenties had to face the possibility of their careers being put on hold.

Bob Feller would later recall, "Most of us were making up our minds during the season what we wanted to do. If you weren't, you had to be living in a cave somewhere."

Dominic's day of reckoning had already come in May. The draft board in San Francisco had notified him that he was to report to Board 18 in Boston for a physical. After the eye exam, he was declared 4F. He protested the classification, to no avail. Vince and Joe, married with children, would be classified 3A.

At the end of the season, Vince returned to Hermosa Beach and Dominic went back to the family homestead. Dominic had told Boston reporters, "Just as soon as we finish the season, I'm heading right for San Francisco. My brother Tom has been tied down all summer at the restaurant, and I want to give him a hand."

Joe stayed in New York—because Dorothy had been pregnant during the season and was due within weeks of the World Series. Weighing in at a lucky seven pounds and eleven ounces, Joseph DiMaggio Jr. arrived on October 23 at Doctors Hospital in Manhattan. Using the baby as incentive, Dorothy persuaded her husband to stay at their West End Avenue apartment indefinitely, maybe even until spring training rolled around again.

A few weeks later, he won his second Most Valuable Player Award. With 291 votes, he beat his younger brother . . . by one vote. More significantly, he edged out Ted Williams by 37 votes. (Bob Feller came in a distant third.)

A couple of weeks after that, on December 7, 1941, the Japanese attacked Pearl Harbor. "In the first days after Pearl Harbor," wrote Dominic, "the question wasn't whether 1941 was baseball's most historic season. Instead, the question was whether it would be the last."

TWELVE

THE PRESS TREATED the arrival of Joe Jr. that October like a royal birth. Headlines around the country heralded the event. Richard Ben Cramer wrote, "Assuredly this was the year's most publicized baby. All the papers had to have pictures. Sometimes, they'd wrap the baby's tiny hand around a tiny bat, and they'd take a picture of Junior, asprawl in the crook of Dad's arm, with the bat propped up next to his lolling head." When sportswriter Dan Daniel visited the DiMaggios' apartment right before Christmas, they presented an image of domestic bliss. Dorothy cradled Joe Jr. in the living room as her superstar husband, dressed as Santa Claus, trimmed the tree.

It was a calculatedly false image. Joe didn't let fatherhood curb his social life in New York. If anything, the arrival of Joe Jr. in the West End Avenue apartment inspired Joe to even more carousing. A man who'd been doted on by his mother and four older sisters and was now treated like royalty himself everywhere he went, was not going to be content at home changing diapers and heating up bottles of milk. Two years into the marriage, he was easily annoyed and often restless.

His favorite escape was Toots Shor's on West 51st Street. His table was in the front right-hand corner of the dining room, where he could observe all who entered, with his back to the wall. Others sat at the table by invitation only. Those usually in attendance were former heavyweight champ Jim Braddock and a cabal of writers that included Ernest Hemingway, sportswriters Grantland Rice and Jimmy Cannon, and war correspondent Bob Considine. Joe was not a drinker, so he spent the night downing cups of coffee and inhaling cigarettes. He wouldn't go home until Dorothy and Joe Jr. were asleep.

When the baby was old enough to be left with sitters, Dorothy wanted to be out on the town with him. She wasn't fond of Shor's, but that was where Joe was comfortable, so there she went. Joe wasn't happy about that. According to Cramer, "The way he saw it, sometimes Dorothy just got in the way—or talked too much, or flirted too much—or was just too goddamn present. So he went out alone. If she got on him about that, he could walk away for days. He could always find a hotel room."

When the Christmastime conversation with Dan Daniel had turned to the upcoming 1942 season, Joe, now 27, had offered, "This should be the year, if everything goes well. I have not yet reached my peak as a ballplayer."

In fact, he had. Joe would never again have a season to equal the production of his first six. He had no way of knowing that Vince would play much more baseball than he would over the next four seasons, or that in several respects Dominic would be the better player of the decade.

On February 1, at its annual dinner, the New York chapter of the Baseball Writers of America honored Joe as the organization's Player of the Year. He had once again beaten out Ted Williams for the award. It was telling that not only the New York but the Boston chapter selected Joe over Ted. Clearly, Ted's relationship with the press there was still frosty.

As the '42 season approached, Joe and Tom held out again for more money. The contract the Yankees sent him was for the same amount he'd made the previous year, despite the streak, the MVP Award, and another world championship. March 1 came and went. "Doesn't he know there's a war on?" Ed Barrow sniped to the press. Finally, he upped the offer to $42,000. It made Joe the highest-paid Yankee since Babe Ruth, who had collected a stunning $80,000 in 1930. It was reported that Barrow beseeched, "For God's sake, Joe, give us a full year's play this time. At these rates, we deserve it." Joe in turn pledged to put 10 percent of his salary into U.S. war bonds. He headed to St. Petersburg—tellingly, not with Dorothy and Joe Jr. but with Toots Shor.

Joe certainly did know there was a war on. Back home in San Francisco, many feared that after Pearl Harbor Japan would target the West Coast. The night of December 7, there had been four air raid alerts in the city. The front-page headline in the next day's *San Francisco Chronicle* was "Japan Planes Near S.F." Later that day people claimed to have spotted enemy aircraft and even submarines. Ships began to arrive carrying military personnel and civilians from Pearl Harbor, some of them wounded. Immigrants and especially people of Asian descent had become suspected spies and were stopped and questioned.

Authorities issued curfews and placed restrictions on foreign nationals, especially those from countries in the Axis. This included Giuseppe and Rosalie DiMaggio, who still were not U.S. citizens, mainly because even after 40 years they couldn't read and write English well enough to pass the test. It was especially frustrating for Giuseppe, who was essentially confined to his home.

The Grotto, like all restaurants in the city, suffered. People were not going out to lunch and dinner. Tom was running an empty restaurant, and Joe would have to make up the difference.

The war had an impact on the 1942 season in many ways. Some players enlisted or were drafted into military service, and others (along with team executives) looked over their shoulders wondering who was next. Bob Feller hadn't waited. On the evening of December 7, he was having dinner with Cy Slapnicka, an Indians executive who had scouted and signed him. (Slapnicka's other key signing for Cleveland would be Roger Maris, in 1952.) Feller announced that he was joining the Navy. Three days later, Gene Tunney, the former heavyweight champion who headed the Navy's physical fitness program, met with Feller and signed him up, and "Rapid Robert" became the first major league player to enlist after America went to war. Hank Greenberg had been drafted into the Army in May 1941, missed the rest of the season, and was then discharged in November. Right after the Pearl Harbor attack, he went back into the Army. He would end up missing four years as a player. Hank Gowdy, a coach with the Cincinnati Reds, had been the first player to enlist when the United States joined World War I. At 53, he would return to the Army in 1942.

When Vince traveled to spring training in February, he worried about leaving Madeline and Joanne behind in Hermosa Beach. By then, fears of a full-scale Japanese invasion had faded, yet many believed that the West Coast was still vulnerable to air attacks. His plan was to get through spring training and then have them join him in Pittsburgh. Joanne would finish out the school year in Pittsburgh, spend the summer there, then return home with her mother when the new school year began in September. It was a pattern Vince and his family followed for the rest of the war.

"It was exciting that my father was a professional baseball player, and my uncles too, but I would miss him when we lived apart," recalls Joanne. "I'd miss his singing. He sang all the time at home. I can still see him in the front room, singing away. I used to sneak down the stairs and I'd peek around and I'd watch him sing. Dad sang Italian love songs, the classic ones."

"Oh, he had a beautiful tenor voice then," says Lee Howard. "Us younger guys used to beg him to sing for us during spring training."

Howard was a Staten Island native who was signed by the Pirates organization as a pitcher and, at 18, was in his first spring training in 1942. He would soon join the Navy, and by the time he made his major league debut for the Pirates in September 1946, Vince had moved on. But Howard remembers a lively personality, quite different from what the public knew about Joe and Dominic.

"Heck of a nice guy, and fun to be around," Howard says. "Now, I was a rookie, even less than a rookie. He was not only a major league veteran, a star, but a DiMaggio. Vince didn't act like it. He was a good teammate who wanted to win. Even with a war going on, there was hope for the Pirates that year."

First, though, there was getting into playing shape. Not only the players but the managers were uneasy, not knowing who they would have on their rosters come opening day—if there *was* an opening day. Vince's skipper, Frankie Frisch, a future Hall of Famer known from his playing days as the "Fordham Flash," spoke for all managers when he said about early 1942, "Spring training was the worst time. The uncertainty—the rumors that the owners would shut down. If we started the season, how far could we go? Were there going to be enough ball players?"

It was a legitimate concern. When the 1942 season began, 61 major league players had already gone off to the war. Month after month, that number would increase. Of the roughly 400 players on big league rosters in '42, a quarter of them were rookies. Many of these rookies were just interchangeable fill-ins, but a few were keepers, like Stan Musial with the St. Louis Cardinals and Johnny Pesky, who joined Dominic in Boston. The former Portland clubhouse boy was now a 22-year-old shortstop showing a lot of promise. He had been the MVP of the American Association the previous year. Joe Cronin was nearing the end of the trail as a player, and with Pesky playing like a veteran right away, Cronin could focus more on managing. Pesky would bat .331 in 1942. (At the end of the season, owner Tom Yawkey gave him a $5,000 bonus.)

As early as spring training, the impact of the war could be seen in the stands too. An estimated 2,000 soldiers—including Sgt. Hank Greenberg—attended a game between the Reds and the Red Sox. Dominic noted that "there seemed to be more fans in uniform than in civilian clothes." By the time the Red Sox opened their season, five of their players were also in uniform. One of them, Earl Johnson, would come back from the war with a Silver Star, a Bronze Star, and a cluster for heroism earned during the Battle of the Bulge.

While many players simply waited for notices from their draft boards, Dominic fought to get into military service. Midway through the season, he accompanied a friend to the Federal Building in Boston and filled out the paperwork to enlist in the Navy. But when taking the required eyesight test, he admitted to the doctor that he could make out only the "E" at the top of the chart. "The Navy's not going to accept you," the doctor told him.

A lengthy conversation ensued, with Dominic making his case for having fine sight with his glasses on and the doctor telling him that wouldn't be good enough for the Navy. When Dom asked about the Army, the doctor replied, "The chances are 40 percent they might take you."

"Well, why can't the Navy take me if the Army's going to? I'd rather be in the Navy."

The doctor offered to write a letter to the War Department stating that Dominic's athletic ability offset his weak eyesight. Dominic agreed to that. He would soon be notified that he had been accepted into the Navy, but that he did not have to report until the season was over. It was back to chasing the Yankees.

Ted Williams started the season with the opposite attitude. "Hitler had been giving Europe fits, and things were looking bad all over, but it hadn't sunk in on me yet," he would later write. "All I was interested in was playing ball, hitting the baseball, being able to hunt, making some money." That winter he had told his draft board that he couldn't go into the military because he was the sole support of his mother. While that was true, the board wasn't swayed and classified him 1A. Ted appealed to the presidential board. That got the attention of the press, and when the season began, Cronin expected his best ballplayer to get an earful on opening day.

There were plenty of men in uniform in the stands at Fenway Park when the 1942 season began. Maybe they came to boo Ted, but he made that hard when, with Dominic on second and Pesky on first, he smacked the ball into the bleachers his first time up. He collected two more hits before the game ended in an 8–3 victory. The following month he finally signed up for the Navy.

Signing up didn't completely silence the boos. On July 1, the Red Sox faced the Senators in a doubleheader at Griffith Stadium. The Senators fans down the left-field foul line got on Ted. He could hear every insult, which, to him, was always louder than any cheer. He made a rude gesture to them that only increased their abuse. In the fifth inning of the second game, admitting later that he wanted to "knock some teeth out," Ted began launching line drives down the foul line in left. "He had those guys in his sights," Dominic said. "Who else would ever do something like that?"

Ted accidentally hit one fair, and it bounced off the left-field wall. Surprised, he was slow getting out of the box and barely made it to second. An enraged Cronin took him out of the game, and fined him $250 to boot.

The war also made its mark on the All-Star Game in a couple of ways that year. In fact, because of the war, there were *two* All-Star Games. The first one began at the Polo Grounds in New York at 6:30 Eastern War Time and had to end at 9:10 so that the ballpark could be emptied out in time for the air raid drill scheduled for 9:30. Dominic was in the AL lineup again with Joe. The AL won. The next day they were in Cleveland, playing a second All-Star Game, a special wartime edition in which the AL team faced off against a team made up of major league players now in uniform. That team included Bob

Feller, Hank Greenberg, and Cecil Travis of the Senators. The AL team won again. The brainchild of the Baseball Writers Association, the two games raised $160,000 for war-related agencies.

AT THE START of the season Joe had looked worth every penny the Yankees were shelling out when he slugged his first home run, a 450-foot blast. But that homer didn't presage anything like his previous year's hitting. Joe struggled through May into June, when his average had sunk to .253 after a 5-for-29 road trip. It didn't help his performance that some fans were booing him, as they did other players, because he hadn't joined the military. It's likely that his worsening relationship with Dorothy was also distracting him. There were items in the New York papers about Dorothy having returned from a trip to Reno, Nevada, which got people wondering what she had been doing there. Barrow and the rest of the Yankee brass became alarmed. If Dorothy divorced him, he would lose his 3A status and might well be drafted. They didn't like that fans were booing him, but they also didn't want to lose him.

Dorothy put the divorce on hold, but she went to stay indefinitely with Lefty and June Gomez. It was probably no coincidence that Joe began, finally, to hit. Four hits in a doubleheader against the White Sox got his average above .300 for the first time in the season. "I'm in a groove now," he told reporters, an uncharacteristic declaration.

The Yankees clinched the pennant in mid-September and finished the season nine games ahead of the Red Sox. Joe had played in all 154 games, the only season he would not miss a game. He managed to finish with a .305 batting average, but his production totals—including 21 home runs and 114 RBI—were the lowest of his career so far.

In the Fall Classic, Joe McCarthy was looking for his Yankees to go seven-for-seven in the postseason during his Yankees tenure; for DiMaggio, defeating the Cardinals would mean six-for-six. St. Louis was a young team, featuring the rookie Musial, right fielder Enos Slaughter, and pitcher Mort Cooper, who had won 22 games. They faced a Yankee lineup full of experienced winners.

In the first game, Joe stroked three hits in the 7–4 victory, with Ruffing collecting a record-setting seventh World Series win (he had been tied with Lefty Gomez). But the Cards surprised them in Game 2 with a tie-breaking run in the bottom of the eighth that held up for a 4–3 triumph. There was an even bigger surprise in the third game, at Yankee Stadium—a shutout, 4–0, by southpaw Ernie White, the first time the Yanks had been blanked in the World Series in 16 years. The Cards won the next game too, 9–6. Now the Yankees faced elimination, something Joe had never confronted before in his major league career. The reliable Ruffing was sent to the mound on October 5. He pitched well, Joe had a hit and an RBI, a red-hot Rizzuto had two hits, the crowd of 69,052 cheered the Yankees on . . . and none of it was enough. The St. Louis Cardinals became world champions by virtue of a 4–2 win, with Johnny Beazley hurling his second complete game. For the first time since the Red Sox in 1915, a team in the World Series had lost the first game, then won the next four.

In his autobiography *Lucky to Be a Yankee*, Joe skips over 1942 entirely.

IN BOSTON, THE YOUTHFUL SOX played well enough to grab the pennant in any league that didn't include the Yankees. Dominic and Pesky formed an excellent tandem with the hit-and-run. They developed a play that was successful for much of the year. With Dominic on first, Pesky in the batter's box would touch his right ear as a signal. He then bunted the ball toward the third baseman, who charged in. Invariably, Pesky would beat the throw at first. Meanwhile, without breaking stride, Dominic rounded second and dashed to third before the third baseman returned to the bag to receive the first baseman's throw. It worked until a game with the Yankees late in the season, when the Yankees' grizzled veteran catcher Bill Dickey got wise. When Pesky bunted, Dickey ran for third base. When Dominic arrived, Dickey already had the ball. "Got ya!" he said, grinning, as he applied the tag.

Ted Williams more than fulfilled his potential this season. He batted .356, hit 36 home runs, and drove in 137 runs, adding up to one of the rarest feats in baseball, the Triple Crown for batting. Incredibly, he *still* wouldn't get elected the MVP of the American League. That honor again went to a Yankee, this time second baseman Joe Gordon. The Flash had lower stats—.322, 18, and 103—but as Ted would point out for public consumption, "The Yankees won the pennant again. And we were second again. The voting tends to go to the team that wins, which is right." Privately, however, he seethed.

The final game of the '42 season was at Fenway Park. Among the crowd were 4,293 boys and girls admitted free for carting in 29,000 pounds of scrap metal for the war effort. The Red Sox downed the Yankees 7–6. Even with the war intensifying in Europe and in the Pacific, few at Fenway could have imagined that this game was the last time they would see Ted Williams, Pesky, and Dominic play there until 1946. In November, Ted and Pesky were assigned to be Aviation Naval Cadets at the training school at Amherst College in Massachusetts. For Ted, the stay at the snow-covered campus was short-lived—while doing exercises one day, he suffered a hernia. He would spend the next two months in the Chelsea Naval Hospital.

THE PITTSBURGH PIRATES did not play well. There had been hopes that a young, aggressive team—catcher Al Lopez was the only player over 30 in the starting lineup—would build on the foundation of the previous year. But there was no one hitting .300 or more on the entire roster. And the pitching was bad. By season's end, Rip Sewell, at 17-15, would be the only pitcher with a winning record.

At least Vince was entrenched in the lineup and still recognized as the best center fielder in the National League. Struggling to keep his batting average over .250, he represented the only power and speed on the Pirates. In late August, he had six RBI in a doubleheader against the Dodgers—and Brooklyn won both games anyway. In several ways, the season couldn't end fast enough for him. Hurlers were pitching around him because there was not much offense in the rest of the lineup, and when he did put runs on the board, Pittsburgh's pitching and defense let the opposing teams back in the game. No wonder, then, that he began to develop ulcers. All he had to do was pick up the papers every day and see that his brothers were on clubs playing winning ball consistently, while he was turning 30 on a club that was sinking back into the depths of the National League. The Pirates were 66-81 in 1942, a woeful 36.5 games out of first. They finished in fifth place only because the Chicago Cubs, Boston Braves, and Philadelphia Phillies were considerably worse.

AFTER THE LOSS in the Series, Joe, Dorothy, and Joe Jr. took a train to San Francisco. They'd no sooner gotten back to the West Coast than Dorothy left for Reno with Joe Jr., establishing residency there. Joe followed her. Her price for a reconciliation was that he had to enlist in the Army. He waffled for weeks. He complained to friends that her idea of saving the marriage was for him to go away for a couple of years, maybe even get killed.

Barrow mailed him his 1943 contract, which he and Tom ignored. There were conflicting press reports through January that Joe would or would not join his younger brother in military service. Finally, back in San Francisco on February 17, he joined the Army. A photo of the ceremony distributed nationally shows him at the front of a group of men, right hand raised, with his expression showing something like terror.

A view of Strada delle Fontane, the street on which Giuseppe and Rosalie DiMaggio lived before emigrating to the United States, as seen from Isola delle Femmine's fish market. *(Courtesy of Margie Cowan)*

Thanks to his brother Vince, Joe DiMaggio became a star in 1933 on the San Francisco Seals, one of the more popular teams in the Pacific Coast League. (*Courtesy of Mark Macrae*)

Team photo of the San Francisco Seals in 1935 with Joe (*lower right*) and their rookie manager, Lefty O'Doul (*center*). (*Courtesy of Mark Macrae*)

Joe was an immediate sensation when he joined the Yankees in 1936. He would take over the leadership role from Lou Gehrig and lead the Bronx Bombers to four consecutive world championships. (*Courtesy of the National Baseball Hall of Fame Library*)

Left: Ted Williams was born and raised in San Diego, and while with the Padres of the Pacific Coast League he and Vince DiMaggio were teammates. (*Courtesy of Mark Macrae*) *Right:* Thanks to his financial success, especially World Series winners' shares, Joe was able to underwrite a restaurant on Fisherman's Wharf in San Francisco operated by his brothers Tom and Mike. (*Courtesy of Mark Macrae*)

Vince (*left*) joined his brother Joe in the major leagues in 1937 when he was signed by the Boston Bees. (*Courtesy of the National Baseball Hall of Fame Library*)

Vince displayed power at the plate with the Boston Bees and was a terrific center fielder, but also led the National League in strikeouts. (*Courtesy of the National Baseball Hall of Fame Library*)

Left: Vince, always a fan favorite, blossomed as a hitter when he joined the Pittsburgh Pirates in 1940. He would become a two-time All Star. (*Courtesy of the Pittsburgh Pirates*) *Right:* Dominic became the third DiMaggio brother to play on the San Francisco Seals, and he credited the tutoring and support of Lefty O'Doul for making him a major-league-caliber hitter. (*Courtesy of Mark Macrae*)

Dominic's rookie season in the major leagues was with the Boston Red Sox in 1940, and he soon intimidated runners who tried to test his throwing arm. (*Courtesy of the National Baseball Hall of Fame Library*)

Joe's 56-game hitting streak came to an end on July 18, 1941, but he still celebrated a 4–3 win over the Indians with manager Joe McCarthy and his teammates, including Phil Rizzuto (*far right*), who had played in the minors with Vince. (*Courtesy of Bettman/CORBIS*)

Left: Despite the intensifying competition between Joe and Ted Williams for best player in the American League, Dominic and Ted became close friends. (*Courtesy of the National Baseball Hall of Fame Library*) *Right:* Vince was back in the Pacific Coast League after his major league career ended, and in 1947 he played for Casey Stengel on the Oakland Oaks. (*Courtesy of Mark Macrae*)

Right: Though not quite the fancy dresser his brother Joe was, Dominic could offer some sartorial splendor as a major leaguer. (*Courtesy of the National Baseball Hall of Fame Library*)

Below: In January 1946, Joe and Dominic were back from World War II military service and were reunited with Vince, then with the Philadelphia Phillies, on Fisherman's Wharf. (*Courtesy of Bettman/CORBIS*)

Though age and injuries hampered him after the war, Joe was still the "Big Guy" on the Yankees with many clutch hits during pennant drives. He is greeted at the plate by Yogi Berra (*left*) and Phil Rizzuto. (*Courtesy of the National Baseball Hall of Fame Library*)

Boston won the American League pennant in 1946 with a potent run-producing lineup that included (*left to right*) Bobby Doerr, Dominic DiMaggio, Johnny Pesky, Rudy York, and Ted Williams. (*Courtesy Bettman/CORBIS*)

This is one of the few times that Dominic and Joe socialized on the field when the Red Sox played the Yankees. By the late 1940s, Dominic was acknowledged as the best center fielder in the league. (*Courtesy of the National Baseball Hall of Fame Library*)

Later in his career, the "Little Professor" schooled a new generation of Red Sox players in hitting and fielding. (*Courtesy of the National Baseball Hall of Fame Library*)

Three of the five DiMaggio brothers—Dominic, Joe, and Tom (*right*)—gathered at DiMaggio's Grotto to celebrate the fiftieth wedding anniversary of their parents, Rosalie and Giuseppe. (*Courtesy Bettman/CORBIS*)

Top: Dominic and his wife, Emily, leaving a Boston restaurant with Joe and Marilyn in January 1955, three months after she had secured a divorce in Los Angeles. (*Courtesy of Bettman/CORBIS*)

Bottom: Marilyn Monroe is flanked by her new husband, Joe, and Lefty O'Doul in 1954 during a tour of Japan, where they were greeted by enthusiastic crowds. (*Courtesy of Mark Macrae*)

The last full season Dominic (*third from right, middle row*) played on the Red Sox was in 1952. He reluctantly retired the following May. (*Courtesy of the Boston Red Sox*)

Their playing days long over, Joe and Dominic together at the wedding of Dominic's daughter, Emily, in 1981. (*Courtesy of Emily DiMaggio Jr.*)

Dominic signing his 1990 book, *Real Grass, Real Heroes*, the introduction of which was written by Ted Williams. (*Courtesy of Emily DiMaggio Jr.*)

The baseball-playing brothers together for the last time, at Fenway Park in Boston in May 1986. Vince (*left*), terminally ill, died five months later. (*Courtesy of the Boston Red Sox*)

According to friends and family, Emily and Dominic were "inseparable" during their sixty-one years of marriage. (*Courtesy of Emily DiMaggio Jr.*)

Dominic (*second from right*) was a member of the freshman class of the Red Sox Hall of Fame in 1995 and was inducted with dear friends Johnny Pesky and Ted Williams, and Charlie Wagner, a former pitcher, executive, and scout for the Red Sox. (*Courtesy of Emily DiMaggio Jr.*)

THIRTEEN

DURING WORLD WAR II, Joe and Dominic would be away from their aging parents and their brothers and sisters for far longer than they ever had before. For the two youngest brothers, there would be no holiday visits to the house on Beach Street, where Giuseppe presided and served his homemade wine while Rosalie cooked up enough food to satisfy everyone.

"My grandmother was a very good cook," remembers Joanne DiMaggio Webber. "My grandparents spoke Italian at the table—pretty much all the time too. At the dinner table we had salad first, then soup, then pasta, then the main course. With nine children, I guess it had been important to prepare several courses."

Vince and his family could still see his parents and most of his siblings, but he wasn't particularly pleased about it: he tried several times to join the military but was rejected because of his ulcers. For the first time since 1936, only one of the DiMaggio brothers would be heading to spring training.

For much of his military career, Joe would tell bunkmates how much he didn't like being in the service and complain about how much money he was losing by earning only $50 a month from the Army. He was a lowly private, but that didn't mean he would be anywhere near the front lines dodging bullets. Only two months later, the Associated Press sent out a story headlined "DiMaggio Stars in Game," about a contest hosted by the Hollywood Stars of the Pacific Coast League. The victorious visitors were a team made up of Army and Navy all-stars, which included Yankees teammate Red Ruffing. Joe might or might not survive his marriage, but there was no doubt he would survive the war.

Joe played baseball so regularly that newspapers kept track of his batting average that spring, which was .333 after a game against the University of Southern California. One account wryly noted, "Private Joe DiMaggio's Spring training has been somewhat different this year." When the major league season began, Joe was roaming the outfield at the Santa Ana Army Air Base. He was one of the best players in a military uniform, but in one game he met his match. His Santa Ana team was playing the Army Air Transport Command squad from nearby Long Beach. Joe managed only to pop up twice and strike out. The opposing pitcher was Ruffing, who at 38 could still bring it. That fall, he would defeat the Camp Pendleton team 4–1 for the Southern California Service Championship.

Dorothy moved to Los Angeles so that she and Joe Jr. could see Joe when he was on leave. It didn't help their relationship. In October 1943, she filed for divorce, charging mental cruelty, and asked for $650 a month in alimony and child support.

Even before the war, Joe had complained of trouble with his stomach. After the divorce filing and the headlines that followed it, his stomach felt worse. By the time the divorce was final in May 1944, the ulcerlike symptoms were chronic. Joe didn't want the divorce, but he didn't contest it, refusing to open up his private life to the press and the court. The terms of the interlocutory decree were a cash payment of $14,000 to Dorothy and $150 a month in child support.

In the early part of 1944, Joe was with the Seventh Army Air Force. Finally, he was to be deployed: he would head a team of former major league stars who would tour the Central Pacific. One of the team members was Dario Lodigiani from the DiMaggios' North Beach neighborhood, who had completed three years with the White Sox. Soon after Joe arrived in Hawaii, he was promoted to staff sergeant.

It was more of the same—play baseball and spend downtime with other players. In August, though, Joe landed in a Honolulu hospital. He was leading the Hawaii League at the time with a .411 average and had recently hit a homer measured at 475 feet. The press reported an unspecified "stomach disorder," but quashed rumors that he was going to apply for a medical discharge and return to the Yankees. Whatever was wrong with Joe's stomach (he insisted the diagnosis was an ulcer, one of the very few times he compared himself to Vince), it was enough to get him a new posting—back to the New York area. He was shipped to the Army Rehabilitation Center in Atlantic City. This trip included a three-week furlough, and it wasn't long before Joe was back sitting at his usual table at Toots Shor's. He also served as a guest referee with heavyweight champion Joe Louis at a series of bouts in Brooklyn.

Joe's little brother had a much more positive attitude toward military service. Dominic enjoyed the Navy. "I wanted to be on the water. I love the water. I guess that comes from being raised in San Francisco." He wouldn't have turned down any branch of the service, though, because "I just didn't want to be at home playing baseball while all my fellow countrymen were out fighting and serving their country. I wouldn't have felt right about that."

Like thousands of others, Dominic found himself at the Norfolk Naval Training Station. It had its own baseball team that competed against teams representing other bases and agencies, even the FBI. The Norfolk squad had dominated in 1942 with a 92-8 record thanks to the pitching of Fred Hutchinson and Bob Feller, who had 19 wins before shipping out to join the crew of the USS *Alabama*. The 1943 edition had Dominic patrolling center field. The team compiled a 75-25 record. The commander of the Norfolk Naval Training Station, Capt. Harry McClure, was also the manager of the ball club. In one game, Dominic chased after a fly ball and crashed into the fence. As he lay there stunned, McClure wanted to check on his center fielder, but it wouldn't do for a captain to go running out to see a lowly sailor. So McClure called for his jeep and was driven out to help Dominic stand up.

The Red Sox sorely missed Dominic and their other young stars that year. The lineup included only two regular starters, Bobby Doerr at second base and Jim Tabor at third. Like most major league clubs, the Red Sox had to rely on retreads and players who might have otherwise retired to fill out their roster. Al Simmons, at 41, could bat only .203 to end what was otherwise a Hall of Fame career. Manager Joe Cronin, who would turn 37 later in the year, was still plugging away at the plate and in fact would establish a still-unbroken American League record of five pinch-hit home runs. The home opener against the Yankees attracted fewer than 7,000 fans. Only 714 people attended the final game at Fenway on September 27. The Red Sox compiled a dismal record of 68-84 and finished 29 games out of first place.

The 1944 season was better, with Boston winding up at 77-77 and 12 games out. But the war was still grinding on, and more good players exchanged Red Sox uniforms for military ones. Doerr had 95 RBI and a .325 average in September, then went into the Army. Tabor and catcher Hal Wagner also went into the service before the season ended. One of the year's few highlights was a 25-game hitting streak by Dominic's replacement in center field, Catfish Metkovich.

Dominic, by then off in the Pacific (stationed in Australia), didn't have time to follow the misfortunes of the Red Sox. "We were part of a team," he said about his Navy service. "You just joined another team—that was all that happened in World War II." Sounding very much the Little Professor, he added, "I do believe that anyone who goes into the service, for even a short period of time, picks up a lot more for their future as far as living and understanding things a great deal better, a maturity, so to speak. It teaches you. It's another avenue of learning."

Ted Williams had fun learning how to fly. "Flying came easy for me," he reported. But not for a teammate who was stationed with him at the Amherst training facility. "Poor Pesky," Ted reported. "He was a great little athlete. A boxer, wrestler, basketball player, he could run like hell and he was a tiger on the obstacle courses. But he couldn't swim a stroke, he'd go right down, and he flew an airplane like he had stone arms."

After Amherst, Ted was sent for further training at a base in Chapel Hill, North Carolina. That July, he and Dominic were together again, not in a military location but back in Fenway Park. Maurice J. Tobin, the mayor of Boston, had arranged an exhibition game to raise money for the city's poor. The Boston Braves would take on an all-star team managed by Babe Ruth. Tobin had enough influence that Dominic could leave the Norfolk base and Ted could visit from North Carolina. Ted met the Babe for the first time and bested him in a home run hitting contest, 3–0. In the game itself, Ted hit a homer that turned out to be the winning run in the 9–8 victory, after Dominic had tripled in two runs.

Ted went for further training in Kokomo, Indiana, and then on to Pensacola, Florida. (Pesky, who just couldn't get the hang of flying, was sent to an operations school in Atlanta, where he could earn an officer's commission while staying on the ground.) Ben Chapman was one of the major leaguers Ted encountered in Florida, where some baseball was being played, "but I didn't have my heart in it at all and I played lousy. By this time I was more interested in flying, and I was also enjoying the pleasures of Florida's fishing for the first time."

Ted was made an instructor at the Pensacola base. In May 1944, when he was promoted to second lieutenant, Ted and Doris Soule, the girl he had met in Minnesota, were married. He would turn out to be about as adept at marriage as Joe DiMaggio was. Ted was eager to see combat, but it was not to be. When the war against Japan ended in August 1945, he was in San Francisco, awaiting transportation to Hawaii. Shipped there anyway, he was reunited with Pesky and a few other major leaguers. Until orders to return to the United States were sorted out, they played baseball under the auspices of the 14th Naval District League. The commissioner was Bill Dickey.

EVEN DURING A WORLD WAR, baseball was still a business. With Joe gone, the Yankees felt free to cut Lefty Gomez loose, even though clubs were keeping many older and damaged players. Gomez had gone 6-4 in the 1942 campaign, but it was clear that his arm strength was declining. He was traded to the purgatory of the National League, the Boston Braves. He didn't last as long as spring training with that club and was sent packing to the Washington Senators. He retired after pitching only four and two-thirds innings for them. His eccentric explanation for his short stint was, "I couldn't speak enough Spanish to make myself understood on that club." The future Hall of Famer had a career record of 189-102, but at least as important to the Yankees was that Gomez had six World Series wins without a defeat (and he hadn't pitched in the 1941 and '42 Fall Classics).

Even with Joe, Phil Rizzuto, Tommy Henrich, and others gone to war, the Yankees won the 1943 pennant by 13.5 games over the Senators. To cap off the season, the Bronx Bombers became world champions again by taking the Series in five games from the club that had taken away their championship the year before, the St. Louis Cardinals. But New York had a dismal '44 season, finishing third behind the usually hapless St. Louis Browns. That year the estate of Jacob Ruppert sold the team to Dan Topping and Del Webb. They brought Larry MacPhail over from the Brooklyn Dodgers as a minority owner and replacement for Ed Barrow as general manager.

The Red Sox had an unhappy '45 campaign. On April 16, the club offered a sham tryout to three black players, Marvin Williams, Sam Jethroe, and Jackie Robinson. The fortunes of the Red Sox might have been dramatically different in the next decade had they signed Robinson, as Branch Rickey of the Brooklyn Dodgers would do six months later. But Boston was not a welcoming place for players of color. The *Boston Globe* reported that near the end of the one-hour tryout someone shouted, "Get those niggers off the field!" It would not be until 1959 that a black player wearing a Red Sox uniform appeared in a regular-season game.

In the opening day game at Fenway Park, the Yankees beat them 8–4, and it didn't get much better—the Red Sox lost their first eight games. In one of them, Metkovich made three errors in one inning—more center-field miscues than Dominic would have committed in half a season. The one highlight of the season was rookie Dave "Boo" Ferriss. As a left-handed outfielder at Mississippi State University, his arm had gone bad, but being ambidextrous, he switched to right-handed pitching. After Boston's eighth straight loss that April, a frustrated Cronin turned to the 23-year-old, who two months earlier had been discharged from the Army Air Corps because of asthma. Ferriss began his first game on April 29 by throwing ten straight balls, then recovered to toss a five-hit shutout. On June 6, he pitched his eighth consecutive complete-game victory. He ended the '45 season with 21 wins. The rookie was feted with a "Boo Ferris Day" on September 23 and presented with a Lincoln Zephyr.

"When I got out of the Army, the Red Sox sent me to their minor league club in Louisville, Kentucky, and I expected to spend the year there learning how to pitch at the professional level," he recalled 66 years later. "No one was more surprised than me when I got called up and told to get out there. Nothing for me to do but give it my best."

FOR THE FIRST TIME since 1936, Vince was the only DiMaggio playing in the major leagues. Early in the 1943 season, he wrote

Dominic, "You fellows left me holding the bag. Now it's up to me to do something about carrying on in the proper DiMaggio style."

He did the best he could. With the wartime depletion, Vince was one of the best ballplayers left in the National League. His third home run of the season, on May 27, was the first one hit at Forbes Field in the '43 campaign, an indication of how poor the rest of the Pittsburgh squad was in the power department. He clouted two homers and had five RBI in a 17–4 rout of the Dodgers on June 3. The next day he raced to the wall to take a homer away from Arky Vaughan.

When Vince was in New York, the reporters were finally able to get past the "wrong DiMaggio" bias. "Likable and affable, Vince has a far warmer personality than either of his brothers," wrote Arthur Daley in the *New York Times*. "Where a brief 'uh-huh' was a full-flowered conversation for the reticent Joe and where Dom was much too shy and retiring, Vince is expansive."

Also for the first time, Vince was chosen for the National League All-Star team. The first Midsummer Classic to be played at night, it showcased just how good a player Vince was. Stan Musial, in his first of 24 consecutive All-Star appearances, drove in a run in the first inning, then the American League scored five runs, helped by a Bobby Doerr three-run round-tripper. Vince led a comeback. After singling in the fourth, he tripled in the seventh off Tex Hughson and scored, then homered in the ninth.

The fans continued to love him in Pittsburgh, never more so than during a game in late July. As the *Pittsburgh Post* reported: "The last of the DiMaggios proved why he is the most colorful and popular of baseball's royal family yesterday. Vince's murderous four-for-four which made the road so tough for the Dodgers wasn't the reason, either. Any hitter has those days. It was rather the Ruthian gesture prior to his second home run of the slugfest. As he trotted in from center in the sixth, 2000 kids in the centerfield bleachers roared, 'We want a homer.' DiMag doffed his cap, nodded and pointed to the leftfield wall. The first batter in that frame, he stepped up and whaled the ball over the fence right at the spot where he had pointed. You should've heard those kids roar! The Babe was never a greater hero at Yankee Stadium."

"For my father, playing major league baseball was always about the fans," says his daughter Joanne. "When there would be things in the papers about he wasn't as good a player as Joe and Dominic, he would shrug and say that the fans get their money's worth seeing him play too."

When the 1943 season was over, Vince finally had his chance to do battle in the Pacific Theater—but on ball fields, not battleships. The commissioner of baseball, Kenesaw Mountain Landis, approved a plan to have 18-player all-star teams from each league go on tour and play games against each other. The managers of the National League and American League squads were Frankie Frisch and Joe Cronin. Vince was one of the five outfielders representing the senior league, the others being Stan Musial, Augie Galan (a fellow Pacific Coast League alum), Dixie Walker, and Ducky Medwick.

During the off-season, Vince and his family spent some of their time in the Bay Area. "I loved being there very much," says Joanne. "My Uncle Tom ran the restaurant, and he was very nice. My father helped some during the off-season. My Uncle Mike was a sweet-heart, and I liked his three kids. My grandfather tried to teach me Italian, but I just couldn't get it. Right down the street from where he and my grandmother lived was the Palace of Fine Arts. Rosalie always gave me pieces of bread, and I walked down there to feed the ducks."

Back from the Pacific tour, Vince took an off-season job at the California Ship Building Corporation. If he wouldn't be allowed to fight, at least he could help build the equipment that did the fighting. The job allowed him to manage a ball club for the first time, helm-ing a team of electrical workers who played in a Long Beach winter league. When he showed up late for spring training in '44—he'd

TOM CLAVIN

wanted to put in as much time as he could at the shipyard—some in the press accused him of holding out for more money. Harvey J. Boyle in the *Pittsburgh Post-Gazette* intoned, "This wouldn't be a very good season for holdouts. Baseball owners are too preoccupied with a variety of manpower problems to get very excited about the hesitancy of a player to accept terms. Beyond the resentment of the owner, there is the fan reaction to be considered."

At spring training it soon became clear that Vince and manager Frisch weren't seeing eye to eye. Watching Vince practice, the Fordham Flash griped to Arthur Daley of the *Times*, "I'm getting tired of telling him to throw that glove of his away. If he could only learn to hit he'd be as great a ball player as his brother Joe." It set the tone for the season. Vince made the National League All-Star team, but with Frisch helming, he rode the bench the whole game. In August he got into a tiff with the organization over his meal allowance. He charged a $9.60 meal to the club. The Pirates sent the bill back to him citing a $4.50 limit. Vince told them through reporters, "If you think I eat too much, trade me."

When the season ended, he had played in only 109 games, his fewest since 1939 with the Cincinnati Reds, with only nine homers and 50 RBI. The Pirates traded him at the end of the season to the Phillies, the worst team in the National League, finishing 43 games out of first. It looked like a punitive move, but Vince had actually requested the relocation.

"He left Pittsburgh because of the problems that happened, and one of the problems was he was having an affair," Joanne says. "He asked to be traded because my mother would not give him a divorce, and he had to get out of the situation. No one said anything to me. I overheard a conversation at my Aunt Frances's house. When I asked about it, I was told, 'Oh no, we're talking about Joe.'" Vince and Madeline would later patch things up.

After exchanging southpaw Al Gerheauser for Vince, Herb Pennock, Philadelphia's general manager, told reporters, "I think

164

Vince will hit a lot of homers over that left-field fence in Shibe Park."
He proved clairvoyant. Vince had his best season since the 1941 cam-
paign. The highlight came on September 1 in a game against the
Braves in Boston, when Vince hit a grand slam. It was his fourth of
the year, and with it he tied a National League record set by Frank
"Wildfire" Schulte back in 1911 (later broken by Ernie Banks).

Vince wound up supplying Philadelphia with 19 home runs, easily the most on the team, and 84 RBI in 127 games. (Jimmie Foxx,
at 37, was back in baseball and also with the Phillies, but he slugged
only seven homers.) Vince also had 12 stolen bases, a career high.
Alas, with 91 strikeouts, he led the league for the sixth time. Not
that it mattered very much, because the Phillies were the Phillies—
they lost 108 games, and finished 52 games behind the surprising
Chicago Cubs.

Vince was now 33. With the war over, many players in their prime
would be returning to the big leagues. He might have to fight to be
a starter in the 1946 spring training camp.

THE SPRING OF 1945 had found Joe as a physical training instructor in the Army Air Forces Redistribution Center in Atlantic City.
Nearby, at Bader Field, that year's edition of the Yankees had begun
spring training. "I'd give anything to be able to take the field with
the Yanks in the American League race," he told Dan Daniel. "But if
I were discharged tomorrow, I would not return to the club. I would
not play ball with the war still on."

This sounds like Joe being patriotic and showing solidarity with
other ballplayers still in uniform. But then he added, "You say the
fans would not hoot a man with a medical discharge. Well, I would
not take the chance. I never will forget the going over some of the
boys in the Stadium gave me before I went into the service."

For the Yankees, Joe couldn't get back from the Army fast enough.
There was no shame in the Detroit Tigers winning the American
League pennant (they would defeat the Chicago Cubs in the World

Series), but finishing fourth, behind the perennial punching bags the Senators and the Browns, was humiliating.

Joe was finally discharged on September 14. Still being treated for stomach ulcers, he had been at the Army Air Forces Don Ce-Sar convalescent hospital in a familiar city, St. Petersburg. Two days after his discharge, Joe was back at Yankee Stadium, but in civilian clothes. He attended a doubleheader against the Browns, accompanied by Dorothy and Joe Jr. In his autobiography, dedicated "To little Joe," Joe Sr. reports that after some fans called out, "Hello, Joe!" and "Glad to see you back, Joe!" his son said, "See, Daddy? Everybody knows me."

He told reporters that he was heading to San Francisco that week to see his family. Reporters wondered about his being out in public together with Dorothy, but Joe wouldn't reveal that he was trying to win his ex-wife back. He wanted to save that news to tell Giuseppe and Rosalie when he saw them again. They were not used to his failing at anything, and that included marriage.

There was another reason to be in New York—to work out a deal for his autobiography. Joe didn't particularly want to do a book, since it would mean talking about himself, even if only to a writer (Tom Meany), but he needed the money. Missing three seasons meant he had missed out on at least $125,000 in salary from the Yankees.

In his biography of Joe, David Jones described Joe's dilemma: "DiMaggio resented the war with an intensity equal to the most battle-scarred private. It had robbed him of the best years of his career. When he went into the Army, DiMaggio had been a 28-year-old superstar, still at the height of his athletic powers. By the time he was discharged from the service, he was nearly 31, divorced, underweight, undernourished, and bitter. Those three years, 1943 to 1945, would carve a gaping hole in DiMaggio's career totals, creating an absence that would be felt like a missing limb."

Joe's appearance at Yankee Stadium signaled that it was time for the traditional order of things to be restored in baseball. Everyone expected that in 1946 the Yankees, with Joe leading them, would win the pennant, then the World Series. Boston had ended the '45 season 10 games under .500 and 17.5 games out. Though the Red Sox had good players returning too, especially the core group of Ted-Dominic-Doerr-Pesky, that had to be too large a deficit to make up in one year.

As it turned out, the Red Sox were about to have one of the greatest seasons in the franchise's history, and Dominic and Joe would square off as two of the best players in the American League.

"All in all, World War II taught me that we're all on the same team working for a common goal and hoping somehow that we could all get back to where we were," said Dominic. "I understood that, being a player. I understood it even better in 1946."

As the two brothers battled for the flag, Vince's lonely struggle to survive in the National League would go virtually ignored.

FOURTEEN

In the 1946 season, Dominic became the best center fielder in the American League, Joe struggled to regain his superstar status, and Vince found himself wearing a uniform he had discarded 13 years earlier. As had happened in the 1930s, the DiMaggio brothers were going in different directions. This time, though, only Dominic was going up.

The much larger picture was that for American society and culture, true baseball was back. According to David Halberstam, "In the years immediately following World War II, professional baseball mesmerized the American people as it never had before and never would again. Baseball, more than anything else, seemed to symbolize normalcy and a return to life in America as it had been before Pearl Harbor."

Anticipating opening day, Arthur Daley wrote in the *New York Times* that a scene "will be enacted in eight major league baseball parks on Tuesday as the long-awaited first post-war season moves off with a gigantic stride. When the first batter steps up to the plate, he will be greeted by roars of anticipation from the stands, echoing off

Coogan's Bluff behind the Polo Grounds in New York and rolling out over the prairies from Sportsman's Park in St. Louis."

Although many familiar names would return to major league rosters in 1946, it was still a significantly changed landscape. There was no longer room for many players who had hung on during the war. Others who had gone off to serve came back a few years older and with their skills diminished. In Boston at the end of the 1945 season, Catfish Metkovich told his teammates, "Boys, better take a good look around you because most of us won't be here next year." (Metkovich did manage to stick with the Red Sox.)

"We had added pressure on us, because we knew that those war years were lost forever," Dominic observed. "Lawyers and accountants coming home from the war would be able to pursue their careers for another 30 years, but the limited number of years available to us in our chosen profession had been reduced to an even lower number. We never knew what that number was because it was going to be a different one for each of us, but we knew that what was going to be a short career anyhow was going to be even shorter now. We couldn't afford to spend a couple of years getting our sharpness back. A ten-year career in the major leagues is far above the average length, and if a player lost three of those ten years because of military service, that's 30 percent of his career."

Johnnie Pesky was not having such dark thoughts. He told the *Boston Herald* years later, "It was a great feeling to be back at Fenway for the opener that year. We had all made it back. A lot of people didn't. We were together again. And we were playing baseball."

Home in San Francisco, Dominic had been having some practical thoughts besides the philosophical ones. He also looked forward to being back with his core teammates, but after returning from the fight to defeat the Evil Axis, he wanted to fight for the rights of players—starting with himself. Decades before it actually became official in baseball, Dominic, after discussing his position with Tom, declared himself a free agent.

He wrote a letter to the Red Sox brass explaining that after spending three years in military service and not signing any baseball contracts, he didn't belong to anyone. One can imagine the impact on baseball—and on America—if other players, especially Dom's brother, decided that their years in a military uniform made them free from ownership as well. But there is no indication that Joe shared his brother's revolutionary ideas about labor relations. Quite the opposite. He couldn't wait to ink his 1946 contract.

Apparently, the Red Sox grasped the potential for disaster. Joe Cronin arrived in San Francisco in a lather. "The veins were popping out of his head," Dominic told Leigh Montville. "He said the Red Sox owned me, and he was there to sign me up for $11,000. This was not the figure I had in mind."

Anticipating that baseball would be more popular than ever, and displaying the business acumen that would make him successful years later, Dominic was maneuvering for a piece of the action. First, he wouldn't take a penny less than $16,000 in salary. Second, he tied additional pay to attendance at Fenway Park—if the club drew 500,000 (it had attracted 603,794 in 1945), Dominic would receive an extra $500, and additional $500 payments for every 50,000 people after that. Cronin relayed this counterproposal to Tom Yawkey, who agreed. Ted Williams would follow Dom's example and work out his own percentage-of-the-gate contract.

A notable returnee who picked up right where he left off after the war was Bob Feller, who had missed more than three seasons and was now 27. He struck out the first batter he faced when the 1946 season began; when it ended, he would have 26 victories and would lead the majors in shutouts and strikeouts. This was especially remarkable given that while seeing combat in the Pacific on the USS *Alabama,* he had suffered an injury to his pitching hand that could have ended his career.

With baseball back in full bloom, the rivalry between the Red Sox and Yankees would achieve a new intensity. When Boston traveled to New York by train through Massachusetts, Rhode Island, and Connecticut, fans lined the tracks to cheer Dominic and his teammates. They jeered Joe and the Yankees when they traveled in the other direction.

One of the insults they could have hurled was "old-timers." The Bronx Bombers were indeed aging. When the season began, Bill Dickey was still catching at 39. He would be spelled by a youngster from St. Louis, Yogi Berra. Tommy Henrich was 33, Red Ruffing was 41, and Spud Chandler was 38. During the season, younger players with potential—including Tommy Byrne, Joe Page, Vic Raschi, and Bobby Brown—would get some playing time, but they weren't ready yet to be stars. Even Joe McCarthy, who had been the manager since 1931, was getting on, with drinking problems speeding the process.

It was generally a good time for Joe. He had left the military far behind. In San Francisco, Giuseppe and Rosalie had returned to their normal lives, though both were getting a bit frail. Customers were showing up at the restaurant on Fisherman's Wharf again, making Tom and Mike smile. It had been good to see Vince and Dominic and hear the latter's stories of far-off Australia.

Joe was ready to resume his role as the Great DiMaggio—the very first edition of *Sport* magazine that year featured a cover story titled "The Story of Big and Little Joe DiMaggio," while *Lucky to Be a Yankee* turned out, not surprisingly, to be a best-seller. He could sit again at his regular table at Toots Shor's whenever the Yankees were not on the road, and even the ulcer wasn't bothering him anymore. Opponents in the American League would fade as the season wore on, and he would be back in the World Series. Life was good—most of it anyway.

"Everybody talked about how he'd changed," wrote Richard Ben Cramer. "Not the way he played. And not physically (though he was still ten pounds underweight). It was the way he smiled, laughed out loud, and talked about anything—Daig was tellin' stories!" (Daig was a nickname, short for Dago.) "And chatting up the writers, and buying dinners: happy as a kid. Hell, he didn't even hold out, but settled on what MacPhail gave him. Same as his old pay: that's what the papers said."

Giuseppe confirmed that his fourth son would have a good year when he told local reporters, "He gonna hit thirty-six home runs."

In his personal life, though, Joe wasn't seeing such success. Dorothy refused to consider his proposal of remarriage. In fact, she had met someone else, a stockbroker named George Schubert. They moved into a suite at the Waldorf-Astoria together. Later in the season they would be married. Joe had no wife, and Joe Jr. had a stepfather.

DESPITE EXPECTATIONS, the Yankees played pedestrian baseball early in the season, while the Red Sox began 1946 like they had been shot out of a cannon. Late in May, Boston took two out of three at Yankee Stadium, and the home team was already five and a half games behind them. The Bombers then went on a hellish road trip, during which McCarthy drank so much that he couldn't attend games. When he did, his drunken exploits embarrassed everyone, like screaming insults at relief pitcher Joe Page. When the team returned to New York, McCarthy vanished. A few days later, his resignation arrived by telegram.

The only major league manager Joe had played for was gone, though he took some comfort in the decision to replace McCarthy with Dickey. But Joe and the team still struggled. The situation worsened when he developed a persistent pain in one of his heels. Then, while sliding into second, he tore cartilage in one knee. He was hitting only .266 at the time.

Because of the injury, he would not be in the All-Star Game. The starting center fielder for the American League was Dominic. At least the injury saved Joe the potential indignity of playing backup to his younger brother.

Dominic later reflected that Boston played better than their New

York rivals that year because "most of the Red Sox players were lucky enough to be able to resume playing at our prewar level of performance. The Yankees, on the other hand, experienced problems." And for the first time in many years, the Sox had an imposing pitching staff. Tex Hughson was back, Boo Ferriss was only 24, and Joe Dobson and Mickey Harris were also under 30. Mel Parnell was an exciting hurler in the minors who might be ready for the big leagues. "Joe Cronin had caught the rest of the league with its pants down," Dominic said. "We just ran away from everyone."

That is precisely what happened. On opening day, President Harry Truman threw out the first ball at Griffith Stadium. Hughson pitched a complete game, Ted Williams socked a 430-foot homer, and the Red Sox won. At their Fenway Park opener four days later, Boston had only two hits, but they were enough to down the Philadelphia Athletics 2–1. The Red Sox were nearly unbeatable the first two months of the season, winning 41 of their first 50 games. A 2–0 loss at Yankee Stadium ended a 15-game winning streak, the longest streak in franchise history. In an 18–8 win over the Browns a week later, after Ted hit a grand slam, he was walked intentionally three times. During the first two weeks of June, the Red Sox enjoyed a 12-game win streak. Both streaks included thrashings of the Yankees in Boston and New York.

Dominic and Joe were able to resume a practice they had begun in 1940, Dominic's rookie season: "Joe and I picked up right where we left off in our brotherly competition." In a game at Yankee Stadium in May, Dominic launched a ball to deep center field. Joe raced after it and climbed the wall to rob his brother of a triple. When the inning ended and the brothers crossed paths behind second base, Joe called out, "It's 32–21," representing the number of times one had taken a hit away from the other. Only the brothers knew that Dominic was leading the competition.

In a doubleheader in June at Fenway Park, Ted proved he was playing as well as ever—or even better. The Cleveland Indians, now managed by shortstop Lou Boudreau, were expected to contend for the pennant. Instead, they were in sixth place. In the first game, Ted hit three homers—the first a grand slam, the second with two on to tie the game, and the third in the ninth won it 11–10. Boudreau had a homer and four doubles in vain.

Between games, he had a brainstorm. After Ted doubled in the second game, Boudreau had his infielders, center fielder, and right fielder shift to their left to blanket the right side against Williams. The third baseman, Ken Keltner, stood behind second base. Boudreau figured that the only way Ted would get more hits was to keep putting the ball in the seats or slap it to the opposite field.

"Gee, I had to laugh when I saw it," Ted later wrote. "What the hell's going on? This was my second time up in the second game. I had doubled to clear the bases in the first inning, giving me eleven runs batted in for the day. In effect, they are now telling me, 'Go ahead, hit to left field, have yourself a single. We'll sacrifice singles to take away your doubles and home runs any day.' They're tickled to death if I go to left because the only thing they're really afraid of is the long ball."

Ted was tickled to death by the shift too. By the end of the season, he had hit .400 with nine home runs against the Indians.

VINCE HAD GONE through Phillies spring training expecting, or at least hoping, to get as much playing time as the previous year. When the team broke camp and headed north to Philadelphia, he was set in center field. But not for long. At the end of April, he got word that he had been traded. The New York Giants were looking to bolster their outfield defense and had purchased Goody Rosen from the Brooklyn Dodgers. Manager Mel Ott thought Vince was the final piece of the puzzle, so he shipped pitcher Clyde Kluttz to Philadelphia. Ott pointed out to reporters that too many balls had dropped in for base hits early in the season, and "DiMaggio, an experienced fielder and fine thrower, should make the going a lot easier for our pitchers."

For the first time since San Francisco, two of the three ballplaying DiMaggios were living in the same city. Between the war and the fact that Vince no longer lived in the Bay Area, he and Joe had seen little of each other the past few years. But the time together in New York was short-lived. The Giants were tanking when Vince arrived, and he didn't help. Ott had wanted some power at the plate along with his defense, and Vince had none left. His last hit for the Phillies, it turned out, was his last hit in the major leagues. He went 0-for-25 for the Giants, and Ott let him go.

Vince managed to grab one dinner with Joe, then packed his bags and headed home. When no major league team picked him up, one in the PCL did—the San Francisco Seals. Lefty O'Doul would now earn the unique distinction of having managed all three DiMaggio brothers.

Like the other teams in the PCL, the Seals had suffered during the war years, hurt by curbs on travel and lower attendance. But O'Doul remained enormously popular in the Bay Area as a manager who could get the most out of his players. In the 1943, '44, and '45 seasons, the Seals did not finish first, but they won in the playoffs to capture three consecutive Governor's Cups. The 1946 team would turn out to be even better.

The season had started auspiciously. The new owner was a successful businessman, Paul Fagan, and his goal was to elevate the PCL to the status of a third major league. His plan was to upgrade his own club to set an example, figuring other PCL owners would follow along. He spent liberally on renovations to Seals Stadium, including innovations like baseball's first glass backstop, uniformed female ushers, and imported turf on the field. Fagan set the minimum annual player salary at $5,000, the same as in the National and American Leagues.

Fagan had a ranch in Hawaii, and that spring he flew the team there for training. During the season, he had the team flown to play games in the more faraway cities, like Portland and San Diego, reducing the wear and tear on them. Fagan wanted to eliminate any differences between the Seals and major league clubs. His efforts would be rewarded with victories and a record 670,563 people passing through the turnstiles. (In 1946 the PCL as a whole set an attendance record of 3,722,843. With the Oakland Oaks drawing over 600,000 fans, that meant 1.3 million people attended PCL games in the Bay Area—higher attendance than most major league clubs could boast.)

When O'Doul learned that Vince was available, he contacted him immediately. Vince was, after all, a DiMaggio, and he would put more fans in the seats. The team had both hitting, led by future Phillie Ferris Fain, and pitching, led by future Giant Larry Jansen. After the disappointments with the Phillies and especially the Giants, Vince found the Seals a very soft and successful landing spot.

Joanne recalls that having her father join the San Francisco club made life less complicated for her. "When I went to school, I would spend part of the year in an eastern school and part of the year in a school in Hermosa Beach, and the east school was so far ahead. My mother would have to school me so I could catch up and be promoted to the next grade. Then when we came back home, I was way ahead so I just slid along."

One of Vince's new teammates was Don Trower, an infielder who had joined the Seals in 1940 and had battled knee problems. He remembers that Vince was "happy-go-lucky," but didn't look completely comfortable at the plate.

"He'd go up there and swing from the bottom of his shoes to the top of his shoulders," remembers Trower, who was 92 when interviewed in 2012. "He was trying to hit a home run all the time. We didn't need him to, because we had a good bunch of boys on a good ball club. And of course, Lefty to steer us."

After games, "Vince just hung around with some of the boys and did some elbow-bending. He liked to talk and laugh. I'd get a kick out of him, though, when he'd strike out and throw his bat down."

Through the season the Seals had to fight off the Oakland Oaks, who had a new manager, Casey Stengel. The Oaks occupied first place for two months, but an injury in July to one of their best players, Les Scarsella, sent them adrift. The Seals went on to clinch the pennant, their first since 1935. Vince had contributed by playing in 43 games and batting .264, but a lone homer showed his power was waning.

The Seals rolled through the playoffs. In the first round, the Hollywood Stars faded quickly, losing four straight games. Next up were the Oaks. They put up a sturdier resistance, but after the Seals won the sixth game in the series, they had their fourth Governor's Cup in a row. Vince had joined a championship team, one that his parents and a few of his brothers and sisters could watch. He proved Thomas Wolfe wrong: you *can* go home again.

TED WILLIAMS CONTINUED to pound the ball, and "everybody was convinced I would win the Triple Crown," he recalled. "Halfway through the season I was hitting .365, I had 27 home runs, 91 runs batted in. I was at peace with the world. I was even doing a column for the *Boston Globe* with a ghostwriter. Fancy that."

Meanwhile, Dominic had become arguably the best combination in the league in manufacturing runs on offense and preventing runs on defense.

"I loved Dom," Pesky told Fay Vincent for his oral history. "I loved Bob. But Dom and I were more compatible to one another because Bobby and Ted came first and then Dom and then me. And we— they said, here are the fearless foursome from the West Coast. We're the fearless foursome, but we got on Ted's coattails, and he knew how to handle it."

By the All-Star break, the Red Sox were an extraordinary 54-23 with a seven-and-a-half-game lead over the Yankees. The game was at Fenway Park, and many of the players who had been All-Stars before military service were back. With Bob Feller starting, the junior circuit held the visitors to just three hits while compiling 12 runs. Dominic was the leadoff batter for the American League and he went 1-for-2. Ted hit solo and three-run homers and two singles. Ted's second home run came against Vince's former teammate Rip Sewell on what he called his "eephus ball," a bloop pitch that achieved a 20-foot-high arc before descending toward the catcher. Boo Ferriss was thrilled in the very first inning when Feller got into a bit of trouble on the mound and "they told me to warm up," he recalls. "Imagine that, [if] they put me in to replace Bob Feller in the All-Star Game. It didn't happen, but I had a great time." It was a magical year for the hurler from Mississippi, who would go on to collect 25 wins against only six losses and complete 26 games.

"You couldn't help but like Dom, and he was clearly a leader," says Ferriss. "You know, he became a top player and everything, but he was just as nice and friendly as one could be. And with Doerr at second base and Pesky at shortstop and Dom in center, that was great up-the-middle strength. That gave our pitchers a lot of confidence."

Ted continued to be hotter than the approaching dog days of summer. In a doubleheader on July 21 at Fenway Park against the Browns, he had seven straight hits and hit for the cycle for the only time in his career. By the end of the month, Boston's record was 70-28. They played even better in August. Dominic and Pesky kept getting on base—the latter established a new Red Sox record of hitting safely 53 times that month—and Ted, Doerr, and Rudy York would drive them in. As the month came to a close, Boston had a .706 winning percentage and had extended its lead over the sputtering Bronx Bombers to 16.5 games.

Joe couldn't recover from injury as quickly as he used to, but he came back after only a few weeks because the Yankees were slipping out of the pennant race. The Great DiMaggio wouldn't let that happen, most fans in the Bronx believed. But it was happening anyway. Dickey was managing well enough. And he was supportive of Joe. The ex-catcher and the younger man had been through many campaigns before. So it was another blow when, late in the season, Dickey was out. He wouldn't agree with MacPhail's personnel demands, so he was replaced by one of the coaches, Johnny Neun.

It was a lost season for Joe. His heel still hurt. He couldn't generate much power and hit only five homers the second half of the season. Then MacPhail unloaded a shocker: he proposed a trade to the lowly Senators, swapping Joe for Mickey Vernon, winner of the batting title that year. Adding insult to injury, the Senators nixed the deal.

The Yankees finished at 87-67, not a poor season but not good enough. They came in third behind Boston and Detroit. In October, Joe listened to the World Series at home in Manhattan, where he was staying because he had custody of Joe Jr. every other weekend.

The 1946 pennant was the first for the Red Sox since 1918, when Babe Ruth had been on the roster. Ted finished with 38 home runs, 123 RBI, and a .342 average. He won the MVP Award in a cakewalk, though he claimed it "surprised the hell out of me because I didn't think I would ever get it."

And how did Dominic's innovative salary structure work out? The Red Sox drew over 1.4 million spectators, third best in the American League. According to the formula, he earned $7,000 above his $16,000 salary, and he would also have a World Series share coming to him. He was catching up to Joe in more ways than one.

Giuseppe and Rosalie came east together for the Series—but this time to watch a different son as the Sox squared off against the Cardinals.

"I met his mother and dad when they came to the World Series," Boo Ferriss recalls. "They were very nice people. You could see where Dom got it from."

The Series went the full seven games, with its share of cliffhangers and heartbreakers. The Sox won two of the first three games, then their pitching collapsed in Game 4 as St. Louis rapped out 20 hits off six pitchers to win 12–3. The durable Red Sox bounced back to win the next game 6–3, with Pesky collecting three hits. But the Cards were tough too. In Game 6, Harry Brecheen pitched a 4–1 complete game as the Red Sox offense slept.

It came down to the final game in St. Louis on October 14. Ferriss pitched a strong game but got nicked for three runs early. Dominic drove in an early Red Sox run, but his team was still down 3–1 at the end of the seventh inning. Rip Russell and Catfish Metkovich began the top of the eighth with pinch-hit singles. There were still men on when Dominic came up with two outs. He drove a 3-1 pitch to right-center. It banged off the wall, and while Enos Slaughter chased it Russell and Metkovich scored easily. Dominic motored from first to second—and his hamstring popped. He staggered to second, then had to leave the game.

With the most important hit of his career, Dominic had just driven in his second and third runs of the seventh game of the World Series, tying it at 3–3. But the player Halberstam called "arguably the most aggressive centerfielder of his era" would not be on the field when the Cardinals came to bat. With Slaughter on first base and two outs, Harry Walker came to the plate. He hit a line drive that got by Dominic's replacement in center field, Leon Culberson. Without Dominic and his powerful arm in center field, Slaughter just never stopped running. In what became known as his "Mad Dash," and with the Cardinals fans roaring, he simply kept pumping, chugging around second, past third, to home. He said afterward, "If they hadn't taken DiMaggio out of the game, I wouldn't have tried it."

With the Cards up 4–3, the Sox offense produced nothing in the ninth, and the Cardinals were the world champions. Dominic had given it his all. Ted Williams had only five hits, all singles, one a bunt. He was so disgusted with himself that he gave his Series check to the loyal clubhouse attendant, Johnny Orlando. "I was shell-shocked. I was so disappointed in myself. Just sick inside." On the train ride back to Boston, "I went into my little compartment. When I got in there and closed the door I just broke down and started crying, and I looked up and there was a whole crowd of people watching me through the window."

It was a long trip back for Dominic as well. He sure would have liked to be the second DiMaggio to wear a World Series ring. Joe already had one for each finger of his right hand.

PART III

Look, I don't interfere with other people's lives. And I do not expect them to interfere with mine. There are things about my life, personal things, that I refuse to talk about. And even if you asked my brothers, they would be unable to tell you about them because they do not know. There are things about me, so many things, that they simply do not know.

—JOE DIMAGGIO TO GAY TALESE, 1966

FIFTEEN

THE 1947 AND 1948 seasons would be turning points for Vince, Joe, and Dominic DiMaggio. Vince, in his midthirties, struggled to keep playing in the PCL. Joe's legend expanded, but his body betrayed him. Dominic established himself as one of the best players in baseball—and found love while he was at it. These two years would also be the last ones of their parents' enduring marriage.

Much is made today of the fierce rivalry between the New York Yankees and Boston Red Sox, which is said to have been burning bright since the Sox sold Babe Ruth to the Yanks after the 1919 season, beginning the "Curse of the Bambino." It makes for good copy and conversation, but it doesn't make a whole lot of sense. It's true that with the acquisition of Ruth the Yankees joined the New York Giants and St. Louis Cardinals as consistent contenders and frequent champions in the big leagues, while Boston went in the opposite direction. There might have been bad feelings in Beantown about the loss of Ruth, but there could be no truly consistent rivalry when one team was routinely in the World Series and the other struggled to stay out of the second division.

The rivalry really ignited in 1947. After the delay caused by World War II, the Red Sox had finally caught up to the Yankees the year before. With their core position players in their prime, it was conceivable that they would now pull ahead. And having the two DiMaggio brothers vying for the league title was a story made for Hollywood. Despite the affection they had for each other, Joe and Dominic would not give an inch in their quest for the world championship.

"He was just like his brother Joe in that regard, in that Dominic badly wanted to win," says Sam Mele, who came up to the Sox from the minors in 1947. "Dominic was a flat-out tough competitor who wanted to win as much as anyone I knew. Every game I went on the field with him, I knew he would give all he had."

On May 26, 1947, Yankee Stadium was filled to bursting with the largest single-game crowd, 74,747, in the ballpark's history. It was no coincidence that the visitors were the Red Sox. The fans knew that this year could well be a watershed for both teams.

Joe had not been ready for spring training; the left heel was still bothering him. The Yankees sent him to Johns Hopkins Hospital in Baltimore for an operation. It was over a week before he left the hospital and headed to St. Petersburg. Not until the first week in April could he begin batting practice. When New York opened the season with a loss to the Philadelphia Athletics, Joe was on the bench.

There were a lot of questions about the 1947 edition of the Bronx Bombers, beginning with the manager. It had become obvious the previous season that not just anyone could replace Joe McCarthy. Larry MacPhail had chosen Bucky Harris, who previously managed the Tigers, Phillies, and Red Sox. At the tender age of 27 in 1924, doing double duty as the second baseman, Harris had guided the Washington Senators to a world championship. But that was a long time ago, New York was a tough town to manage in, and success with the Yankees depended on how Harris could get along with the man teammates called "the Big Guy."

Yogi Berra, the veteran of D-Day who had been mostly a catcher in the minors, would find playing time in right field, with Aaron Robinson doing much of the catching and Ralph Houk as his other backup. (Dominic had played with Berra when both were stationed in Norfolk during the war and had written Joe Cronin about his great potential.) Bobby Brown was still a newcomer at third base. Two outfielders, Joe and Henrich, were aging and injured. Their best pitcher, Spud Chandler, was 39. The Yanks would have to see what Bobo Newsom had left in the tank (not much) and if new arrival Allie Reynolds and untested Vic Raschi could contribute. Frank Crosetti was still on the team, though he got into only three games. True, there had been a war on, but the fact was that the Yanks hadn't won a pennant in the previous three seasons, a gap not seen since the 1933–35 period.

Finally, as May began, Joe was back. He celebrated with a three-run homer during a doubleheader sweep of the Athletics. Just in time too, because as Lester Bromberg reported, "The Red Sox are coming, by appointment, but it surely will be a surprise to Dom DiMaggio to find Brother Joe a reasonable facsimile of his peerless self, instead of a dugout-haunting convalescent." However, about the first game of the twin bill Bromberg noted that Joe didn't look like the graceful outfielder of old: "In the fourth he clutched at Mickey Guerra's hit after a slow approach, and a run scored from second. In the eighth he collided with bulky Berra. Nobody hurt, though." Only Joe's pride, no doubt.

There were more comments that Dominic had emerged as the better center fielder, which meant the best in baseball. "We, his teammates, certainly thought so," says Sam Mele, who was playing his first season in Boston.

"He covered a lot of ground," Doerr recalled 65 years later. "And he was so smart. When every game was about to start in any ball-park we were, Dom would check the wind, then call Pesky and me to a meeting at second base. He'd tell us if the wind was blowing in, we had the pop flies. Blowing out, we leave them to him. Nothing escaped him."

Later in the season, Red Smith reported, "Joe himself has declared that his kid brother, Dominic, is a better fielder than he. Which always recalls the occasion when the Red Sox were playing the Yanks and Dom fled across the county line to grab a drive by Joe that no one but a DiMaggio could have reached."

But soon it became clear that reports of Joe's demise were premature, at least at the plate. In fact, at 32 he returned to prewar form. After a doubleheader in early June in which he had seven consecutive hits, Joe was leading the league with a .368 average and had batted .493 in the previous 16 games. He explained to Dan Daniel, "My heel mended, my timing came back, and I began to find pitchers I could hit."

A week later Joe had 36 runs batted in, first among four Yankees with over 30 RBI on the season. The Bombers were back at the head of their division.

The Red Sox put a powerful lineup of their own on the field, enhanced by several additions—Eddie Pellagrini at third, Mele and Wally Moses in the outfield, and Birdie Tebbetts as a reliable backstop. If the pitching staff could have a season anything like '46, clearly the Sox would be at least as good as the team that had come within one inning of a world championship.

Passing on that experience and preparing younger players to be part of a winning club became a priority for Dominic. Though only 30, he was one of the older members of the lineup and he embraced the role of tutor. His easygoing personality was a clear contrast to Joe, whom young players often found chilly, even intimidating.

Mele became a willing pupil. During spring training, the Associated Press ran a story that Dominic and the 25-year-old from Astoria, Queens, were "closer than Damon and Pythias, ham and eggs or a dead heat. It is Dom (the little professor) and young Sam

Mele—on and off the field, find one and you have the other. Mele credits much of his success to the bespectacled Dom and the way he passes out baseball wisdom, which has done so well by all the DiMaggios."

Dominic had made the transition to being a veteran player, and rather than becoming aloof, he tried to raise the young Red Sox the right way. Mele recalls, "I think it was my first road trip. We go to Philadelphia. All the players run into the lobby of the hotel, to the front desk. What the hell, I don't know what's going on, so I see an empty chair in the lobby and sit in it. I'm waiting and waiting. The players are getting their room keys and telling bellboys to take their luggage. The last guy left is Dom DiMaggio. And me. He says to me, 'Okay, rookie, you need a roommate? I'm it. Let's go.' So we roomed together on the road. In the rooms we talked not just baseball, like how to play different positions, but how to dress, how to present yourself to other people, especially fans. That was very important to establishing and maintaining a winning tradition."

In their season opener, led by Dominic's three hits, Boston beat the Senators 7–6. They won their next three games too, and the most hopeful Sox were already figuring out World Series shares. When Tex Hughson pitched a two-hit 1–0 win over the Yanks in New York on April 24, it looked like the Red Sox could still succeed even when their offense took the day off. Two days later, tragedy was averted when first baseman Rudy York was pulled unconscious from his Boston hotel room. His careless cigarette smoking would cause a second hotel room fire in August, after he had been traded to the White Sox. Ironically, after his retirement from baseball York became a fire prevention officer in Georgia.

Ted Williams was off to the races, hitting for both average and power. He was 2-for-3 in an 8–7 win over the Yankees at Fenway on May 12, though the winning run came when Dominic drove in Doerr. In a 19–6 demolition of the White Sox the next day, Ted hit two opposite-field homers at Fenway (while Doerr hit for the cycle), and three days later his grand slam powered a 12–7 victory over the St. Louis Browns. Three days after that, on a 3-0 count, Ted clobbered a two-run walk-off homer against the Tigers. In June the Red Sox, playing their first night game at Fenway, defeated the White Sox 5–3.

Boston struggled, though, to put together the kind of long winning streak that separates a team from the pack. A big problem was that Dominic had pulled a ligament in his shoulder and had to sit on the bench while it healed. Mele was pressed into service in center field. The team missed Dominic's speed and base-running smarts. But after winning many of the tough games they had to win, the Sox were within a few games of the leading Yankees when the All-Star break came.

THE SEALS DID NOT CALL Vince back in 1947, despite his contribution to their 1946 championship season. "My father was very proud to have played on that championship team in San Francisco," says Joanne. "The rings in those days were comparable to what they were giving in the big leagues to World Series winners. Unfortunately, that ring didn't lead to another baseball job right away."

Vince took a job as a sporting goods salesman. It was his first sales job since hawking the *Call-Bulletin* on San Francisco street corners as a boy. He wanted to play baseball, not sell them. He was still confident about his abilities. It was true that he was turning 35, but he had played in two All-Star Games and been among the top ten home run hitters in the National League six times. He would later tell Dave Larsen of the *Los Angeles Times*, "I never felt I played in the shadow of either [Joe or Dominic]. Joe was a better batter, but I could play rings around him as far as knowledge of the game and being in the outfield. I could smoke those throws. If you put a dime on second base, I could hit it from the outfield."

Finally, he did get a call from a PCL team—from Casey Stengel, his 1938 manager with the Boston Bees. The Oakland Oaks needed an outfielder. Vince confessed that he could "uncork only one good throw a game." Stengel replied, "That's good enough. It's better than my other outfielders can do."

Though making consistent contact bedeviled him again—he batted .241—Vince went on to a solid season for the Oaks. His 22 home runs would be third in the PCL, and his 81 runs batted in would help the Oaks into the playoffs in Stengel's second year as manager. Two other key players were one of Joe's former teammates, Nick Etten, and neighborhood pal Dario Lodigiani.

Playing for a Bay Area team, Vince could keep tabs on the DiMaggio clan, even though his own family still resided down in Hermosa Beach. (Joanne now had a baby sister, Vicki Rose.) Postwar crowds were packing the Grotto, keeping Tom and Mike happily busy. Giuseppe and Rosalie were a worry, though. They were in generally good health, but with Giuseppe at 75, a very ripe age for a man in the 1940s, that could change at any moment.

WITH DOROTHY REMARRIED, Joe was a free man in 1947, and one of the most eligible bachelors on both coasts and in all the cities in between where the Yankees played. He wasn't looking for another wife, just companionship. Women flocked to him. He was a high-roller again, a regular at Toots Shor's, always with a beautiful woman in tow. The problem was, he couldn't afford it. He had lost a lot of money in missed salary during the war. Then there was an expensive problem with the IRS that had to be resolved. He needed help, and naturally he turned to the family. But when Dominic bought out his share of Joe DiMaggio's Grotto, the first serious rift between Joe and his brothers occurred. The embarrassment of having his baby brother bail him out might not have been so bad, but Joe felt that the family ganged up to gyp him out of a fair price for his share. He angrily instructed Tom to take the "Joe" off the restaurant's name, which Tom did. Still, for decades afterward, diners would believe that part of what they paid went into Joe's pocket.

It wasn't just the DiMaggio family angering Joe that summer. His Yankee family outraged him too. One night when Joe wasn't at Shor's, Red Sox owner Tom Yawkey and Yankees co-owner Dan Topping were there, and they got into a legendary drinking competition. At some point in the long, drunken night they struck on what seemed at the time a brilliant idea: they would swap their superstars, with Ted Williams going to the Yankees and Joe DiMaggio to the Sox. Joe could bang balls off the Green Monster in left at Fenway Park, and Ted could threaten Ruth's single-season home run record year after year given the short right-field porch in Yankee Stadium. The next morning a sober Yawkey realized three things. First, Joe was four years older than Ted. Second, Ted's homers trumped Joe's doubles. And third, even with Ted's rocky relationship with the press and fans in Boston, Yawkey would be tarred and feathered if he traded Ted away and broke up the Red Sox core. He called Topping and canceled the trade. But Joe heard about it and greatly resented that ownership would even consider pulling the Yankee uniform off his back. Even so, DiMaggio-for-Williams scenarios remained a staple of off-season speculation for years afterward.

While Joe was squiring beautiful ladies around, Dominic was looking to settle down. With his shy ways, short stature, and eyeglasses, he did not cut such a dashing figure as his big brother. He had to find the right woman, one who saw him for his many good qualities.

In 1947 he did. He had first met Emily Frederick in 1943 when his Navy team played an exhibition game in Boston. After the game, he and his friend Jimmy Ferretti went out to Wellesley to visit another friend, Albert Frederick. There he met Albert's daughter. They had a pleasant conversation. Dominic was impressed by her humor and intelligence as well as her looks, but she had no interest in baseball and he was due back to resume his Navy duties in Norfolk, Virginia. For the time being, that was the end of it.

Four years later, Ferretti asked him for an autographed baseball. Dominic wondered if it was for Emily. When his friend said yes, Dominic said he would have all his teammates sign it and then deliver it personally. The 24-year-old Emily had just broken up with a boyfriend, and Dominic was ready to seize the opportunity. They went out to dinner and dancing. Dominic drove her home, and before Emily got out of the car she hid the signed baseball in the glove compartment. Of course, he had to see her again to return it. They started dating frequently.

IN THE SECOND HALF of the season, Joe's legs swelled regularly, with pain in his heel, knees, and hamstrings. "I feel like a mummy," he told reporters about his heavily taped limbs. Even his throwing arm hurt for some unknown reason. Bucky Harris repeatedly offered to rest him, but Joe wouldn't allow it. There was no McCarthy or Dickey or Ruffing or Gomez anymore—Joe was the senior man. New York fans had seen what happened to their Yankees when Joe didn't lead them. In 1947 he insisted on a world championship, nothing else, whatever the personal price. Boston writer Ed Rumill added incentive when he wrote, "Joe'd better get that heel fixed up or there'll be a new king in San Francisco's #1 baseball family."

Joe played hard the rest of the season, leading by example. No member of the Yankees could contemplate taking it easy when the team's star, legs heavily bandaged and wincing before and after games, was giving 100 percent. And Joe wasn't about to let his brother Dominic wear the crown yet as best center fielder—in 319 chances, Joe made only one error. The Yankees finished the 1947 season at 97-57.

If Joe could carry the Yankees on his back, Ted Williams thought maybe he could do the same for the Red Sox. It didn't pan out. The main problem was that Ted couldn't pitch as well as slug homers, and the Sox pitching staff just did not deliver that season. Boo Ferriss recalls that while hurling a 1–0 win over the Indians, he felt something snap in his shoulder. "My arm was never the same again," he says. "I was out for a while, then I came back and continued to pitch, but my velocity was gone. I was only 25 years old and lost my arm strength."

The Boston defense tried to make up for pitching deficits. The left side was especially strong, with Pesky at short, Eddie Pellagrini at third, Ted in left field, and Dominic in center. Ted was not considered an excellent left fielder, but Dominic more than made up for that, which Ted acknowledged. They were an unlikely pair: the bombastic, often cranky, tall, powerful "Kid" from San Diego and the shy, short, fast, bespectacled "Little Professor." Yet in their second season back from the war, they had grown close as friends as well as players.

Ted never passed on an opportunity to praise the man he often called "Dommie" during their playing days and afterward. "The wolves in left field were always yelling how he was playing his position *and* mine," he wrote in *My Turn at Bat*. "I could have been a little miffed at that, but the fact was Dom and I got along good. He was quiet, but he was great to play with because he'd talk under a fly ball, holler good to let you know what was happening. And he *was* a great outfielder, he could get better position on the ball to left center, so I made it a point to concede to him."

It was frustrating for Dominic not to be giving the kind of performance at the plate he had in 1946. There were very good days, like the grand slam he hit on August 19 to beat the Browns, but there were no hot streaks and in too many games he wore the collar. For the first time his durability was suspect. Dominic collected only 145 hits, batted .283, and had 8 homers and 71 RBI.

Apparently, Pesky didn't get the memo about having an off year. His third year in the majors was his third one with more than 200 hits—he would lead the league at 207. He also scored 106 runs and batted .324. And of course, there was Ted. It is incredible to think that his .343 batting average was 63 points *lower* than his best year; it was still good enough for the batting title. He also smashed 32 homers and had 114 RBI—good enough for his second Triple Crown—and 125 runs scored.

Ted did everything he could to keep his club in the pennant picture and was more responsible than anyone for the 83 Red Sox wins. But that was good enough for only a third-place finish, behind the Yankees and Tigers. A disappointed and worn-out Joe Cronin resigned as manager.

Ted was denied the Most Valuable Player Award again—deservedly so, it could be argued, but it happened in the most bizarre fashion.

Joe DiMaggio won it, his third MVP. He had indeed shown his value to a pennant-winning club and played the best he could through injuries. His leadership in the '47 season was unquestioned. That he won the MVP by a vote of 202 over Ted's 201 was unremarkable—it should have been that close. What was remarkable was that one of the voting writers—the *Boston Globe*'s Mel Webb—not only didn't vote Ted number one, but didn't even vote him into the top ten, leaving Ted's name completely off his ballot. If Ted's name had appeared in even the tenth slot on that ballot, he would have won the award. Clearly his combative relationship with Boston sportswriters had come back to bite him again. For Ted, it was another bitter end to a season. "It wasn't the first time Williams earned this award with his bat," Red Smith observed, "and lost it with his disposition."

Dominic did not head straight home to San Francisco as usual. He had a girl in Boston he wasn't keen on leaving behind. In fact, he was pretty sure he was going to marry her. When he did eventually head west, he had Emily with him to present to the DiMaggios. He had been the last in the family to be born, he was the last to go into baseball, and with the approval—or at least without the opposition—of Giuseppe and Rosalie, he would be the last DiMaggio to marry.

* * *

JOE WAS BACK in the World Series, his first since 1942, and his first without Joe McCarthy as the skipper. Perhaps McCarthy watched it on television—it was the first one broadcast to sets in several markets. If so, he saw one of the best Fall Classics in baseball history. The Yankees faced a young and exciting Brooklyn Dodgers team whose core group of players would elevate the "Bums" to greatness in the next decade—Jackie Robinson, Pee Wee Reese, Gil Hodges, Duke Snider, Ralph Branca, Carl Erskine, Don Newcombe, and Carl Furillo. That Robinson was the first African American to play in a World Series was just one of the many highlights in 1947.

Game 1 was played September 30 at Yankee Stadium. Johnny Lindell and Tommy Henrich batted in two runs each as the Yankees beat Branca and Brooklyn 5–3. Game 2 was a laugher. Joe collected only his second hit of the Series, but his teammates piled up ten runs to Brooklyn's three as Allie Reynolds struck out 12 Dodgers. At Ebbetts Field for Game 3, the Dodgers jumped out to a 9–4 lead after four innings and held on for a 9–8 victory. Joe's two-run homer wasn't enough.

For the next game, Harris decided to start Bill Bevens, whose record was only 7-13, with a lackluster 3.82 ERA. Harris hoped he would keep the Dodgers off-balance long enough for the bats of the Bronx Bombers to do damage.

Bevens set a World Series record by walking ten batters—but through eight innings he didn't give up a hit. The Yankees eked out a 1–0 lead in the first inning when Harry Taylor, afraid to give Joe anything good to hit with the bases loaded, walked him. Joe walked again next time up but was thrown out trying to score from first on a throwing error. New York went up 2–0 in the fourth. The Dodgers scored a run in the fifth on two walks, a sacrifice, and a grounder. The score remained 2–1 into the top of the ninth inning.

Lindell singled. Phil Rizzuto reached on a force. Bevens, with a no-hitter on the line, was allowed to bat. When he bunted, Dodger catcher Bruce Edwards failed to nab Rizzuto at second. Now the bases were loaded, Snuffy Stirnweiss dumped a hit to center, and Rizzuto held at third. When Henrich came up, the Dodgers brought in Hugh Casey, the same confrontation as in the 1941 World Series, when Mickey Owen had muffed strike three. This time, "Old Reliable" hit into a double play.

The Dodgers went to the plate, bottom of the ninth, trailing by one. Edwards flew out. Furillo walked, and Al Gionfriddo was sent out to run for him. Spider Jorgensen fouled out to first. With Pete Reiser up, Gionfriddo took off for second and beat Berra's throw. Bevens walked Reiser. Cookie Lavagetto was sent up to pinch-hit for Eddie Stanky. On an 0-1 count, with Bevens just two strikes from immortality, Lavagetto smashed a double off the right-field wall and both runners scored. On that pitch, Bevens lost the no-hitter and the game. He never started again in the major leagues—the Oregon native's next stop was the Pacific Coast League.

The Series was tied. In Game 5 at Ebbetts Field, the Yankees' Spec Shea faced the home team's Rex Barney, starting for the first time since July. Barney gave up runs in the fourth and fifth innings, the second on a solo shot by Joe. The Dodgers could manage only one run. The Yankees were returning to the Bronx with a 3–2 edge.

Game 6 was another nail-biter, with the two teams trading scores in front of the biggest crowd of the Series, 74,065. Pitchers came and went as players crossed the plate. It was one of the most famous games in Joe's career. In the sixth inning he came up with two men on and the Yanks trailing 8–5. He launched a long drive to left. Most everyone in the ballpark thought it was a game-tying homer. But Gionfriddo, not known for flashing leather, snared the ball over the railing atop the 415 feet sign, then tumbled over the short wall into the bullpen. He reappeared with the ball in his glove. Rounding second, Joe kicked the dirt—a natural reaction for any ballplayer, but a startling one from the relentlessly stoic DiMaggio.

"The reason I let my feelings show then was that I'd never had a Series where I'd been lucky," he told reporters after the game, barely suppressing his anger. "That catch by Gionfriddo was the straw that broke the camel's back."

The Dodgers won it 8–6.

In Game 7, New York scored a run in the second, two in the fourth, one in the sixth, and one more in the seventh to beat the Dodgers 5–2 and win the Series. Joe would get his sixth Series ring, his first in five years. Curiously, even as the players celebrated, MacPhail announced that he was resigning as general manager.

After a few weeks relaxing in New York, Joe headed back to Baltimore for another operation at Johns Hopkins, this time on his right arm. A small bone near a nerve was removed, and he was expected to make a full recovery. His financial situation was starting to look healthier too. He wanted a big raise, and with the Series and another MVP to back him, he got it. His 1948 contract would be for $70,000, the most the Yankees had paid a player since Ruth. (Still, it was only the third highest in baseball: Ted Williams got $75,000 and Bob Feller $85,000.)

IN THE PCL PLAYOFFS, Lefty O'Doul's second-place Seals faced Casey Stengel's fourth-place Oaks. Vince was looking for one more championship. Things went well for Stengel's squad when they took the first two games. In the third game, Vince scored to put the Oaks up 3–1, but the Seals won it in the 11th. Vince had two homers, a double, and five RBI in his team's 8–4 victory in the next game, then Oakland closed out the series with a 4–0 blanking of O'Doul's squad.

The Oaks then faced the Los Angeles Angels for the Governor's Cup. They lost the first three games. In the fourth, Vince, going 3-for-6 with three RBI, powered the Oaks to an 8–7 victory. But the Angels took the fifth game and the cup. Thankfully, Vince had a hit in that losing effort, because it was his last game in a Pacific Coast League uniform.

SIXTEEN

To rebound in 1948, the Red Sox needed to retool their pitching staff. Hughson and Ferriss were questionable at best, and Boston lacked a minor league system as well stocked as those of the Yankees and Dodgers. So the club engineered one of the largest trades the major leagues had ever seen, with the St. Louis Browns, who after the war had returned to their accustomed place in the depths of the second division. Raiding Tom Yawkey's piggy bank, the Red Sox sent $375,000 and nine players west for pitchers Jack Kramer and Ellis Kinder and a shortstop, Vern Stephens. This would turn out to be one of the better deals in franchise history.

Joe Cronin had now moved up from manager to general manager. Who would replace him on the field? None other than Joe McCarthy. Though he had a lot of mileage on him at 62, McCarthy had recovered from his alcohol-fueled flameout with the Yankees a couple of years earlier. Cronin wanted a manager with a winning track record, and no one in baseball had a better one. Cronin wanted him to bring to Boston the Yankees' disciplined behavior, which included players wearing ties and being clean-shaven off the field, no pipe smoking, plenty of hustle, and most of all a hatred of losing.

A game between the teams on March 29 showed how intense their rivalry was getting. It was only an exhibition game, but neither McCarthy nor Bucky Harris would accept a loss. At the end of nine innings, the score was 2–2. They kept playing. Finally, after battling over four hours and using 33 players, the combatants agreed to the tie.

Already the Red Sox player representative, Dominic was now elected the player rep for the whole American League. His free agency gambit had marked him as a player not intimidated by management. Other players had great respect for the Little Professor's intelligence and ability to communicate. No matter how highly regarded Joe was as a player, he would never have been elected a spokesman.

"In addition to being an outstanding player, Dom was really well liked by everyone who knew him," says Cot Deal, who earned a spot on the Red Sox starting pitching staff in 1948. "He just had such a good personality, and he was viewed as a completely trustworthy guy."

Dominic played an important role in negotiating issues that would lead to the formation of the Major League Baseball Players Association. In the 1970s, what Dom started would result in free agency and other labor advances for players. He and National League player representative Marty Marion, the Cardinals shortstop, put together a list of concerns that included "conditions on the field. Probably meal money, that sort of thing." (Perhaps Vince, still smarting from his experience with meal money, put his brother up to that part of it.) "And a pension. We felt that a pension was very much desired." Though professional baseball had existed since well before the turn of the century, the professionals who played it still did not get a pension when they retired.

On opening day against the Philadelphia Athletics at Fenway Park, the Sox lost both ends of a doubleheader. Boston got its first win on opening day at Yankee Stadium, 4–0. In the stands was Babe

Ruth, who, many in New York knew, had been diagnosed with throat cancer. As usual, Joe and Dom did not socialize in front of the fans. "You have to remember that the umpires were pretty strict back then about opposing players," says Yogi Berra. "The funny thing is, though, I can't imagine any umpire stopping brothers from talking to each other. But Joe and Dom just didn't do that."

"Dom was quiet, but compared to Joe he was an extrovert," says Cot Deal. "But both brothers were total professionals, and standing around chatting just wasn't something that either one of them would feel right doing."

At the end of May, the Sox were a frustrating 14-23, 11.5 games out of first, and fans were already calling for McCarthy's head. But in June they caught fire, and they blazed white-hot into September, going 69-24. Dominic would have the best year of his career.

Dominic and his teammates had become television stars in early June when WBZ broadcast its first game from Fenway Park, where the francise had finally installed lights. The first night game was played there on the thirteenth. Another, and bigger, milestone for the American League was that it saw its first African American player, when Larry Doby was brought up by the Indians.

Cleveland was clinging to first place and looked to separate itself a bit from Boston when the Sox arrived for a three-game series in mid-June. But they were rudely manhandled by the visitors, with the final insult being Dominic's home run that broke a 6–6 tie and ensured a series sweep. Boston now had won 11 of 14 games.

The Red Sox celebrated Independence Day at Fenway Park at the expense of the Athletics. The score was 5–5 when Ted walked, and then the floodgates opened. Dominic doubled and walked, driving in a run and scoring three in the same fourteen-run seventh, which ended only when Ted grounded out his third time up in the inning.

Disaster almost struck later in the month. Doing some restless sparring on a train, sophomore outfielder Sam Mele punched Ted, and the rib injury put him on the sidelines. He missed 13 games, but the Red Sox kept rolling. An 8–0 blanking of the Tigers in Detroit was the team's thirteeth consecutive victory. They had leapfrogged over the Athletics (still skippered by 85-year-old Connie Mack), Yankees, and Indians into first place. However, an indication of how tightly bunched the top teams were was that a doubleheader loss to Clevelend on August 1 dropped Boston to fourth place.

Boston fans took to singing altered lyrics to the "Joltin' Joe DiMaggio" tune Les Brown had written in 1941:

Who hits the ball and makes it go?
Dominic DiMaggio.
Who runs the bases fast, not slow?
Dominic DiMaggio.
Who's better than his brother Joe?
Dominic DiMaggio.
But when it comes to gettin' dough,
They give it all to brother Joe.

Brother Joe and the Yankees spent the early summer chasing the Indians and Athletics for first place. Joe's bat was hot again. On May 20, he duplicated a feat from 12 years earlier, when he had been just 21. The Yankees were in Chicago to face the 4-18 White Sox. In the first inning, Joe hit a three-run homer. In the third, he singled. In the fifth, he hit a solo shot. In the sixth, he tripled in three runs. And in the ninth he doubled, for the second (and last) cycle of his career. He would have gone 6-for-6, but in the eighth his long fly was grabbed against the fence. On June 20, in a doubleheader against the Browns, Joe hit three home runs, powering his team into second place, three and a half games behind the Indians.

But the heel started bothering him again, and both knees. Joe DiMaggio was still shy of 34, but some days he felt 74. As the season progressed his body played him a symphony of aches and pains. There were days when he simply couldn't stand the thought of suiting up to play, but he did: the Yankees were in a tight pennant race, and he hated the thought of not being the Big Guy.

"There were occasions this year when DiMaggio must have felt he was through," wrote Jimmy Cannon, who continued to be one of Joe's buddies at Toots Shor's. "He was sick with doubt and irritable. The heel was full of pain. On payday when he picked up his check he was ashamed of himself. Seldom does any athlete feel he is fleecing an employer when there is a contract to guarantee him a salary. The inactivity changed him. It made him a recluse. The telephone was shut off in his apartment. He ducked intimates. He sat home and played jazz records endlessly. At the Stadium, he gave me the impression he felt himself an intruder."

But he played, game after game. In midsummer, he had hits in 25 of 27 straight games and batted .493. With all his physical and mental agonies, the Big Guy still put the Yankees on his shoulders and carried them toward September.

VINCE COULDN'T CATCH on with a PCL team for the 1948 season. For a time he resumed peddling sporting goods. It could not have been easy that his sales calls took him around to PCL clubhouses, including Oakland's. Still, he just couldn't quit baseball completely. He went down a notch in the minors to the California League, signing a contract with the Stockton Ports, who that year were affiliated with the Oaks.

It was a pretty good contract. The owner of the team, Al Spreckens, had enlisted Vince to manage the team as well as patrol center field. Given his outgoing personality, managing and coaching could turn out to be the best way for Vince to stay in baseball. With an eye on the drawing power of the DiMaggio name, Spreckens declared that Vince's salary "will be the highest ever paid to a California League manager." It sure beat hawking bats and gloves.

Vince had his hands full. Besides himself, only one player had been a major leaguer. The other players were on their way up to or down from the Pacific Coast League. For his own part, facing California League pitching rejuvenated Vince at the plate, and he could still play center field at a major league level. "It was great fun playing for the Ports, because Billy Herbert Field was so well kept and Vince DiMaggio had a lot of room to catch fly balls hit to center field," remembered Lou Bronzan, a pitcher then spending his first of two years with the club. At the end of the season, Vince's 30 homers led the league, and he was fifth in runs batted in.

But Spreckens, facing financial difficulties, would decide not to renew Vince's costly contract. Once again, Vince had to wonder if he was finished in baseball while his two younger brothers were making headlines every day.

JOE CONTINUED TO DRAG himself out onto the field game after game—he would miss only one the entire season. Despite the pains in his legs and a worsening pain in his throwing arm, he played magnificently, especially when he came to bat with runners in scoring position. The Yankees kept winning and kept chasing the Indians, Athletics, and now the Red Sox, who were surging. The way the three rivals were playing, Joe couldn't afford to take his bat out of the lineup, even when his own manager suggested it.

As in Joe's magnificent season of 1941, when Lou Gehrig died, the franchise experienced a great loss in 1948. On August 16, Babe Ruth died. The cancer treatments had proven ineffective, and by the early summer it was common knowledge that the greatest baseball player ever was not going to make it. Weak and wan, he managed to attend the premiere of *The Babe Ruth Story* that June, with William Bendix rather uncomfortably playing the Sultan of Swat, but he was barely able to speak to fans and reporters. He was hospitalized soon after.

He was only 53 when he died, another Yankee champion taken too soon. His funeral filled St. Patrick's Cathedral in New York (with 75,000 more mourners standing outside on Fifth Avenue in the rain). Before the season was over, the team would retire the Babe's number 3. As a man who had declared himself "lucky to be a Yankee," and who had often been mentioned in the same sentence with Ruth, Joe had to feel the loss to the club.

The doubleheader on August 20 was an example of how relentless the Red Sox had become by late summer. They were down 4–1 to the Senators in the ninth inning. Then the hometown fans were thrilled when a three-run shot by Vern Stephens tied the score, and a walk-off homer by Stan Spence won it. In the second game, Dominic's grand slam led the way to a 10–4 win. In a victory the following day, Stephens socked a grand slam. And on the twenty-fourth, the Sox scored three runs in the ninth to defeat the Indians 9–8 and reclaim first place.

The finish to the 1948 season remains one of the finest in American League history. Three tough and talented veteran teams battled down to the last regular-season out and beyond before the pennant winner was left standing. No wonder the Yankees, Red Sox, and Indians established new attendance records—combined, the clubs drew 6.5 million spectators to their home parks.

Even better, as David Halberstam points out in his book *Summer of '49*, "The best player on each of the three teams was having a remarkable year." Ted continued to hit almost every pitch on the nose. His average was the best since the 1941 season, over .400, and again he surpassed 100 runs batted in. Somehow, despite the pressure of being skipper of the Indians, Lou Boudreau was hitting almost as well as Ted. He would be voted the American League MVP. And even with the nagging injuries, Joe was having one of his best years, especially as an RBI machine.

At times it was as if they were competing directly against each other, even though there were 16 other men on the field when two of the rivals played. In a late-season doubleheader, Indians catcher Jim Hegan made the mistake of teasing Ted about Boudreau's having inched ahead of him in the batting race, saying that "the

Frenchman's got you beat this year." Ted responded, "The hell he has," and knocked out six hits in his next seven at-bats. When he stepped up to the plate for the eighth time that day, he said to Hegan, "This one's for Lou." The next pitch went over the right-field wall.

Dominic was also having a fine year. No one was playing the outfield better. He covered an enormous amount of territory between Ted in left and Mele, Wally Moses, or Stan Spence in right. In 1948 Dominic set an American League record for center fielders with 503 putouts, a record that would stand until Chet Lemon of the White Sox broke it 29 years later.

"Dom was a fantastic fielder," Buddy Lewis of the Washington Senators told *Baseball Digest* in 2006. "He would play in about 20 to 30 yards closer to the infield than other center fielders. You try to hit the ball over his head in Fenway Park and you couldn't do it. It would just make you sit down and cry after you saw Dom race back and catch a ball you hit and thought was a sure double or triple." (When Lewis died at 94 in 2011, he was the last player to have been present at Lou Gehrig's farewell speech at Yankee Stadium in 1939.)

"He was a terrific center fielder," says Bobby Brown, who played for the Yankees as an infielder and outfielder from 1946 to 1954. "Dom was a very good hitter too, but he *made* that Boston outfield defense. Ted Williams was an average fielder, and Dom helped him greatly by covering some of left field as well as all of center."

Mele remembers that during "one game at Yankee Stadium, Joe hit a ball toward left-center. No way Williams was going to get to it, but Dominic streaks across and makes a tremendous backhanded catch. Inning over, rally snuffed out. Dom, Ted, and I are running in and Joe's running out to center. 'Nice catch,' he said. Dom kept running. That is what he did, another day of doing his job. But I'm sure an 'outburst' like that from Joe meant a lot."

The fans in Boston began to hope that for the first time since 1915 the World Series would feature both of the city's teams. The perennial punching bags the Braves, recovered from their days as the

Bees, had grown into genuine contenders, led by Warren Spahn, Bob Elliott, and Eddie Stanky. They fought off the St. Louis Cardinals to nab the National League title, their first pennant since 1914. Now if the Red Sox could only gut it out. . . .

Dominic was doing his part—getting on base, driving in a lot of runs for a leadoff batter, and playing center field brilliantly. He was getting banged up but refused to sit out a game. He also refused to be distracted by his impending wedding. All the DiMaggios were making plans to be at the ceremony in the Boston area. He was certain that Emily was the one. According to Halberstam in *The Teammates,* Emily's "lack of interest in baseball did not bother Dominic at all. Nor was there any problem of ethnicity, as might have happened in an era when ethnic divisions were considered more important. Her grandmother, Carlotta, seemed to be rather proud of the fact that, although she was Italian, she was not Sicilian, and she had said something along that line one night at dinner, a snide zinger aimed at Sicilians, and Dominic had said, quite gently, 'Carlotta, *I'm* Sicilian,' and Carlotta, not one to back down, and not quite ready for political correctness either, looked at him and said, 'Well, that's your problem.'"

The Red Sox clung gamely to first place during the first, then second, then third week of September—including a thrilling 10–6 comeback win over the Yankees on September 9 in which Dominic went 3-for-3 and made what the *New York Times* described as a "breathtaking catch" in center. The Yankees and Indians howled at their heels.

During the 1948 season, Joe went from the Great DiMaggio to something like an immortal who awed even his teammates. Richard Ben Cramer offered a description of his daily entrance:

"When Joe walked into the locker room, it was like the lights came on, as if a voice on the PA had announced: *the team is here.* Of course, he was impeccable: not just in a suit and tie, but the best suit and tie in America. He had a pal from Seventh Avenue who'd make the suits—whatever Joe wanted—and his tailor, of course, to put the finishing touches. And no hat: might obscure the face.

"He'd stride in, across the new carpeted clubhouse, with the paper under his arm. If there were fellows already getting dressed, Joe wouldn't stop. 'Good morning.' 'Good morning, Tom,' he'd say as he passed—like an executive greeting secretaries on the way to his office. By the time he had his coat hung perfectly, Pete Sheehy would be running with the 'half-a-cuppa-coffee.' Joe didn't have to ask anymore.

"DiMaggio would sit in his undershirt with his half-a-cup and a smoke, one leg thrown over the other. He'd open up the paper. The other players would sneak glances, to see if Dago was gonna say anything. They'd never talk to him first. . . . The Big Guy could sit in stillness till he was ready to visit the trainer, get himself taped. After that, it was BP. Joe hit first. When Joe stepped into the cage, that's when BP started."

For Vince and Dominic, it would be unthinkable to act in such a way. But they had remained mere mortals, while their brother had ascended to Mount Olympus. This would be a facet of their relationship for the rest by their lives. "Normal" for Joe would always be the veneration of others—and the isolation. Tommy Henrich shared the outfield with him every year from 1939 to 1950 except during the war. No one on the team knew Joe better or admired him more, yet during all those years the two men never once went out to dinner.

Remarkably, the Indians, Red Sox, and Yankees had identical 91-56 records with one week left. Four games later, as the tireless Bob Feller won again, the Indians had a two-game lead with only three games left to the season, all against the Detroit Tigers, who had sunk to fifth place. When Cleveland lost the first game in the series, a window opened for the other two contenders.

In the past, this would have been the moment for Joe to lead the Yankees through that window. But he had been younger then, and the injuries didn't linger as long or hurt as much. As the season progressed he had tried walking on his toes to take pressure off his heel, which was inflamed again. But that strained his leg muscles, so that before every game he had to be wrapped tightly in ever more bandages. Jimmy Cannon lived in the same building as Joe. One day in late September, Cannon caught a grimacing Joe coming down a flight of stairs, putting both feet on one step before he could lower a foot to the next. When Joe noticed Cannon staring at him, he begged him not to write about how much pain he was in. This wasn't about him, Joe explained, it was about not letting opponents know how gimpy he was.

In the last week of the season, a *Time* reporter visited the bruised and battered hero. "The center-fielder of the New York Yankees had the worst charley horse he could remember. He wore a thick bandage over his left thigh (to support the strained muscles) and a second bandage around his middle to hold up his first one. On any ordinary day such aches & pains would have put Center-fielder DiMaggio out of the line-up. But no day last week was an ordinary one in the American League. The Yankees were fighting for survival in the hottest pennant race in history, and they needed DiMag." The article also reported that Joe was up to a pack of Chesterfields a day, probably an underestimation. The article dismissed "bespectacled Dom" as the "family pet."

Showing a surprising lack of faith in his team's chances, Dom and Emily had set the date of the wedding for October 7. "I'll see that Dom is free to get married on the seventh," Joe told Rosalie over the phone.

The last games of the season were on October 2 and 3, with the Yankees in Boston against the Sox. The Yankees had to win the first one for a shot at the pennant; failing that, they could at least force the Sox into a playoff by winning the second. Saturday morning before the first game, Boston fans were in the streets to jeer the Yankee players as they left the nearby Kenmore Hotel to go to the ballpark.

In the game, before a packed crowd, Ted socked his 25th home run in the first inning, which helped propel the Red Sox to a 5–1 win, with Jack Kramer pitching a complete game. For only the third time in nine seasons, Joe would not be in the World Series.

Dom and Joe drove straight from the game to Wellesley, where the DiMaggio family was meeting for dinner near the church where the wedding would take place. For most of the ride, Joe was too disappointed to speak. Dominic didn't know what he could say to console his brother. Finally, Joe told him, "We'll get back at you tomorrow, we'll knock you out. I'll take care of it personally." Dominic recovered with some bravado of his own: "I may have something to do with that. I'll be there too."

"Joe and Dom absolutely had a good relationship, and they were also very proud men," says Babe Martin, a backup catcher on the 1948–49 Boston teams who became one of Dominic's close friends. "They wanted to show everybody that they would go ahead and play hard against each other. They didn't want people to think that they would favor each other under any circumstances. They would not do that. They would play hard against each other and show everybody the competitiveness they had."

"They were DiMaggios, and that name was golden in baseball," says Bobby Doerr. "They had to do their best because they were the best baseball-playing brothers in the game."

Harris tried to talk Joe out of playing in a game that was really meaningless to the Yankees. The Big Fella deserved a rest. But Joe told his manager, "My brother's with the Red Sox, and nobody in Cleveland or anyplace else is going to say I rolled over and played dead so Dom's team would have a better chance. I can't do that."

On Sunday, the Tigers trounced the Indians 7–1. The door was left open for Boston.

"They had come to see Yankee blood," Joe said about the 31,304 fans at Fenway Park that day. He was in a strange position—even his own family was not pulling for him. In the stands were Giuseppe and Rosalie and their seven other children and various in-laws. They weren't exactly rooting against Joe, but they wanted Dominic to have another shot at a world championship. "Are you rooting for either of your sons, Mr. DiMaggio?" a reporter asked. After one of his daughters translated the question, Giuseppe replied, "I hope Dominic win this time. Giuseppe, he win all the time."

In the first inning, Joe doubled in a run. The Yankees were still in front in the third inning when the Sox scored five runs. In the fifth, Phil Rizzuto singled and Bobby Brown doubled. Joe stepped to the plate and doubled off the Green Monster. It was 5–4 Sox in the sixth when Dominic and Stephens took over and produced four runs with homers. The score was 10–5 in the ninth and Joe stood in the batter's box. Both he and his brother were 3-for-4. Joe sent another ball off the left-field wall, but it was only a single—he could barely make it to first base. Harris sent Steve Souchok in to run for him. As Joe limped toward the Yankee dugout, the Red Sox crowd cheered him in a way that rivaled anything he had experienced at Yankee Stadium. Anyone who glanced into center field saw that Dominic had doffed his cap as a salute to his brave brother.

Afterward, Joe told reporters, "I'll never forget that crowd. It was standing and roaring like one man. I tipped my cap but it didn't stop. I looked up at the stands at this ovation they were giving a guy who had tried to beat them."

For the first time in American League history, two teams finished tied, with the Red Sox and Indians both at 96-58. The Indians traveled to Boston the next day for the playoff.

There were 33,957 anxious people at Fenway Park. In a decision that would haunt Sox fans for years, McCarthy bypassed his established starters to choose 36-year-old journeyman Denny Galehouse to take the mound. He only made it into the second inning, having given up four runs. The Indians broke the hearts of Boston fans yet again with an 8–3 win. They would go on to beat the Boston Braves in six games for the championship.

Dominic and Emily were married on October 11—a just-in-case last-minute change of date—at St. Paul's Catholic Church in Wellesley. Though the crowd wasn't as rowdy as the San Francisco one had been for Joe and Dorothy's wedding, there was enough commotion that extra police were called out. "Most of the fans were a trifle disappointed as the cops hustled Dom and his bride through a back door of the church at the conclusion of the ceremony."

Unlike Joe's marriages, Dominic and Emily's would endure for 61 years.

SEVENTEEN

The DiMaggio clan welcomed Dominic and Emily to the Bay Area. Unlike Joe, Dominic was not going to bring his wife to live in the house on Beach Street. The couple rented an apartment in San Francisco from November through February 1949, when Dominic would report to spring training. They both missed Boston, where Emily's family lived and where Dom had come to feel at home. But the San Francisco sojourn gave him time to be with his family, and there was work to do at DiMaggio's Grotto. Dom also wanted to spend time with Giuseppe, who at 76 was moving slower and getting fragile. Rosalie, who turned 71 in February, still ran the kitchen and household with help from her daughter Marie. In 1947, the couple had celebrated their 50th wedding anniversary with all nine children in attendance.

"After my wife and I got married that November, we went to the West Coast for our honeymoon," remembers Boo Ferriss. "Dom and Emily invited us to stay a couple of days at their apartment. That was a generous gesture, because they were newlyweds too, and we didn't have much money to spend on a honeymoon. The two of them couldn't have been nicer, and we had a great time."

In the spring—having successfully dickered with Cronin over his contract—Dominic headed to Sarasota. After coming within one game of the World Series and eliminating the previous world champions, the Red Sox looked liked the American League favorites for 1949. A lot depended on the pitching. The outfield would be more than solid with Dominic, Ted, and Mele. The infield was iffy—Bobby Doerr and Johnny Pesky continued at second and third, but Vern Stephens was only an okay fielder at short and Walt Dropo was untested at first. Then again, the Sox had the best hitter in baseball in Ted Williams, who had become a father in the off-season.

Cleveland, of course, could repeat. And what about those Yankees? The front office had done the right thing by Joe after his courageous '48 campaign—they made him the first $100,000 player. "Thus, the 34-year-old son of an Italian immigrant fisherman, who used to sell newspapers for a dollar and a half a day on the streets of San Francisco, becomes the highest salaried player in Yankee history and perhaps all of baseball," John Drebinger commented in the *New York Times*.

But a question lingered: could Joe and Casey Stengel get along? The 58-year-old had been plucked from the Oakland Oaks by GM George Weiss to skipper the Yankees. McCarthy and Harris had been as much Joe's fans as his managers. Stengel had been around too long to idolize anyone—and he'd never managed a star of Joe's magnitude before. How much he could get out of the Big Guy could well define the Yankees' season. For his part, Joe might not have much faith in a manager with a lifetime .439 won-lost percentage in the Major Leagues.

Mainstays Tommy Henrich, Johnny Lindell, and Charlie Keller were back. Phil Rizzuto and Jerry Coleman made for an excellent keystone combination, and Bobby Brown was still at third. Bill Dickey was working with Yogi Berra to turn him into a solid, everyday catcher.

The Yankees would surely struggle, though, if Joe wasn't healthy.

After the '48 campaign, he'd had another operation, this time on his right heel, to remove bone spurs. He'd been slow to heal. Except for the occasional foray on crutches to Toots Shor's or to visit Joe Jr. (the seven-year-old was a student at the Walt Whitman Progressive School in Manhattan), Joe holed up in his fifth-floor suite at the Hotel Elysee on East 54th Street.

When the reporter Will Wedge visited him a few weeks after the surgery, Joe told him, "I sit around and smoke and listen to the radio and read. No exercise. That's what's been tough. As a result, my appetite is no good now. I'm irregular about ordering my meals up. Often I'm content just heating up a can of soup for myself in the kitchenette, and making coffee. I'm a kinda loner, as you know." The ulcer pains had returned, and on top of everything else he was plagued by insomnia. He'd had bouts of it before—the chronic coffee-drinking sure didn't help—but not as bad as this.

When spring training began in St. Petersburg, Joe was there, but suiting up was all he could do. When he tried to run, the pain in his right heel was intolerable. Mostly pinch-hitting, he went just .226 in exhibition games. The worried front office, fretting over the six-figure salary they had committed to him, shipped Joe back to Johns Hopkins in Baltimore for more treatment. Once again, he would miss the start of a regular season.

And more than that, as it turned out. According to a *New York Post* headline, "Joe DiMaggio Reconciled to Long, Drawn Out Comeback Process." Week after week went by, and at the end of April he was still out of commission. The Yankees didn't fall apart. While Boston and Cleveland struggled, the Bronx boys won enough to be in first place.

Joe was well enough at least to make an unhappy trip west when Tom called to say that Giuseppe had died, on May 3. The funeral was in San Francisco. Joe, with his bad heel, was the only son who couldn't serve as a pallbearer. At the reception afterward at the Fisherman's Wharf restaurant—where Papa DiMaggio's boat was still docked—his children agreed that he'd had a good life, made unexpectedly better by baseball, the most American of games. Tom would assume the role of the head of the family.

AT 36, VINCE still couldn't stop playing the game, even after the Stockton Ports cut him loose. He stepped down another rung to the Class D Far West League as player-manager of the Pittsburg Diamonds. Pittsburg, about 30 miles northeast of San Francisco, was largely Italian immigrants and first-generation Italian-Americans. Martinez was next door, where people knew the DiMaggio family back in an earlier era and would turn out to cheer a favorite son. And he could earn extra income working for Tom (and his youngest brother, Dom) at the family restaurant.

Vince found managing frustrating. "I thought playing was tough," he said. "Try to please a couple dozen athletes." But as a player, he was a former major leaguer facing minor league competition. His arm wasn't the same, but it was still better than most, and he simply knew the game from now having been playing it professionally for 18 years. That he still hit with some power and drove in runs was not a surprise, but finally he was enjoying not striking out as much. His average stayed above .300 as the season progressed.

One might think that with Joe sidelined indefinitely, Dominic would have relished being the only DiMaggio in the spotlight. But that wasn't his personality. He felt awful about his brother's woes. At best, he would shrug when favorable comparisons were made. When reporters asked him about his own exploits, he often turned the subject to Joe or to one of his teammates.

Yet, at 32, he was having an MVP season. After a rocky start, Boston was playing very good ball, and Dominic was propelling them. He was hitting well, and his fielding was so good that most opponents had given up on running against his arm.

"I never saw a guy go from first to third on a base hit against

Dominic," says Babe Martin. "Never. To try it was like giving us an automatic out."

"During my career, I played with Joe and against Dominic, and each in his own way was a great guy and a great ballplayer," says Charlie Silvera, another Italian-American ballplayer from San Francisco who had joined the Yankees the previous September. "Dominic didn't get all the recognition he deserved, but just like Joe he went out and played hard and never complained."

James O'Francis of *The Sporting News* tried to get at least some chest-thumping out of the man he described as "the fellow who looks more like a school teacher than a ball player," but found that he was "modest to a point of irritation to an interviewer and reluctant to discuss his feats on a diamond." Dominic attributed his hot pace to "a lot of luck," and his boldest statement, echoing what Vince had said during the war, was that while Joe was recovering, "I'll do my best to carry on the family name in the best DiMaggio tradition."

The Little Professor used an advantage he had over his brother—his brains. Joe studied pitchers, but Dominic went a step further. "When we were in a room together or with a few of the other guys, he would take out his little black book and we'd study it with him," remembers Mele. "Dominic had notes on all the pitchers on all the other teams in there—how they throw, what they like to throw in certain situations like the strike count, how you could tell what a pitcher was about to throw. That was way out of the ordinary back then. And every time we'd go to another city, he'd say, 'Remember this or that when you go up to the plate.'"

"Dom was a well-organized guy, he was always prepared to play," says Doerr. "He was a really good *team* ballplayer, and how he collected and shared information on pitchers was just one good example."

When the Red Sox were at Yankee Stadium on April 30, Dominic went 3-for-4, but New York won, 4–3. Boston was hitting and playing well, but Stengel's Bronx Bombers were playing better.

Dominic was still not chatty on the field with players. Berra was one of the few catchers with whom he exchanged pleasantries. "I knew from Joe that I had a lot in common with the DiMaggios," the Yankee Hall of Famer recalls. "Whenever Dom came up to the plate, we said hello and such, how you doing, where you going to dinner that night." Berra had been born to Italian immigrants in St. Louis. His mother never learned English. His father supported the family as a factory worker, and the last thing he wanted was for his son to be off playing baseball. As Berra recalls, "I sold newspapers on the street, just like Vince, Joe, and Dom, and we used to crack jokes about that while Dom was in the batter's box." Berra also didn't look like a gifted athlete. Like Dominic, he had to prove through hard work that he was the best at his position.

Boston got an opportunity to gain on the Yankees with a three-game series beginning June 28. It also marked the return of the Yankee Clipper. That Friday Stengel put Joe in the lineup for the first time in the '49 season. After months of pain, Joe had gotten out of bed one morning and the right heel felt fine. Almost afraid to believe his good fortune, Joe walked on it, then ran, then went through some drills and batting practice at Yankee Stadium while the team was away. From there he went to join his team in Boston. He was weak from inactivity, but he was going to play.

"I tried to talk him out of it," Dominic told Dave Anderson of the New York Times in 1982. "I didn't think he was ready. I told him his health came first. But he played. And he was ready."

Yes he was. After awkwardly fouling a few off, Joe lined a pitch over short for a single. His next time up, he hit a two-run homer, and some Boston fans couldn't help cheering. In the bottom of the ninth, with the Yanks leading 5–4, Ted launched a long fly that Joe hauled in to end the game. Perhaps distracted, Dominic was hitless.

On Saturday, Boston jumped out 7–1 after four innings. Then

Joe clubbed a three-run homer. In the eighth inning, with the score knotted at 7–7, Joe put one over the Green Monster, and the Yankees held on for an improbable 9–7 victory. On Sunday, the Yankees led only 3–2 going into the top of the eighth. Joe cracked a three-run homer, and the final score was 6–3. Joe didn't need Dominic or anyone else to carry on the DiMaggio tradition—in the three games he had batted .455, slugged four round-trippers, and driven in nine runs.

The Sox went into a long slump after that. By the first week of July, they were at 35-36 and a full dozen games behind New York. Stengel broke a cardinal baseball rule when he declared, "That's it. The Red Sox won't bother us."

Ebbets Field hosted the 1949 All-Star Game, and the American League presented an especially strong starting outfield: Ted Williams, Joe DiMaggio, and Dominic DiMaggio. Dominic wound up with two hits and two runs scored, but his brother stole the show with three RBI, the biggest hit being a sixth-inning double. Stan Musial had a homer, two singles, and a walk, but the American League took an 11–7 win. It was the first All-Star Game to feature not just one but four black ballplayers: Jackie Robinson, Roy Campanella, Don Newcombe, and Larry Doby.

The Red Sox rebounded after the break. Leading them at the top of the order was Dominic. As his hitting streak reached 30 games, the press wondered if he'd match his brother's famous streak.

"Dom was a nightmare for third basemen," recalls Bobby Brown. "If you came in, he'd smack the ball past you. If you stayed back, he'd drop the most beautiful bunt. And of course, once he got on, he was an excellent base runner."

The streak was at 34 games when the Sox went to the Bronx. Dominic was 0-for-4 when he came up in the eighth inning. It has gone down in legend that Joe made a sensational catch to stop his brother's streak. But as Dominic described it for the writer Alan Schwartz: "I smacked a line drive right up the middle so hard that it passed Raschi's ear! He ducked to get out of the way of it! As soon as I hit it, I said, 'O.K., that's 35.' But the ball wouldn't drop. The ball refused to drop. Joe is standing out there in center field, and he didn't have to move. He said it himself later—if he hadn't caught the ball, it would have hit him right between the eyes. So there was no effort on his part. I just hit the ball too damn hard!"

One might think that the dinner the two brothers had that night would be strained. But as disappointed as Dominic was, it wasn't in him to hold a grudge against his older brother. The dinner was probably Joe's treat. When the Red Sox were home against the Yankees, at least one night Dominic would bring his brother home and Emily would cook dinner. In New York, Joe brought his brother to Toots Shor's, where Dominic could rub elbows with regulars like Jackie Gleason and Frank Sinatra.

"My father was there the night Gleason came in and announced he had just gotten the job to host a variety show," says Paul DiMaggio, the eldest of Dominic and Emily's three children. The show was *Cavalcade of Stars,* which helped make Gleason a star. "My father was not a big party guy, but he told us there was a huge party that night, with Gleason buying drinks left and right."

The Red Sox offense ran rampant through August. Playing the Senators helped Boston's surge—doubleheader losses on the twelfth and fourteenth. (They would roll over again in a twin bill on September 5.) In the game in between, Stephens hit a walk-off grand slam. Though he cost the Sox a few runs because he wasn't nearly the shortstop Pesky was, Stephens was having another strong offensive year. In the rotation, Ellis Kinder was a pleasant surprise. The righty had begun the season as a 34-year-old with an underwhelming 21–25 career record and was known more for his partying and curfew-breaking than pitching, but he was leading the Boston staff in almost every category. He would end the season with a totally unanticipated 23–6 record. Parnell was having another strong season too. When he defeated the White Sox on the twenty-sixth, it was his twentieth victory. During August, Parnell and Kinder were each 6–0, Jack Kramer was 3–0, and Chuck Stobbs was 3–0. In the middle of September, with his team still trailing New York, Ted Williams once more lifted the Sox on his shoulders. He was putting himself in the record books again: from July 1 through September 28, he had reached base in 84 consecutive games, which remains a major league record.

As the Red Sox clawed their way back into the pennant race, the Yankees weren't rolling over for them. The club was beset by injuries, most significantly to Berra, Hank Bauer, Rizzuto, and Vic Raschi. But even though injuries cost each playing time, the team managed to keep winning enough to hold on to first. Most important, the team had a healthy Big Guy. In the first week of September, Joe had five RBI, four from a grand slam, in a game in Philly. The Yankees and Red Sox were like two racehorses making the turn into the home stretch. The Sox were two games behind. It got closer as the month went on.

Then it happened again—Joe was sidelined. He had contracted a cold, which turned into something like the flu. When he reported for the September 18 game with a 102-degree temperature, Stengel benched him. It was pneumonia, and Joe went back to the hospital.

Many people believed that the Yankees-Sox game on September 25 would be the big showdown of 1949. Despite all the injuries the Yankee players had suffered and a manager untested in major league pennant races, New York had clung to first place day after weary day. With Joe listening to the game at the hospital, the Yankees sent out the veteran Allie Reynolds against Mel Parnell, who was 15-3 at Fenway that season. Beating Boston at home and going two games up with a week left would be huge. But Parnell surrendered just one run, the equally worn-out Red Sox pushed four across, and the teams were tied for first. It was Boston's ninth victory in a row.

The two teams hopped trains for the Bronx to make up a game that had been rained out earlier in the season. Now the stakes were even higher. Certainly that was apparent to the 67,434 who piled into

Yankee Stadium on the afternoon of the 26th. Was it too much to ask of the Sox to win ten in a row? Initially, it looked to be. The Yankees jumped out to a 6–3 lead. But in the eighth inning, Boston tied it up, and Pesky was on third. Doerr executed the squeeze. Henrich, playing first, picked up the ball and tossed it to Ralph Houk. The catcher applied the tag, but Pesky was called safe. Stengel, his hair on fire, charged out of the dugout.

The two teams seesawed back and forth during the final week of the season. Boston had gone 59-19 and needed only one more win to be back in the World Series. "Sox and Parnell to Clinch Flag Today," the *Boston Herald* optimistically proclaimed on its October 1 front page.

But they would have to do it on Joe DiMaggio Day at Yankee Stadium. He had climbed out of his hospital bed but had been a reclusive figure at the Elysee suite, 18 pounds lighter and still struggling to catch his breath. With so much at stake, Joe couldn't stay out of the lineup. He could have done without the attention and the extra effort of having to respond to the press and the 69,551 fans at the ballpark. The hardest part was standing through the speeches and ceremonies before the game began.

Thankfully, Dominic was there. "He made his whole speech leaning on me," Dominic told Dave Anderson in 1982. Not wanting to take anything away from Joe in the spotlight, he asked Joe if he wanted him to leave. "No," Joe croaked.

The newly widowed Rosalie DiMaggio had made the tiring trip from San Francisco with her son Tom. Dominic recalled, "When she came out onto the field, she walked right by Joe and came over to hug me, the baby of the family. I think people wondered why she ignored Joe, but she had seen Joe the night before. She hadn't seen me until she came out onto the field."

Joe, with Joe Jr. also on the field, choked back tears and managed to give a speech to the adoring crowd. He called the Yankees "the gamest, fightingest bunch of guys who ever lived" and ended with what is probably his most famous quote: "I'd like to thank the Good Lord for making me a Yankee." Then he dragged himself out to center field, having told Stengel he would try to play three innings.

Dominic led off the game with a single. Pesky's bouncer should have been a double play, but Dominic took Rizzuto out at short before the relay to first. Williams singled, and a sacrifice fly by Stephens made the score 1–0. In the bottom of the inning, Joe struck out to end it with Rizzuto on third. In the third inning, Reynolds walked Pesky, Williams, and Stephens, and Doerr's single made it 2–0. Joe Page came in and walked Al Zarilla (who during the season had taken over right field when Mele was traded). Then he walked Billy Goodman. The Sox had a 4–0 lead going into the fourth.

Then Joe doubled to right, and Bauer drove him in with a single. In the fifth, the Yanks made it 4–3. They went on to a 5–4 win. Joe played the entire game.

Rosalie was escorted down to the Yankee clubhouse. When it appeared there would be a wait to see Joe, Frank Scott, then the Yankees' traveling secretary, offered to bring her to a room upstairs. With a sad smile, she said, "No, take me to Dominic, he lose today."

As MUCH AS he wanted to see his brothers go down to the wire for a league championship, Vince had not accompanied his mother east. He had his own season to finish up in the Far West League. Pittsburg's attendance got a boost in July from a special "Vince DiMaggio Night." It was a very modest affair compared to the one that Joe would have to endure. A highlight of the game was the gimmick that Vince and his rival player-manager, Ray "Little Buffalo" Perry of the Redding Browns, played all nine positions during it. Vince's Diamonds enjoyed an 11–2 victory.

His team was on its way to a celebration dinner at the Los Medanos Hotel when they came upon a building on fire. The Diamonds joined the volunteer firefighters, and while he helped battle the blaze Vince cut his hand. He recovered quickly, however.

By season's end, Vince had had a great year at the plate. He slugged 37 homers, drove in 117 runs, and hit a very satisfying .367. And he was again a fan favorite. Spectators enjoyed the way he sang arias in the outfield during lulls in games, as well as what was routinely described as his "affable personality." But the Pittsburg Diamonds as a whole didn't do too well, finishing fourth in the eight-team league.

Still, ownership was happy enough with attendance and Vince's rapport with the fans that they hired him back for the 1950 season.

THE NATIONAL LEAGUE race was going down to the final day too. The winner of the American League's 154th game would face either the Brooklyn Dodgers or the St. Louis Cardinals.

Raschi took the mound for New York and Kinder for the home team Sox. The Boston hurler surrendered a run in the first inning on a Rizzuto triple and Henrich groundout, but he gave up nothing after that. The score was still 1–0 in the top of the eighth when McCarthy sent up pinch hitter Tom Wright for Kinder, who walked. But Dominic bounced into a double play, and there was no threat. The Yankees capitalized against Parnell. Henrich homered. After Berra singled, Hughson came in to pitch. Before the inning ended, he had yielded a three-run double to Coleman. In the top of the ninth, the Red Sox were in a 5–0 hole.

Pesky fouled out. Ted walked. Stephens singled. Doerr tripled—a wheezing Joe was unable to catch up to the fly to center—to bring Ted and Stephens home. It was 5–2. Joe, spent, removed himself from the game, replaced by Cliff Mapes. Mapes caught Zarilla's fly ball, and his throw home froze Doerr at third. Goodman singled, and the score was 5–3 with two outs. Henrich, drifting away from first, gloved a foul fly by Birdie Tebbetts, and the Yankees had won their 16th pennant, stunning even their own fans.

The Boston locker room was like a morgue. Stephens tried a couple of cheering-up comments, but nothing worked. "That phrase, 'You could hear a pin drop,' I never really knew what that kind of silence was like until after that game," the Sox catcher Matt Batts recalled 63 years later.

"The whole team was heartbroken," Williams later wrote. "Sick. To come that close twice in a row was an awful cross to bear. I remember sitting at my locker and seeing McCarthy come in and wondering where he had been. He had been over to congratulate the Yankees. He had perked up pretty good, but I know it hit him hard. I don't think he ever got over it completely."

"Very, very painful," remembers Doerr. "We couldn't look at each other."

The Red Sox had the dubious distinction of becoming the only team in major league history to finish a game out of first in two consecutive seasons. Once more, Ted had done all that could be asked of him, and in a few weeks he would have his second MVP Award to corroborate that. Dominic had been the best leadoff man in the league, batting a career-best .307. He drew 96 walks and scored 126 runs, both the second-highest totals of his career. It just wasn't enough.

When a devastated Dominic skipped the World Series, he missed a very good one. The Dodgers had won the NL pennant. They had a talented outfield of Duke Snider, Gene Hermanski, and Carl Furillo and an excellent infield with Gil Hodges at first, Robinson at second, Pee Wee Reese at short, and Spider Jorgensen at third. Campanella had become the full-time catcher; his three MVP Awards were still ahead of him. Don Newcombe, Preacher Roe, Ralph Branca, and Carl Erskine were formidable hurlers. Charlie Dressen's team seemed to have the advantage over Stengel's exhausted, injury-riddled roster.

But as the Bronx Bombers had proved before, especially during the DiMaggio years, the Fall Classic was a different season, one in which the Yankees elevated their game. In the first game, at Yankee Stadium, Newcombe pitched brilliantly, striking out 11 and giving up one run. But Reynolds pitched a two-hit shutout. The second game produced the opposite result, as Roe blanked the Yanks 1–0.

Joe scratched out a hit, then would go hitless until the final game.

At Ebbets Field on October 7, the Yankees earned a 4–3 victory. Brooklyn, needing to even the Series up, sent Newcombe out again, this time against Eddie Lopat. A winded Joe wore the collar once more, but the Yankees were up 6–0 after five innings. Lopat surrendered four runs in the sixth, then Reynolds, the Big Chief, shut the door. After the 6–4 loss, the Dodgers faced elimination in Game 5. Rex Barney and five other hurlers were slapped around by the seemingly inexhaustible Yankees. Joe finally contributed with a solo home run and two RBI, Coleman had three RBI, and Brown two more in the 10–6 triumph. The Subway Series had not been much of a contest.

When Stengel was asked if his first world championship as a manager was the biggest thrill in his life, he replied, "No. I'd say the biggest thrill came when we got in there. If we hadn't won the pennant we wouldn't be here. Winning the pennant took some doing, after all we'd been through."

The press noted that in the clubhouse celebration, with his son beside him, Joe, though having gone 2-for-18 in the five games, smiled for the first time since the Series began. He admitted to reporters that he was wiped out by the season. It had been the worst of his career.

Did Joe have more celebrations planned? No, he was too tired. He just wanted to go home to San Francisco. He took Rosalie to the airport for her return trip and followed her two weeks later. Her home cooking would restore him. If not, since he was about to turn 35, maybe it was time to consider retiring.

EIGHTEEN

WHILE JOE SOUGHT to be restored in San Francisco and Dominic and Emily began living full-time in the Boston area, Vince prolonged his career in Pittsburg. After a strong 1949 season, and with the fans behind him, he didn't want to retire. He simply loved the game too much.

The Far West League had begun in 1948 with nine teams: two in Oregon—the Klamath Falls Gems and the Medford Nuggets (soon renamed the Rogues)—and six in California besides Pittsburg: the Marysville Braves (renamed the Peaches), Oroville Red Sox, Willows Cardinals, Santa Rosa Pirates, Roseville Diamonds, and Redding Browns. When the 1950 season began, the Santa Rosa and Roseville clubs were already history and a Vallejo club had quickly come and gone, as had one in Chico.

The Pittsburg club seemed relatively stable, not least because the marquee DiMaggio name kept bringing fans in. They flocked to watch him when the Diamonds were on the road too.

"My father fully believed in the saying, 'If you can't say something nice, don't say anything at all,' and that included even when he was a manager," recalls Joanne, who was by now a teenager. "One time at dinner he mentioned something about talking to an umpire, and I said, 'Dad, how can you talk to him after he called you out in the game?' He said, 'That's his job to make a call, but otherwise we're friends.' He always tried to be good to people, and I never heard him curse. Never."

During the off-season, Vince continued to work at DiMaggio's Grotto and still sold sporting goods as well. Yet, Joanne says, "with all the jobs he had, my father always kept time for fishing. Nothing got in the way of that. He loved it so much. I remember one time my mother and I went out on the water near Pittsburg with him and all of a sudden the weather changed. Large swells were striking the boat. My mom turned green. My dad was fine, so I was too. I had no worries that he would get us back to the marina. I thought he'd probably done this lots of times and the boat was big enough. I found out later that there were plenty of people he had rescued out on the water in bad conditions because he knew what he was doing and they didn't."

From time to time at his brothers' restaurant a patron would ask him to sing, and when he did he demonstrated that he still had a fine operatic voice. Family gatherings were an occasion for songs too. "I remember that most about Vince, his wonderful voice," says Emily DiMaggio, who had heard him sing the first time Dominic brought her to San Francisco. "He sang for me at the dinner table, and I could understand why Dom had wanted him to pursue training in the opera."

The most important performance for Vince, though, was still on the field. To some extent he was carrying the entire Far West League on his shoulders. He was 37 when the '50 season began, but he looked pretty spry feasting on D league pitching. By the end of the season, having played in 125 of the team's 130 games, he had a .353 average, 26 home runs, and 129 RBI, with a whopping .624 slugging percentage. He even stole 15 bases. And no one in the league was a better outfielder. Unfortunately for the Diamonds, their pitching was weak, and the club wound up with a 67-73 record.

The Far West League had always struggled, and it folded in the middle of the 1951 season. Vince still tried to hold on. He signed with the Tacoma Tigers, a step up to the Class B Western International League. Vince could focus on playing the rest of the season because the Tigers already had a manager, Jim Brillheart, who at 47 still pitched occasionally. The team wasn't very good, though. Vince could contribute only a .225 average with five homers in 74 games. When the 63-82 season ended, so did the Tacoma club.

For the first time in over two decades, Vince had to face a future without baseball. He would not be picked up by any organization in 1952, neither as a player nor as a coach-manager. While his brother Joe's retirement would produce nationwide headlines, Vince's departure went unnoticed except by his family. Unlike the Yankee Clipper and the Little Professor, Vince was the DiMaggio who never got a nickname. In addition to his various Pacific Coast and minor league stints, Vince had played in ten major league seasons and had compiled a .249 career average, 125 home runs, and 584 RBI. He had been a two-time All-Star and would have been selected more often if more weight had been given to excellent fielding and rapport with the fans.

SAN FRANCISCO WAS GOOD for Joe. Rosalie's home cooking helped him heal. Away from the New York spotlight and expectations (though no expectations were ever higher than his own), Joe relaxed at the Grotto with his brothers and visited with his sisters and various nieces and nephews. He kept fit by taking up golf as a gift to himself when he turned 35, with Lefty O'Doul as his regular partner. When the Yankees sent a contract in January, he signed it immediately. He hadn't looked forward to spring training this much since he'd returned from the Army.

He did not go to New York before heading to St. Petersburg,

instead fielding phone interviews from the team's beat writers while in San Francisco. He told them that he once again tipped the scales at over 200 pounds, and that he still wore the smile that had finally appeared in the clubhouse after the World Series win. "Maybe it would be tempting fate to go popping off," Joe said. "Nevertheless, the way I feel now I can't see any reason why there should not be three or four more good years ahead of me."

Asked how the club would do in the '50 campaign, he responded, "If a fellow doesn't expect to finish first, what's the sense of him being a Yankee?"

At Casey Stengel's request, Joe took it easy in the early weeks, then played more games. By the time the Yankees broke camp, Joe had batted .403. Old Reliable Henrich was a bigger concern for the team. He, Joe, and Phil Rizzuto were the only remaining prewar starters. Henrich had returned too soon from a back injury the previous season and still wasn't right. Chronic knee problems were flaring up again. Henrich was smart enough to know that most likely this was his final campaign. He wanted to go out the way he'd always been—a winner.

For much of the 1950 season, the press and fans tracked milestones for Joe to reach. In an 8–2 win over the Indians, he cracked his 2,000th hit, a single to center. But it was clear that Joe was slower in the outfield. Stengel wanted him to try playing first base, but couldn't bring himself to talk to Joe directly about it, so co-owner Dan Topping did, one Saturday night in Boston in early July. To the press it was announced that DiMaggio would cooperate. "Joe is willing to go along with the idea," Arch Murray reported in the *New York Post*. "DiMag, who doesn't want to reach the sunset any quicker than his bosses want him to, will go along with anything that may stave off the encroaching years."

But Joe hated the idea. Henrich noted that when Joe returned to the locker room after a practice session, he was drenched in sweat—not because the workout was that intense, but because of his fear of embarrassing himself in front of the fans, especially the ones in New York. Joe played first base exactly one game, handled 13 chances flawlessly, then told Stengel he was finished as a first baseman. The official reason offered was that an injury to Hank Bauer left the Yanks one outfielder short.

It was, of course, as a center fielder that Joe was selected to play in the All-Star Game. Joining him at Comiskey Park in Chicago were Yankees Yogi Berra, Rizzuto, Jerry Coleman, Vic Raschi, Allie Reynolds, and, for old time's sake, Tommy Henrich. Joe and Dominic were starters in the outfield again. Also from the Red Sox were Ted Williams, Walt Dropo, and Bobby Doerr. The brothers went hitless—in his only appearance, Joe hit into a double play. The National League prevailed in the 14-inning battle, 4–3.

AFTER THE CRUSHING disappointments of the previous seasons, it would take a lot for Dominic and his teammates to pull themselves together for another pennant drive in 1950. If consistency was a key, Boston had a good chance, as they had pretty much the same lineup and pitching rotation as before, with Joe McCarthy back as the skipper.

Opening day at Fenway Park began on a festive note, with commissioner Happy Chandler presenting Ted with his MVP Award. The Sox leaped to a 9–0 lead against the Yankees. But in the eighth inning, the visitors exploded for nine runs of their own. Billy Martin, a Pacific Coast League product, set a record with two hits in one inning in his first major league game. With Henrich tripling twice, the Yankees won, 15–10. Dominic went 2-for-5 with two runs scored, and Joe went 3-for-6 with an RBI. Despite this loss, by the end of the month the Sox looked good, burying the Athletics 19–0 in one game and dusting the White Sox 11–1 the following week. Dominic inspired his teammates with his consistent hitting and ability to get on base. He himself may have been inspired by a happy occasion in his private life: on April 28, Emily gave birth to a seven-pound, 13.5-ounce boy, Dominic Paul DiMaggio Jr. They'd call him Paul.

Through June, Boston kept bashing opponents—demolishing the St. Louis Browns 15–2, 20–4, and even 29–4, going 11–5 over the Indians, and thrashing the White Sox 17–7 and 12–0 in consecutive games. In one nine-game stretch, the Red Sox scored 119 runs, and they would plate a record-breaking 1,027 that season.

The output wasn't enough, however, to cheer McCarthy. He had not been able to recover from the bitter disappointments of the 1948 and '49 seasons. Drinking heavily again, he quit the Red Sox after 59 games. Joe Cronin replaced him with Steve O'Neill, a coach who fingered rosary beads in the dugout. His prayers were heard as Boston kept pounding the ball. The Sox feasted on the Yankees' Whitey Ford when he made his major league debut on July 1 at Fenway Park. The young lefty lasted four and two-thirds innings, giving up five earned runs on seven hits and six walks as the Sox lashed the Yanks 13–4. Yet for all their phenomenal hitting, the Sox were giving up too many runs and still trailed the Yankees and Tigers.

The All-Star Game was a dark day in Boston. In the first inning, while making a fine catch of a Ralph Kiner drive to left, Ted Williams collided with the left-field wall and broke his elbow. Somehow he played nine innings, even hitting a single in the eighth, but X-rays the next day told the tale. He would not play again until mid-September.

The gutty Red Sox did not fold. On July 18, their 12–9 win over the Tigers at Fenway Park brought them to .500 at 39-39. In the next 59 games they went 47-12. On September 12, when they beat Chicago for their 24th victory in 27 games, Boston was a game behind the Tigers and a half-game behind the Yankees. Three days later, Ted was back in the lineup. He celebrated by going 4-for-6, with a homer and three singles in a 12–9 win over the Browns. On the 18th, defeating the Tigers 3–2 in Detroit put Boston ahead of the Tigers and a game behind the Yankees.

Then Boston's pennant hopes died, rather abruptly. On the 20th, the Indians beat them twice. They lost five of their next nine games. The late-season swoon proved fatal. The Red Sox finished with 94 wins, but four games out of first.

Dominic had clearly been their most valuable player. He might have won the American League MVP if the pitching hadn't let the team down.

"He was valuable off the field too, which people didn't see," says Jimmy Piersall, who at only 20 had been called up in September as a backup outfielder. "He was fine with young players asking him about playing in this park or other, against this hitter or that hitter. I talked to him as much as I could and watched how he played center. He badly wanted the Red Sox to win, and sharing his knowledge was part of that."

THOUGH THE YANKS were in first place for much of the season, Joe and Stengel were not getting along. No doubt Casey did not hold Joe in the same respect, even awe, that Joe McCarthy had. Bucky Harris had seen Joe produce some great performances when he was hurting. But Stengel had inherited a fading star who wasn't making the great catch or getting the key hit often enough to warrant special treatment. Joe could understand that. But it angered him that Stengel still couldn't bring himself to speak to him directly.

For his part, Stengel knew that to keep his job in New York he had to win championships. Joe's ego and past exploits weren't going to make that happen. The Yankees were winning with a team effort that balanced hitting and pitching. Berra had settled in as one of the league's best catchers and with a few stints in the outfield would play in all but three games in the 1950 season. Billy Martin was a restless utility man in the infield. Reynolds, Raschi, Eddie Lopat, and Tommy Byrne were workhorse hurlers, leaving little room for the untested lefty Ford and righty Lew Burdette, and Joe Page still ruled the bullpen.

The Yankees were strong across the board, but by August it looked like the Yankee Clipper didn't have the three or four good years left he had suggested to sportswriters before the season. His average was near .300—respectable, but nothing like in his healthy years. Every so often his legs cramped for no apparent reason. A really good fastball could be in the catcher's mitt before he got around on it. He ceded more of left-center to Gene Woodling, a former San Francisco Seal. He was humiliated when Stengel benched him for six games that month. Joe spent most of those games in the tunnel leading from the dugout to the locker room, silently and sullenly smoking cigarettes.

When the Yankees even lost to the Senators, Berra composed a poem for Joe: "Roses are red. Violets are blue. Ted Williams can hit. Why can't you." The next day Joe was back in center field and walloped his 22nd homer. He went on to hit .442 in the next 11 games. A four-game sweep of the Indians put the Yanks two games in front of the Tigers and two and a half ahead of the Red Sox.

Joe's knees were acting up again, and Stengel rested him when he could. When he couldn't, Joe delivered. On September 10, he became the first player to slug three home runs in one game at Griffith Stadium; he also doubled for a perfect day in the 8–1 triumph. Joe hit his 28th home run two days later, but the surging Tigers moved into first by half a game. The Bronx Bombers took their case directly to Detroit and beat the home team there on September 14, with Joe blasting number 29. By the time the Yankees arrived in Philadelphia for a season-ending series, Joe had 118 RBI, 32 homers, and a 19-game hitting streak. At season's end, his slugging average of .585 led the league.

The pennant was New York's again. The Yankees ended the season with 98 wins and a winning percentage of .636. The surprising star of the team was the diminutive Rizzuto. He had played in every game, had 200 hits with a .324 average, his 66 RBI were very good for a leadoff man, and no one played a better shortstop. When the voting was done, "the Scooter" was the American League MVP.

The World Series, against the Philadelphia Phillies, was a mere formality. For the ninth time since Joe joined the team, the Yankees became world champions as they swept the Phillies.

After the Series, Lefty O'Doul asked Joe to accompany his San Francisco Seals on a trip to Japan. O'Doul's fascination with the country had never faded since his 1934 visit. When the Seals had ended their season in 1949, and with the war over by four years, O'Doul and his team had gone across the Pacific. "The San Francisco Seals arrived today to a thunderous welcome for their 'bicycle series' with Japanese and GI baseball teams," reported the *New York Times*. "Tens of thousands lined some five miles of city streets to cheer the visiting Pacific Coast Leaguers—first athletes to come here since the war. It was a bigger throng than even Emperor Hirohito has attracted in recent years."

The tour had lasted six weeks and included a luncheon with Gen. Douglas MacArthur, who had ordered Korakuen Stadium emptied of the ammunition stored there so it could again be a ball field. The 11 games drew an estimated 500,000 fans and raised over $100,000 for various Japanese charities.

The 1950 trip with Joe included exhibition games in Korea for U.S. troops who were part of the United Nations forces, commanded by MacArthur, fighting there after North Korea had invaded South Korea the previous June. In Japan the highlight was a ten-day home run contest between the Great DiMaggio and Makoto Kuzuru, labeled the "Babe Ruth of Japan." Japanese fans were thrilled when during the first three days the hometown hero outslugged the Yank. Joe did not have his own bats from home and was trying to make do with a shorter, lighter one made of soft wood that he said "felt like an Italian sausage." On the fourth day, however, "I got my hands on a [Louisville] Slugger that had been left over there on O'Doul's trip the year before. I managed to win the home run derby over the next seven days."

NINETEEN

FOR THE 1951 SEASON, Joe Cronin and the Red Sox made changes to the roster they hoped would help them dethrone the Yankees. Birdie Tebbetts was sent to the Indians. Joe Dobson and Al Zarilla were dealt to the White Sox. After Lou Boudreau was axed as Cleveland's manager, the Sox signed him to be their starting shortstop, bumping Vern Stephens to third and putting the popular Pesky on the bench. The resulting team was weaker defensively in the infield—not good for a club with chronically shaky pitching.

Boudreau homered in his first game at Fenway Park, and again Boston had a potent offense, but they gave runs back as soon as they scored them. On May 15, the franchise marked its 50th anniversary with a 9–7 loss to Chicago. When they could get consistent pitching (Parnell won 18 in 1951), the Red Sox were unbeatable—a twin-bill sweep of the Yankees on Memorial Day gave them ten victories in a row. Dominic, though 34, had fresh legs and a quick bat.

In June, he got news he and his siblings had been dreading: Rosalie was close to death. When Dominic had visited just before Christmas, doctors told him his mother had cancer. The 73-year-old matriarch had been failing since then. When she slipped into a coma, Tom tracked Joe down in New York and Dominic in Boston. Both left immediately for San Francisco. Joe arrived early on the morning of June 18. All four sisters and three of his brothers were there at the house on Beach Street. Three hours after Joe joined them at their mother's bedside, Rosalie died. Dominic arrived a half-hour too late, thwarted by plane schedules.

As they had done two years earlier for Giuseppe's funeral mass, the DiMaggio brothers and sisters gathered at Saints Peter and Paul Church. Rosalie was buried next to her husband at the Holy Cross Cemetery, in a mausoleum the family had purchased. The next day Joe and Dominic boarded a plane together for the trip back to the East Coast.

Dominic returned to a blazing hot Boston team. After taking both ends of a 26-inning doubleheader in Chicago, the Red Sox were in first place with a 49-29 record. The Yankees eased into first ten days later, but the resilient Red Sox kept pummeling most of their opponents. Dominic had five hits in a 13–10 win over the White Sox. Boston hovered near first through August and into September. The ageless Ellis Kinder put together a string of 29 scoreless innings. With a 12–5 victory over Chicago, the Red Sox were just two and a half games out of first.

And then, as they had before, Boston imploded. They lost two games, won one, then lost their last nine contests, closing the season with the Yankees sweeping them in five straight games. They finished the season in third place, 11 games out. For Dominic, it was a miserable end to a season that had shown he remained an elite player—a .296 average, 72 runs batted in (two more than in '50), and 113 runs scored, again tops in the American League.

That winter Dominic pondered another run in 1952. He learned that any new campaign would be without one of his longtime comrades. During a cold night in Cleveland late in the season, Doerr had hurt his back charging in to field a slow grounder. If he wanted to continue playing, he would need surgery to repair disc and vertebrae damage. At 33, he decided instead to call it quits. That would leave Dominic, Ted, and Pesky of the original West Coast group to tilt at windmills.

JOE HAD FELT GOOD at spring training in 1951, telling the *World Telegram and Sun*, "I am out to surprise those who believe I am finishing up my career." However, he also told reporters, "This year might be my last." A "flabbergasted" front office issued a statement: "We regret to hear anything like this. We hope he will have the sort of season which will cause him to change his mind."

He didn't. Joe's batting average stayed at a journeyman level, and he suffered from a chronic power outage. He couldn't stay in the lineup for long stretches. When on June 8 he pulled a muscle in his left leg chasing a fly ball, it was already the third time in the season an injury had exiled him to the bench.

Adding to his frustration, the Yankees had introduced a teenager from Oklahoma already touted as the next Big Guy. So far, though, Mickey Mantle was still struggling to figure out American League pitching and left field at Yankee Stadium. On May 30 he whiffed five times in a doubleheader swept by the Red Sox 11–10 and 9–4. On July 13, he would rack up four strikeouts and be shipped down to the Kansas City Blues.

The Red Sox were in the hunt again. Heading toward July the White Sox held on to a slim lead atop the league. When the Yankees beat Boston 5–2 on July 1 (with Doerr collecting his 2,000th hit), the Red Sox were three and a half games behind and Chicago and New York were tied for first. Joe was back in the lineup, sore leg and all. Maybe he was prodded by columns like one from his friend Jimmy Cannon, who, being somewhat unkind to both brothers, wrote, "DiMaggio may be in his last season. Time has warped the great gifts. You must take such as his brother, Dom, over him."

For the 13th time in 13 active seasons, Joe was an All-Star. But with the left leg still bothering him, Stengel didn't play him. Dominic started in his place in center field. Ted was the only other Red Sox starter. The National League found the confines of Briggs Stadium in Detroit friendly as homers by Gil Hodges, Stan Musial, Ralph Kiner, and Bob Elliott powered the senior circuit to an 8–3 victory.

The second half of the season wasn't much easier for Joe. In addition to the nagging injuries and anemic hitting, the New York press ran pieces that were critical of Stengel for not handling the aging superstar correctly, and critical of Joe for seeming to need special handling. Milton Gross wrote, "On Friday I did recognize a profound difference in the personal climate which surrounds DiMaggio and the Yankees this season. It is a frigid one, all because Joe, who always was a strange man, difficult to understand, is now living in a shell that is virtually impenetrable."

In a rare, Ted Williams–like outburst, Dominic had a "strong beef" with reporters. Visibly angry, he told them that his brother "was being crucified by New York baseball writers for no good reason."

Joe didn't comment, but Dominic's opinions clearly meant a lot to him. An anecdote from that season illustrates this. In 1951 Babe Martin was back in the minor leagues, catching for a team in San Antonio. Before an exhibition game against the Yankees, Joe emerged from the dugout and said to Martin, "Babe, are we going to have sandwiches and coffee after the game?"

"I was thrilled to death that Joe DiMaggio would come out to see me, a minor leaguer who had been only a third-string catcher in the big leagues," Martin recalls 61 years later. "During that game, the pitcher knocked me down. I got up and hit a homer on the next pitch. Later, Joe and I are eating together and he says, 'Babe, that's the way you're supposed to do it.' Why did Joe go out of his way to see me? Because he knew Dom and I had become close friends, and for Joe, there wasn't a better recommendation about a man than that."

It's hard to say what gnawed at Joe more in the summer of '51.

From the days at the Horse Lot he had been a gifted athlete, and now more than injuries were conspiring against him. His skills had seriously eroded. Since his first full season in the Pacific Coast League 18 years earlier, he had enjoyed a generous to adoring press, and now reporters and columnists were turning on him. He had just lost his mother, who with his sisters had doted on him. His marriage was long over, he was more a loner than ever, and he didn't see his son nearly enough (which was not only Dorothy's fault). His immediate future looked to be a choice between eking out one more year on the field and possibly humiliating himself or trying to find out what life was like without putting on a uniform. He had bled pinstripes, the good Lord had made him a Yankee, yet the club might not even want him back—if this Mantle kid straightened out, the weight of the team might shift to his shoulders, just as Joe had once assumed it from Gehrig.

No surprise then that after he hit a homer and a triple but the Yankees still lost to the lowly Senators, Joe lashed out at reporters. "You are darn right that I wanted to make you writers look bad. I'll always try to make you look bad. Just because I have had a bad day, you guys want to fire me. Some of you guys are the ones who had me washed up in 1946. But here I am, five years later. How are you going to explain the hits I made today? Are they going to fire me every time I have a bad day?"

As the Yanks battled the Red Sox, White Sox, and revived Indians, there were a few more flashes of the old Yankee Clipper. In the first game of a twin-bill sweep of the White Sox, Joe blasted two home runs. Gradually, day after day, the rivals fell back in September. Berra led the Yanks in RBIs, and Woodling and a returned Mantle did their parts. Pitching again made the biggest difference, with Reynolds, Raschi, Lopat, and whoever Stengel thought would give him innings bearing the burden. (Whitey Ford had been drafted into the Army.)

Reynolds pitched many big games in his career as both a reliever and a starter, but perhaps none was bigger than the one on September 28 at Yankee Stadium. He already had a no-hitter in the '51 season, beating Bob Feller and the Indians 1–0. This Friday the Yankees needed two wins to secure their third consecutive pennant, and they had to do it against the Red Sox. Dominic, irritating Reynolds by taking time to wipe his glasses, worked a walk to open the game—he would like nothing more than to beat Reynolds and at least delay another title for New York. But Pesky lined into a double play, and Ted struck out. Reynolds retired the next six batters. Ted walked in the fourth but was left stranded. After four innings, it was 4–0 Yankees. A Woodling homer in the eighth tacked on one more run. In the top of the ninth, with one out, Dominic walked again. Pesky whiffed, bringing up Ted. He popped out, and Reynolds became the first American League pitcher to hurl two no-hitters in the same season.

Taking the second game of the twin bill would give the Yankees the pennant. They were leading 7–3 when Joe came up with two on and launched one into the left-field seats. The Sox were finished. In his last at-bat of the season, Dominic flew out to Woodling, who gave the ball to Joe. That would be the souvenir he kept for his tenth American League pennant.

The New York Giants, left for dead midway through the season, were the opponents in the '51 World Series. Winning relentlessly in August and September, Leo Durocher's team had tied the Brooklyn Dodgers and forced a playoff. The Giants earned entry into the Fall Classic on what remains one of the most famous home runs in history, Bobby Thomson's three-run walk-off wallop. New York newspapers speculated that if the Yankees took the Series, Joe would be back in '52 so he could repeat his 1936–39 feat of four consecutive world championships.

But in the first three games it looked like the Clipper had already outworn his welcome. He was 0-for-4 in a 5–1 Game 1 loss, 0-for-3 in a 3–1 win (in this game, Mantle went down with the first of many serious leg injuries), and 0-for-4 again in a 6–2 defeat.

Joe just wasn't feeling comfortable at the plate. He was unhappy enough with his regular-season average of .266, but this was worse. He had tied Babe Ruth for most World Series appearances with ten, and he wanted to go nine-for-ten in championships. (He had not been a member of the 1943 championship team.) The Yankees had always looked to the Big Guy to lead the way, but an 0-for-11 collar in three games wasn't getting it done.

He was blunt to Louis Effrat of the *Times:* "I've just been lousy . . . I still think the Yankees will beat the Giants if I give the boys some help. Maybe I'll do better. It's a cinch I can't do worse."

As luck would have it, Lefty O'Doul was in New York trying to put together a team of major leaguers for another trip to Japan. Joe said he'd join the team if Lefty helped him out of his slump. It was 1935 again as O'Doul became Joe's hitting instructor. "You've been pressing, lunging at bad balls, and your body is ahead of your arms so that you're pushing the ball," he told Joe. O'Doul also pointed out that Joe was swinging so hard that he was taking his eye off the ball. He needed to correct that immediately, go back to being a patient batter who swung at the last moment.

Against Sal "The Barber" Maglie in Game 4, Joe made it look easy. He singled in the third inning, and in the fifth he sent the ball into the upper deck in left for a two-run homer, powering the Yanks to a 6–2 victory. The Big Guy had evened things with the Giants with what turned out to be his last Series homer.

The Yankees won Game 5 too, 13–1, with Joe batting in three runs. In the finale, a 4–3 win, Joe was 1-for-2 with a run scored. His last hit in the major leagues was a double.

BECAUSE HE COULDN'T say no to his former PCL manager either, Dominic joined Joe as a member of the troupe that went to Japan in the fall. The visiting Americans played 16 games against

Japanese all-star teams. Among the American players were Yankees Billy Martin and Ed Lopat and Mel Parnell of the Red Sox. The "Yanks" won the first 11 games, but in the one on November 10, Japan's Central League All-Stars led 1–0 going into the top of the eighth. The 50,000 fans in attendance at Meiji Park in Tokyo "were clamoring for what they hoped would be the first Japanese victory over an American visiting team of major leaguers since 1931," reported the United Press. But the DiMaggio brothers were playing together for the last time, and they would go out winners. In his final at-bat as a professional, in a Yankee uniform, Joe belted a 400-foot home run high into the left-field stands.

"They kept changing pitchers every few innings," recalled Dominic. "I hit before him, and he came up to me and he wanted to know, 'What's this guy doing? What's he throwing?' I told him I had him 3-0 and 3-1 and he threw me a screwball each time. Joe said, 'Okay.' He got up and I think it was 2-0, and he threw him a screwball and Joe hit it into the seats. He came back into the dugout and said, 'That's it, gentlemen. That's my farewell. I'm not playing tomorrow.'"

For O'Doul, the success of the trip and the adulation of the Japanese fans—"Banzai O'Doul!" was their favorite chant—took some of the sting out of being fired by the Seals, who had finished the 1951 season in last place. In '52 he would be managing the San Diego Padres, and two years later would skipper them to first place in the PCL.

Dominic would have preferred to return from Japan to San Francisco, but Emily had other ideas about that. "One of the biggest fights of their life was where they were going to live," says Paul DiMaggio. "My mother really disliked San Francisco, it was too damp and dreary for her. She'd been very homesick there years earlier when they lived there for a few months, so instead, my parents settled into an apartment in Wellesley, and the Boston area was home for the rest of their lives."

Dominic also returned knowing what his brother was about to do: Joe retired from baseball on December 11, 1951. The Yankees arranged a press conference at their offices at 745 Fifth Avenue attended by a tearful Dan Topping, Casey Stengel, and several team-mates. "I once made a solemn promise to myself that I wouldn't try to hang on once the end was in sight," Joe said. "I've seen too many beat-up players struggle to stay up there, and it was always a sad spectacle." He explained that the injuries in recent years had been too numerous and painful. "And when baseball is no longer fun, it is no longer a game. So I've played my last game of ball."

Somewhat indelicately, Topping told reporters, "I don't know why he had to quit. Sick as he was last season he did better than most of the players hanging around." Obviously, the co-owner still didn't understand—Joe had never seen himself as *just another player*. If he could no longer be the Big Guy, there was no sense playing.

A superstar professional career that had begun with the San Francisco Seals almost 20 years earlier was now over. As the writers asked Stengel how he was going to compensate for the loss in center field, Joe left to begin the rest of his life, which included contracts for TV and radio broadcasting, corporate affiliations, and various prod-uct endorsements.

He ended his career with inarguable Hall of Fame credentials: a .325 batting average, 361 home runs, 1,537 RBI, and the still unsur-passed string of nine world championships in ten appearances. His number 5 was retired immediately by the Yankees, joining the numbers of Gehrig and Ruth, and his home uniform and the glove and bat he used in his last game were sent off to Cooperstown. Joe would remain very much in the spotlight, however, thanks to dating another actress.

TWENTY

Joe's retirement made him the second DiMaggio brother to end his professional baseball career in 1951. For Vince it wasn't voluntary. The phone just wouldn't ring anymore.

That left only Dominic on the stage. He turned 35 in February 1952, and it was clear that his chances of getting back into the World Series were dwindling. The upcoming season looked the least promising since he'd broken in as a rookie in 1940. Bobby Doerr had retired. In January the Marine Corps announced that it was going to recall Ted Williams to active duty, and he could be sent to fight in Korea.

"In my heart I was bitter about it," Ted confided in his autobiography, "but I made up my mind I wasn't going to bellyache. I kept thinking one of those gutless politicians someplace along the line would see that it wasn't right and do something."

Johnny Pesky was still in Boston, but not for long. Starting alongside Dominic would be such untested players as Sammy White at catcher, Dick Gernert at first, Faye Throneberry in right, Jimmy Piersall and Ted Lepcio in the outfield, and Ike Delock in the bullpen. Mel Parnell, Mickey McDermott, and Ellis Kinder remained on the pitching staff, joined by young hurlers and castoffs from other teams.

And there was a new manager. During the off-season, Steve O'Neill was let go, despite a 150-99 total record; he would wind up managing the Philadelphia Phillies in 1952. The Red Sox installed Lou Boudreau. "I'm sorry to see Steve O'Neill go, but we're glad to see Boudreau named the new manager," Dominic told the United Press.

He wouldn't be glad long. Boudreau said he wanted to give the younger players more time, and Dominic was not a young player.

"Boudreau was not eager to have veteran players roughly his own age on the team, especially ones with deeper roots in the organization," wrote David Halberstam in *The Teammates*. "Dominic DiMaggio was immediately suspicious of Boudreau, sensing that he wanted to bring up his own people. He sensed his own time was limited now and warned Pesky to be careful."

Boston got off to a good start with the youngsters playing well, Ted still on the roster (though with an ailing calf), and Dominic leading the charge. They jumped off to a 10-2 record. But the last day of April was Ted's last game. He homered in a 5–3 win over the Tigers at Fenway Park. It was Ted Williams Day in Boston, and before the game the Detroit and Boston players had joined various politicians and club officials on the field to sing "Auld Lang Syne." Ted admitted later he was genuinely touched. He stood at home plate during the song, his right hand on the shoulder of a wheelchair-bound Korean War veteran, his left hand clutching Dominic for support. At least Ted could report for duty in style, as the Red Sox presented him with a new Cadillac as a going-to-war gift.

Remarkably, the Sox were in first place on June 2. The next day, for some veteran punch, they obtained third baseman George Kell from Detroit. But among the players given up was Pesky, leaving Dominic as the only remaining member of the four core West Coast players in the lineup. It was a lonely time. He didn't even have Joe anymore to dine with when the Yankees were in Boston, though they tried for get-togethers when the Red Sox visited New York.

"Dominic was in a tough position, because he had all these new guys around him, and he could easily have ignored us. But he wanted the Red Sox to win, so he was always there with suggestions based on his experience," says Gernert. "Ted was good too, but then he was gone, and that left Dominic as senior member of the team. He had to handle a situation like Piersall coming after him with questions, the guy who wanted center field."

"I talked to him a lot," Piersall says. "Yes, a lot of questions. He never told me to get lost. But one day he did say, 'Don't ask me any more questions, you're already better than I am now.' That shocked me, but also made me realize I belonged in the big leagues."

A 4–3 loss to the White Sox pushed Boston out of first. The club would not return there for the remainder of the season. It became as hard to win games as it was to recognize teammates. During the season the Sox would use 48 players, more than half of them putting on a Boston uniform for the first time. Dominic heated up toward the end of summer, clubbing his last major league grand slam on August 2, but the team wasn't following his lead. They clawed to within three and a half games behind the Yankees and Indians, then went 8-24 the rest of the way. They were no match for the Yankees in the stretch drive. In their worst season since before World War II, the Red Sox finished below .500 at 76-78, an embarrassing 19 games behind the Yankees.

AFTER RETIRING FROM major league baseball, the biggest event in Joe's life was falling in love with Marilyn Monroe—just what he needed, another actress ill-suited for domesticity. That Marilyn was on her way to movie stardom made it even odder that Joe wanted to have anything to do with her. He was greatly relieved to be out of the limelight. He wanted to be respected for being one of the greatest sports stars ever, but he didn't want to bake in the glare of the press and public attention. As Bobby Brown said, "Joe's biggest fear was being asked for an autograph. His second-biggest fear was *not* being asked for an autograph." Dating Marilyn would leave him little of his desperately preserved privacy.

Granted, Joe could not have known how big a star Marilyn would become, or understood at the time how much his being with her contributed to that. They met in March 1952 on a blind date at the Villa Nova restaurant on the Sunset Strip in Los Angeles. He was in the area to play in a charity baseball game involving other retired players and the Philadelphia Athletics. Marilyn arrived two hours late, establishing herself immediately as the only person on the planet who could get away with keeping the Great DiMaggio waiting. As usual, Joe was dressed perfectly and said little during dinner, even when Mickey Rooney left his own table to discuss baseball. The couple dining with them supplied most of the conversation. They dated again a week later, without another couple this time. Even before they sat down at their table, the columnist Sidney Skolsky announced that the two were an item.

Marilyn had had a horrendous childhood in Los Angeles that included foster homes and being a ward of the state—very different from Joe's family-oriented upbringing to the north—and up to that time she had played supporting roles in good films such as *The Asphalt Jungle* and *All About Eve,* along with a bunch of not-so-good films. Not knowing the business or anything about the "buzz" in the gossip columns about her, Joe had no idea that Marilyn would soon take off in such pictures as *Niagara, How to Marry a Millionaire,* and *Gentlemen Prefer Blondes.* Joe was not as careful an examiner of people and situations as his brother Dominic. The best explanation is, he simply fell in love with her.

And there was lust, for both of them. Marilyn told the screenwriter Ben Hecht, who wrote her "autobiography," that she and Joe slept together on their first date, which may have been their *first* first date or that second one when it was just the two of them. Joe had had many willing partners during his career, and he was still a great catch, but he had never met anyone as alluring as Marilyn.

"The gossip press following Joe and Marilyn during the early 1950s quenched a national thirst and kept their names constantly before the public," wrote Roger Kahn in *Joe & Marilyn*. "This generally pleased Marilyn and delighted her bosses at 20th Century-Fox. DiMaggio's comment on the furor sounded like a remark at Toots Shor's bar: 'Never mind the publicity, honey,' he told Marilyn. 'Just get the dough.'"

Joe was making some pretty good dough himself, enough to support a comfortable lifestyle and the ongoing child support payments to Dorothy. He often had to travel to earn his pay. He was in Florida as a special hitting instructor for the Yankees during spring training in 1952, and then he had his broadcasting duties. He told the press that he was "as jittery as a scared hen" when he did his first 15-minute interview program before New York's game on April 11. His guest was Charlie Dressen, manager of the Brooklyn Dodgers, and to help him prepare Casey Stengel presented Joe with a dictionary. He wanted it back eventually, though, because "I haven't finished reading it."

But as often as he could, Joe returned to Marilyn, whether she was in Los Angeles or on location making a movie. She liked and admired the man she called "Slugger," and she told friends that the sex was great. Still, there's no doubt he fell a lot harder for her than she did for him. When she had her appendix out in April, she woke up to find her hospital room filled with flowers. The following month she flew to New York so Joe could introduce her to the gang at Toots Shor's, who had become more of a family to him than his own family was.

A library's worth of books have told the tale of the doomed movie star. All agree that Marilyn was exactly the wrong woman for Joe. In all likelihood, the only advice he sought in the matter was from

Dominic, who didn't try to talk his older brother out of it. During their early courtship, Joe and Marilyn saw Dominic when they were in New York; later, Joe brought her to visit Dominic and Emily in Massachusetts. According to Dick Flavin, a longtime friend of Dominic, "Emily and Dom liked Marilyn Monroe very much. They saw her as a vulnerable woman who was, beneath all the glamour, very sweet. And they marveled that she could keep Joe waiting for hours and he wouldn't say anything. No one else kept Joe waiting for even thirty seconds and got away with it. So it was love for sure.

"There is a wonderful photograph of Joe and Dom just emerging from Locke Ober, one of Boston's great old restaurants. It's a winter night and in the foreground ahead of the brothers, in fur coats, are Emily and Marilyn. I once said to Dom, 'Those were two pretty good-looking girls you had with you.' Dom smiled and said, 'I'll take Emily over Marilyn any day.' Not for a moment did I doubt he meant it."

And so, with Dominic's approval, the courtship continued. He just wanted his brother to be happy, and if this actress was the one, so be it.

Lou Boudreau made it clear that he would continue to give playing time to the younger Red Sox in the 1953 season. Obviously this didn't bode well for Dominic, now 36. Still, he had no idea how difficult things would get. He suffered from an infection in his right eye during the off-season that was bad enough to require a stay in Beth Israel Hospital in Boston, and his vision still wasn't quite right when spring training began. His eye doctor had advised him to delay going to Florida and suiting up, but Dominic believed his job was in jeopardy. How right he was. He struggled through the exhibition season, with Boudreau trying different lineup combinations and using players ten or more years younger.

Ted was flying and fighting in Korea. Given that he was seeing actual combat, some in Boston feared he might never return. On February 19, he had crash-landed his bullet-riddled, flaming F-9

Panther jet and jumped out before it could explode. He would not be back in a Boston uniform until that August, having been in 37 combat missions, half of them with future astronaut John Glenn as a wingman. Billy Goodman and George Kell were still effective players, but Vern Stephens was gone, traded by Joe Cronin to the White Sox. Piersall, who had struggled with well-documented emotional problems in 1952, was back and healthy. And Boston still had Dom, its All-Star center fielder, on the roster.

But not on the field. On opening day, the Boston center fielder was Tom Umphlett. "That really hurt Dominic, not being in the opening day lineup," recalls Gernert. "He kept mostly to himself after that."

According to Lepcio, "Dominic was pissed off and his ego was shattered. Did us young guys feel bad for him? Well, sure, but we also knew that Dominic and the other veteran guys had not won a thing since 1946, and maybe Boudreau was right to give us a try. It wasn't handled in the best way, though."

Dominic continued to ride the bench through April. It was insulting that Boudreau did not even talk to him about the benching—this from a guy Dominic had roomed with the year before. Boudreau told reporters that Dominic "has been retarded by cold weather and heavy fields" and that he couldn't play in night games because of his eye problem or in both games of doubleheaders because of his age.

Dominic wasn't playing at all. He wouldn't complain to the press, though he did go as far as to tell a few Boston reporters, "I retain the right to change my mind, but the way I feel now this is the end of the baseball trail for me."

Being a smart man, Dominic figured out another reason he was being eased out. "In the insecure Boudreau's mind, Dominic was a threat," Flavin states. With Dominic's intelligence, his service as the league's player representative, and the respect he commanded from players, other managers, and the Boston front office, Boudreau knew, Flavin says, that Dominic "was the manager-in-waiting." But

"Dominic didn't want the job," he added. "He wanted to play baseball."

Behind the scenes, Dominic appealed to Tom Yawkey, who said he couldn't overrule his manager. He then asked Joe Cronin to trade him or at least give him his release so he could sign with another team. Cronin refused. Out of options, and not willing to earn his $35,000 salary on the bench, Dominic retired.

"I believe I could have played at least one more year of good baseball," he told the press at Fenway Park before the May 12 Red Sox–White Sox contest, "but under the circumstances I prefer to turn my interests elsewhere rather than be a hanger-on."

"I was sorry to see him go, because he was someone us young guys could go to for advice on hitters, he was generous that way," recalls Ike Delock. "His career was ending, but he wasn't taking it out on anyone. One day he was there, then the next he wasn't, and that was it."

As most writers pointed out at the time—and Dominic would readily admit then and for the rest of his life—he had always played in Joe's shadow. Indeed, that would be the headline of his obituary in the *New York Times*. But it can still be argued that from the time Dominic arrived in the major leagues—that is, after Joe's remarkable 1936–39 seasons—he was the better ballplayer. In the 1940–1942 and 1946–1952 seasons, *no one* in baseball had more hits than Dominic, and that includes Ted Williams, Stan Musial, and Joe DiMaggio. He also scored more runs than any other player with just one exception: Ted. Dominic did not have Joe's power and RBI production, but the simple fact was that Dominic was the best in baseball—or very close to it—at his strengths: getting on base, scoring runs, and almost never costing his team a run in the outfield.

And he knew it. "Dominic is regarded as a nice guy, and he was, but he had a big ego too," says Lepcio, who had a ten-year career in the major leagues and was involved in Red Sox events after he retired. "He gave 100 percent, and he expected his teammates to do the same, just like Joe did in New York. And you couldn't bullshit Dominic about taking a backseat to Joe."

He finished his career with a .298 average, 1,680 hits, 1,046 runs scored, and 618 RBI. Like Ted and other very good players in the 1940s, serving in the military for three years had kept his statistics from being even more impressive—and in Dominic's case, worthy of election to the Hall of Fame. Though he was very much appreciated by the fans in Boston and had the respect of other players—especially the runners he gunned down from center field—Halberstam could write legitimately that Dominic was "probably the most underrated player of his day."

And so, in 1953, for the first time since 1935, there was no DiMaggio playing major league ball.

Dominic was not about to sit around and mourn the end of his career. He had been casting about for business opportunities to pursue at the end of his playing days, wanting to go beyond his investment in DiMaggio's Grotto. The end had come a year or two earlier than expected, that was all. He and two partners formed the American Latex Fiber Corporation. It produced padding for cars, furniture, and other products. Next he bought an automotive supply firm, and the two companies became the Delaware Valley Corporation; eventually he would buy out his partners to become sole owner. He had a growing family. Life was good.

This wasn't much comfort to Dominic's many fans in Boston, especially those who had grown up watching him play. "Dom DiMaggio had been my hero since boyhood, ever since the day I became the only boy in the fourth grade of Merrymount School in Quincy who had to wear glasses," recalls Flavin, who would become the "poet laureate" of the Red Sox. "I was by then already a baseball nut and was fully aware that he was the only position player in the American League who wore glasses. Dom gave hope to me, as he did to countless other four-eyed kids. If he could do it, maybe I could too. . . . My whole life I've believed that Lou Boudreau hurt the Red

Sox more in a Boston uniform than he ever did wearing an Indians uniform."

AT THE BEGINNING of June 1953, Joe and the newly retired Dominic were in San Francisco for another funeral, a totally unexpected one—their brother Mike had died. On May 30, he had fallen off his fishing boat. His body was found in Bodega Bay, between his boat and the dock. Devastated family members believe that even though he was only 44, he'd suffered a heart attack, then gone over the side.

"I was close to my cousin Rosalie, and I felt awful that she had lost her father at such a young age," says Joanne DiMaggio Webber. "My Aunt May, Mike's wife, was still so young herself and now had three children to raise and support alone. But she did a fantastic job, and Mike's brothers and sisters did what they could."

Ironically, Joe had been on a boat off the coast of Mexico fishing when Mike died. When Dominic learned of the tragedy, he made calls and sent telegrams trying to locate Joe. "That was a terrible experience for Dom," Emily recalls, "adding to what was a tough year. Mike was the first sibling to die. No way to prepare for that."

George Solotaire, a member of the Toots Shor crowd, was able to track Joe down and deliver the awful news. Tom, Vince, Joe, and Dominic were among the pallbearers. The funeral was in the familiar confines of the Saints Peter and Paul Church. Mike was buried in the DiMaggio plot next to his parents.

Marilyn was at the funeral too, though under the circumstances the press was more respectful than usual. She was surrounded by Sicilians as friends, in-laws, and cousins showed up with food and wine.

"It was different after my grandmother Rosalie died, because there weren't really family get-togethers after that," Joanne says. "Mike's death began the exceptions—the remaining DiMaggios gathered for funerals each time one of them died. It was the toughest on Uncle Dominic. He was my favorite uncle, he took care of everybody, and I know it hurt him a lot to watch them go one by one."

Vince was not having an easy time of it being away from baseball. It wasn't like he'd fallen from a great height. No club would be retiring his number. But Vince had played hard, done the best he could, and had done well by his family. Now he found he didn't have much going for him outside of baseball. Joe would always be able to make good money just being Joe DiMaggio. Dominic had a head for business and immediately took to it. Smart guy like that, he would never have a problem making a living.

But Vince was neither a superstar like Joe nor as smart as his youngest brother. He just knew how to apply himself. The problem was, to what? He moved from job to job. He spent six months as a bartender in Pittsburg. The owner was a friend who taught Vince how to make ten basic drinks. After that, he went to work for another friend who owned a dairy business. Starting the day at 4:00 A.M., he drove his route delivering milk, eggs, and butter. By noon he was done and dropping his hook into the Sacramento River—making a living would not interfere with fishing.

Then it was back to liquor, this time as a salesman peddling cases and bottles to stores and bars. This he liked because he could sample some of his wares and make his own hours. Still, it was reported that "Vince has had to scramble to survive."

Vicki was still very young, but Joanne was in high school and displaying real talent on the ball field. "I was a very good softball player," she says. "I began to think about playing semipro ball. And of course, no one was more encouraging than my father."

Vince saw little of his brothers other than Tom. Growing a business, Dominic had little time for West Coast trips, especially after his daughter Emily was born in September. And Joe, well, he had his hands full.

As 1953 progressed, Joe became more involved in Marilyn's career. He thought he knew what was best for her. And being something like business partners allowed them more time to be together. When she was filming *River of No Return* with Robert Mitchum in Canada, Joe was there. When she got the script for a sure stinker of a movie titled *The Girl in the Pink Tights,* Joe told her she didn't have to make crap like that anymore.

"The title made me nervous," Marilyn "wrote" in *My Story,* her autobiography actually written by Hecht. "I was working with all my might trying to become an actress. I felt that the studio might cash in on exhibiting me in pink tights in a crude movie, but that I wouldn't."

When the studio suspended her for rejecting the picture, Joe's solution was for the two of them to get married in Reno and the hell with the motion picture business. She wasn't keen on that. They argued, and Joe left for New York. He didn't stay long.

"After much talk, Joe and I decided that since we couldn't give each other up, marriage was the only solution to our problem," Marilyn/Hecht wrote.

Joe was delighted. He told Dominic, then took Marilyn to San Francisco to visit his sisters, who had gathered for Tom's birthday party. His hometown was Joe's favorite place to bring Marilyn. He shared fond family memories with her, they went fishing on his boat, the *Yankee Clipper,* and the attention they received was much more manageable than in New York and Los Angeles. Marie, who was divorced, lived in the Beach Street house; when Joe and Marilyn stayed there, she gave the actress cooking lessons. They were there that January 1954 when Joe wondered, why wait?

When Joe, 39, and Marilyn, 27 and a true movie star by then, married on the 14th at San Francisco City Hall, it was a fairy-tale event for the gossip-lovers in America. No one from Hollywood attended, and even more curiously, it was not the typical DiMaggio family affair either. Joe's best man was Reno Barsochinni, the manager of DiMaggio's Grotto, and the witnesses were Lefty O'Doul, Lefty's wife, brother Tom, and his wife. No Vince or sisters, no Dominic and

Emily. Joe wore a blue suit and the blue polka-dot tie he had worn on their first date. Marilyn wore a brown suit with a white Peter Pan collar. Municipal court judge Charles Peery married them in a simple ceremony in his chambers. No church wedding for Joe this time, as he was a divorced man. He and Marilyn even passed up on a wedding reception to escape the aggressive reporters and photographers. They drove south until eight o'clock, when they checked into a motel in Paso Robles. The next day they drove on to a mountain cabin in Idyllwild, 50 miles from Palm Springs.

After the fairy-tale wedding, grim reality set in. "What went wrong so quickly?" Kahn mused. "He was neat. She was sloppy. He was repressed. She was hyperactive. Each was willful. Each had a temper. Each was a star. Stars in collision. Marilyn liked older men, *successful* older men, DiMaggio liked younger women, *blonde* younger women. But when it came time to play house, reality came crashing all about them, shattering dreams into so much shrapnel."

Things started out well enough. With Marilyn still suspended by her studio, she could accompany Joe on the next exhibition tour of Japan organized by O'Doul. She was, of course, a sensation in Japan. Joe was still popular there too, but he was no longer an active player. She was the blonde bombshell from Hollywood. An oft-repeated story is that after a side trip with Jean O'Doul to visit troops in South Korea, Marilyn returned to Japan and commented to Joe, "You never heard such cheering." His rueful response was "Yes, I have."

Bobby Brown, who by then had a medical degree, had served for a year with the Army in Korea and was still there when the DiMaggios arrived. He got permission to accompany them on the tour. "To me, he was Joe, and Marilyn was a real nice gal," Brown said. "We had a great time together. We would give clinics, and the Japanese would entertain us at night. The Japanese just went wild. At that time, the two biggest things in their lives were baseball players and movie stars, and you had the two biggest right there."

In the months ahead, Marilyn had to spend most of her time in

Los Angeles resolving her problems with 20th Century-Fox and its head man, Darryl Zanuck. Joe was traveling a lot, pitching products and fulfilling his broadcasting contract with the Yankees. After the suspension was lifted on April 13, it was back to work for Marilyn. Next on the docket was another musical, *There's No Business Like Show Business*, which would be followed by a Billy Wilder comedy, *The Seven-Year Itch*.

Joe was set in his ways. He liked to watch television and have dinner in front of it. He didn't like to be out in public or go to Hollywood parties, especially accompanied by one of the hottest actresses in the world. He was unhappy with the salacious attention his wife received from men. Joe wanted to live in San Francisco. His idea of fun was golf, cards, and playing the horses with a few fellows.

There were more and more arguments and fewer sightings of Joe and Marilyn together in public. One of the most iconic of Hollywood photographs caused a huge rift. In the fall of 1954, Marilyn was in New York shooting scenes for *The Seven-Year Itch*. One would involve her cooling off in the breeze blowing up through a subway grating. Joe was at Toots Shor's that night. Walter Winchell insisted that Joe go with him to watch Billy Wilder direct the scene. When the breeze gusted and her dress lifted up to her shoulders, Marilyn seemed to be undressing in front of the 1,500 spectators who had surrounded the set on Lexington Avenue. With each take, Joe became more furious. Finally, he stalked off the set.

The night went downhill from there. Joe returned to Shor's, and Shor tried to sympathize: "Joe, what can you expect when you marry a whore?" Joe left. He and Shor would never be close friends again. Joe and Marilyn's battle in the St. Regis suite later, during which Joe struck her, convinced them both that their marriage was badly broken.

Where were the other DiMaggios? Of the sisters, Marie was the most concerned. The other sisters had their own families to look after. Marie and the much younger Marilyn had formed a sincere friendship.

Tom had the family business to run. Vince had little to contribute—what Joe was going through was alien to him, and he had his own struggles just making ends meet, something Joe could do easily.

The one who understood Joe best was his younger brother. Dominic had been lucky in love. He knew how stubborn Joe could be and the temper he had. He genuinely wanted his brother to be happy with Marilyn. But was there anything he could do?

"Joe did come to Dad seeking advice on Marilyn," states Paul DiMaggio. "First of all, Dad was the kind of person who gave counsel to a lot of people because he was sympathetic and smart and direct. With Joe, we have at least one letter in a safe-deposit box that Dad wrote to Joe with advice. He hoped for the best, but things didn't go well."

In an interview, Dominic said he realized that "her career was first. Joe could not condone the things that Marilyn had to do. Joe wanted a wife he could raise children with. She could not do that."

In October, Joe was back in New York to cover the World Series. (For the first time in six seasons, the Yankees weren't in it. The New York Giants and Cleveland Indians were.) Joe went to Marilyn, apologized for his behavior, and asked her to reconcile. She asked for a divorce. A few days later, humiliated in front of the press, Joe moved out of their Los Angeles home. "I'm going to San Francisco," he told them. "San Francisco's my home. It's always been my home."

With incredible speed, Marilyn was granted a preliminary divorce on October 27, 1954. The public explanation was "conflicting career demands." The fairy-tale marriage hadn't lasted a year. Less than a month later, a "pale and drawn" Joe was hospitalized in New York with a bleeding ulcer.

He had loved her deeply. He always would. Joe would live for 45 more years and never remarry. He could not feel that way about any other woman—or about anyone, for that matter. According to Dominic, "Joe had wanted that relationship to work. He held on to it for the rest of his life."

TWENTY-ONE

THE THREE DIMAGGIO brothers, together again on a ball field. This had always been a rare sighting, but with Vince, Joe, and Dominic out of professional ball for years now, it was a sight many fans thought they would never see again. But there they were, in Wrigley Field in Los Angeles. On a sun-dappled day in August 1956, they wore San Francisco Seals uniforms. All three had been Seals, though not at the same time.

The reunion had taken some doing. Ordinarily the brothers' paths rarely crossed. Without Marilyn, Joe had few reasons to be in Los Angeles. Most of his time was spent in New York and San Francisco and traveling for paid special appearances. Dominic was the hands-on owner of a thriving business back in the Boston area, and Emily was expecting their third child. (Peter DiMaggio would be born later in the month.) When Dominic traveled to the West Coast, he went to San Francisco—to check on the restaurant, look after new commercial real estate investments, and say hello to his sisters, Tom, and Joe if he was in town. But he and Joe had made this trip to L.A. for Vince and Lefty O'Doul, who really wanted a Seals alumni gathering.

Even though he was soon to turn 44, there were times when Vince felt he could run out to center field and play ball again. He was fit and trim, still at his playing weight, his hair still dark (unlike Joe's, which was showing streaks of white). With their Pacific Coast League memories intact, the DiMaggio brothers wanted to watch the Seals-Angels game that would follow the three-inning exhibition featuring the alumni. The Angels were having a sensational year. Led by Steve Bilko, who would win his second of three consecutive MVP Awards, the Angels would finish the season at 107-61, 16 games ahead in first for the PCL championship. (Governor's Cup playoffs had ended two years earlier.) It was their last moment of glory: the following year Phil Wrigley sold the team and the ballpark to Walter O'Malley. By 1958 the entire PCL would be extinct and the Brooklyn Dodgers would have moved west to debut in Los Angeles.

Since a 1956 Old-Timers' Day was scheduled for August 4 at Wrigley Field, and the San Francisco team was to be the opponent in the regular game, someone had the bright idea of having a squad of former Seals play former Angels. Vince was all for it. He reached out to Joe and Dominic. They realized that this would mean a lot to Vince, who had ongoing problems adapting to life after baseball, so they agreed to show up. When the Seals old-timers took the field, Vince trotted out to left, Joe headed to right, and Dominic was the center fielder.

It was a wonderful day for Vince. Before and after the game, Joe, the tallest and broadest of the three, posed for one photo after another, his left arm across Dominic's shoulders and his right draped around Vince's. The brothers were entering middle age, but in the three-inning game they played like youngsters on the sandlots again. Dominic patrolled center field seemingly as fast as ever. Joe singled twice in two plate appearances. And with a man on, Vince reminded fans of his power by launching one into the stands. The Seals alumni won, 3–2, thanks to that two-run homer.

The fans at Wrigley Field loved it. Vince had a great time being with his brothers. It would be six years before they got together on a ball field again, and Joe would regret it.

As their playing days receded into the past, Vince, Joe, and Dominic grew increasingly distant from one another. We might compare them to their fictional second-generation Sicilian-American counterparts, the Corleones—with bats, baseballs, and gloves their weapons instead of guns and bullets. Vince was like Fredo, the well-meaning, endearing brother who lost his way and needed some looking after because he was too vulnerable to other influences. Joe was Sonny, the stud middle brother. He lived an increasingly reclusive life, looking out for himself and no one else (including his own son). Dominic was like Michael, the youngest Corleone son, the smart and decisive businessman who became the caretaker of the DiMaggios, his sense of old-world obligation matched by the compassion of a man with a big heart in a comparatively small body.

Vince and Madeline continued to live in Pittsburg, which, fittingly, became the sister city of Isola delle Femmine, with a replica in its downtown area of the fisherman's statue in the Isola town square. Joanne got married and had children. Vince held on to the liquor sales job for 15 years. Through the 1950s and 1960s, he drank and smoked too much and was angry a lot. He never got ahead with money. It didn't help that he gambled away too much of what he did earn. He was frustrated that he hadn't become a professional singer, that he hadn't been a better baseball player, that Joe didn't bother with him anymore even when he was in San Francisco. If it hadn't been for Vince, there wouldn't have been a Great DiMaggio, yet he was the DiMaggio no one knew, and that was never going to change.

What little contact he had with Joe was in its way humiliating.

"When Joe got tired of his clothes, he'd send them to my dad," recalls Joanne. "My dad would send them to a tailor and get them fitted. Dominic, the same thing. Times when my father had to get dressed up, he could look pretty sharp."

Vince even had a bone to pick with Dominic. As the American League player representative, Dominic had helped persuade the baseball owners to create a pension plan. It took a lot of pushing and pulling, but it happened. However, the owners wouldn't make it retroactive, because suddenly giving pensions to all the players since at least 1900 would have cost many millions. The compromise agreed to was every player on a major league roster from the 1947 season on was entitled to a pension. That was the year after Vince last played in the majors. Vince, the one brother of the three who could have really used the pension, couldn't have one. He felt his little brother had not looked out for him, and it rankled.

By 1970, both Joanne and Vicki were married, and Vince and Madeline had four grandchildren. They lived in Daly City, having moved from Pittsburg so Vince, soon to turn 58, could be closer to DiMaggio's Grotto, where he now worked mostly in the basement, handling the buying and receiving for Tom. Reporter Dennis Lustig found him there that July. Vince claimed that he was 42 and that "I sing three times a week and I plan to sing for money and soon." Lustig told readers that Vince went upstairs to sing at the restaurant every morning at eleven, and "Joe D. probably will be there too." Sometimes it was even true.

The following year Vince's life changed dramatically. In May he was at home listening to a speech by the evangelist Billy Graham. "I got up from my chair—I don't think I did it on my own—and got on my knees immediately and accepted the Lord and prayed the sinner's prayer. And I shed tears—oh, man—without any problem. Ever since then—why, I'm with the Lord."

For the rest of his life, Vince would tell or write anyone who would listen about becoming a born-again Christian, contending that his wife had undergone a similar conversion six months before he did.

He gave up drinking, smoking, and gambling and claimed his marriage was stronger than ever. In an article in 1977, Vince reported that his daily routine was to watch Christian-based television shows until 10:00 A.M., then go to church for two hours, then return home to watch more religious programs. By then, Vince and Madeline were back in Southern California. The job at the Fisherman's Wharf restaurant had ended, and Vince had wanted a fresh start away from San Francisco. They found a small house in North Hollywood. He sold cleaning products door to door for Fuller Brush as he waited for Social Security to kick in.

For a time, he was a burlesque star—but this was news to Vince. In a bizarre twist, an edition of the *Cleveland Plain Dealer* in 1976 had captioned a photo, "Vince DiMaggio, one of the members of baseball's most famous families, with his wife and co-burlesque star Ezrulle Sabie, now at the New Era Theater." Ezrulle, it was reported, was really Joyce Caldwell from Alabama, specializing in onstage antics with snakes, and had been Vince's wife of six years.

They were, of course, phonies. The man impersonating Vince had first surfaced in Dallas a few years earlier as a partner in a restaurant. When the DiMaggio con was discovered there, he disappeared. He began to show up at burlesque theaters around the country, with Caldwell in tow. Their booking agent, Jerry Murphy of Baltimore, never suspected that he wasn't Vince DiMaggio. He had even advanced money to "Vince," to be paid back after the gig at the New Era, a striptease joint. A follow-up article in the *Plain Dealer* included a quote from the real Vince: "I don't know what law he's breaking, but I wish he'd stop. I found out he was doing dirty shows. That's an abomination to our Lord Jesus. It's 100% antagonistic to my nature."

No one pretended to be Dominic. He did a fine job, better than Vince or Joe, of just being himself. He worked hard at the manufacturing business in Lawrence, and it began to be successful. He watched Red Sox games because he believed they would always be his team, especially with Ted and a couple of his other friends still playing. He accepted invitations to franchise special events. He especially enjoyed being a father to his three children, though his patience could be tested.

"As children, we always had lots of baseballs and bats around the house, so the DiMaggios' place was the go-to yard for an afternoon pickup game," reports his daughter Emily. "In fact, the shape of the front yard was reminiscent of a baseball field, so it was easy to lay out the bases.

"One day, there were no balls in the bin, so we went into the den and grabbed a ball off the bookshelf. It was Dad's 1946 pennant reunion ball with the autographs of his teammates. At the end of the game, we returned it to its proper place on the shelf. When Dad came home, he went into the den. He picked up his prized possession, turning it over and looking at the grass stains and bleeding signatures. We held our breath. He looked over his glasses and asked, 'So, did you win?'"

"He was an old-fashioned father, I guess, but to me he was just Dad and this must be how all dads are," Paul DiMaggio remembers. "I spent almost every night with him watching TV, we were big on that. Red Sox games, of course, but other programs. He was not a modern father necessarily, but I remember one time when I was 18 and I took him on a long car ride because he challenged me on something and I wanted to explain the facts of life as I saw them. He was cool with that. I knew it was not something that would've happened between him and his father."

Emily Sr. became a relentless fund-raiser for charities, and she was especially devoted to the Dana Farber Cancer Institute in Boston. Dominic helped when he could, and Ted couldn't resist pitching in when Emily asked him. Ted retired after the 1960 season—slugging that thrilling homer in his last at-bat at Fenway Park—and after a stint as manager of the Washington Senators in the late '60s, he spent much of his time fishing in Florida. When Emily called, Ted came running. He thought the world of her and referred to Emily affectionately as "the Queen."

"I don't really know why he called me that," she says. "But he was always ready to help in any way he could when I asked him. Mostly, I remember Dom and me being with Ted and his wife and laughing and having many happy times together."

By the end of the 1950s, Dominic's company was doing so well that he could branch out into other interests. One was football. In 1960 he was part of a group of local businessmen who founded the Boston Patriots in the new American Football League, which would evolve over time into the New England Patriots.

In 1962 Dominic was diagnosed with Paget's disease, which causes enlarged bones. Sometimes, to tolerate the intense pain, Dominic had to bend over, even at work and in public. Ted, still a strong and powerful man in his forties who would become even closer to Dominic as they aged and the Paget's persisted, told David Halberstam, "It's a real mean son of a bitch of a disease, but he's the proudest human being you ever met. Anyone else with a goddamn disease like that loses dignity. Not Dommie. Dommie doesn't lose his dignity."

It didn't slow him down either. In 1966, at the invitation of Red Sox officials, Dominic was a spring training special assistant. The following year, after consulting with Cleveland general manager Gabe Paul (who once wrote a glowing report on Vince with the Reds) and the former Indians star Al Rosen about the success of their Wahoo Club, Dominic and 49 other businessmen founded a similar booster group, the Bosox Club.

Now if only the Red Sox themselves could field a winning team. The 1965 edition had been the first team since 1932 to lose 100 games. The next year was only a bit better, with Boston at 72-90 and finishing in ninth place, 26 games behind the Baltimore Orioles. The club hired Dick Williams to be their manager, and his 1967 opening day lineup included good young players like George Scott,

Mike Andrews, Rico Petrocelli, Reggie Smith, Tony Conigliaro, and their lone star, Carl Yastrzemski.

An even bolder step, Dominic thought, would be new ownership, and he knew just the man for the job—himself. He put together a syndicate with the goal of raising $8 million to buy the Red Sox from Tom Yawkey. To this day it is rare that a former player owns a club; the exceptions are Michael Jordan, who owns the Charlotte Bobcats in the NBA, and Magic Johnson and his group, who purchased the Los Angeles Dodgers in 2012.

The news that Dominic might own the Red Sox caused a lot of excitement among fans and the press, who were desperate for the team to return to its winning ways of the 1940s. Things looked good. As one newspaper reported, "Owner Tom Yawkey has indicated he would consider selling the team if he gets the right offer from the right group." Dominic had proved he could make and raise money, and who better than the Little Professor to create a contending club?

Imagine returning to the old neighborhood not just as a player, as he'd already done, but as an owner of a major league club, one with a long legacy. "My father would have liked that, to show what he'd achieved through hard work, realizing the American Dream," says Paul DiMaggio. "I enjoyed going with him to San Francisco. My dad and Tom went over business matters. Dad was phenomenal with figures and finances. Tom was a great guy, I really liked him, but Dad was the brains of the DiMaggio business interests."

Dominic sold his 10 percent share of the Boston Patriots, which he had purchased for $25,000, for $300,000. He was also exploring building a greyhound racing track outside Boston. He and Emily had bought a home in Florida for getaways on winter weekends. A *Sporting News* profile in 1967 concluded: "Husband, father of three, businessman, former exec of the Patriots, prospective owner of the team—Dom is all of these things. He also is the proud bearer of one of the greatest names in baseball history."

Then things fell apart. Yawkey resisted selling, especially after the "Impossible Dream" season the Red Sox had in 1967, when they captured the American League pennant and lost to the St. Louis Cardinals in seven games in the World Series. Dominic was disappointed, but happy his team was winning again. He would just have to be patient.

TWO PIVOTAL EVENTS in 1955 directed the course of the rest of Joe's life. One was the divorce from Marilyn becoming final. It did not close his heart to her, but it did close his heart to any other woman and just about every other person. The second was the crowning achievement of his baseball career: induction into the Baseball Hall of Fame. For the rest of his life, he would be an American sports immortal.

Oddly, when Joe's name first appeared on the ballot, in 1953, he received only 44 percent of the 75 percent necessary. Apparently a majority of the Baseball Writers Association of America members felt it was too soon to enshrine him. Joe still didn't make it in 1954. Finally, in 1955, 89 percent of the writers felt he had waited long enough.

The induction ceremony was on July 25. Also being inducted that day were Gabby Hartnett, Ted Lyons, Dazzy Vance, Frank "Home Run" Baker, and Ray Schalk, the latter two voted in by the Veterans Committee. On hand to welcome the new Hall of Fame members were 87-year-old Cy Young, Bill Terry, Mel Ott, Frankie Frisch, and Joe's onetime contract negotiator, Ty Cobb.

But Joe didn't hang around Cooperstown to celebrate with his peers. He drove back to New York to have dinner at Toots Shor's. When he finished, he left, by himself. Watching him go, Toots said to a sportswriter at the bar, "There goes one of the loneliest men in the world."

As he had done with Dorothy, Joe continued to court Marilyn, hoping she would come back to him. "Joe was very distressed, and he and Dom talked a lot about Marilyn," remembers Emily Sr. "When Joe was down, he reached out to Dominic."

When Joe and Marilyn did get together, they tried to stay out of public view. This was hard to do, even at Dominic and Emily's house in Wellesley in the middle of winter. When Joe and Marilyn were there in January 1955, the press was tipped off and a crowd of reporters and photographers were waiting outside. When the couple emerged, they climbed into Joe's Cadillac and set off back to New York. To elude the press vehicles following him, Joe floored it, passing through some towns at close to 100 miles per hour with a parade of speeders behind him. Finally, the Caddy simply outdistanced its pursuers.

For more than seven years, Joe waited for Marilyn to come back to him. During that time, she had numerous romances, and a marriage to the playwright Arthur Miller, and the films *The Seven-Year Itch* and *Bus Stop,* and a brilliant performance in *Some Like It Hot* had made her a household name. But as has been well documented, the increasingly intense battles with depression and drugs took their toll. She managed another remarkable performance in *The Misfits,* but was unable to complete the film *Something's Got to Give.* Her marriage to Miller was over. She was in a bad way and needed a lot of help.

Joe came to the rescue. He wanted to get her away from Frank Sinatra, John and Bobby Kennedy, and all the other men he considered creeps and bloodsuckers who just wanted to use Marilyn.

"He wanted her to feel safe with him—and that meant showing her he'd changed," Richard Ben Cramer analyzed. "He could take care of her without taking over. He didn't remonstrate about her habits, her friends—never said a bad thing about her work. Anyway, she didn't have any work. She didn't seem to have enough energy to get work, or even to want it. The years since their marriage had changed Marilyn too."

In July 1962, Joe asked Marilyn to marry him again. She saw that he hadn't changed completely—but he'd changed some. Thinking maybe he really could save her, she said yes. The wedding was scheduled for August 8. Joe was ecstatic to be getting a second at-bat with the woman he couldn't help but love deeply. He had to fly to New York on business, where he found it hard not to tell his pals the great news—this was to be a quiet affair, with just a few friends in the backyard of Marilyn's L.A. home. When he returned to the West Coast, he had to detour to San Francisco that Saturday, August 4, to reunite with his brothers for another Seals old-timers' game. The plan was that he'd fly to L.A. the next day, get together with Marilyn on Monday, and they would be married two days later.

Joe didn't even tell Vince and Dominic, or Tom, who was also at the game. The crowd loved seeing the brothers together in Seals uniforms, and the Hall of Famer was more outgoing than usual. That night Joe went out on the town with Lefty O'Doul and several others. Finally, everything was going to be right with Marilyn again.

The phone woke him at the Beach Street house early the next morning. Marilyn had been found dead in her bed.

Joe flew to L.A. immediately. At the morgue, he identified the body. He realized that if he hadn't been talked into attending that reunion in San Francisco, he would have been with her. He sent a telegram to Marilyn's sister asking permission to handle the funeral. He would take care of his wife one last time.

The funeral was held at Westwood Memorial Park. On the afternoon of August 8, accompanied by Joe Jr., who was now 20, Joe buried Marilyn instead of marrying her. He had arranged it so that none of her Hollywood crowd or members of the Kennedy family were allowed to participate. When their complaints were relayed to him, Joe rasped, "Tell them if it wasn't for them, she'd still be here." Later, Joe instructed that fresh flowers be placed on Marilyn's grave "forever."

"Dom was always ready to comfort and support Joe, but right after Marilyn's death, Joe wanted to be left alone," Emily Sr. says. "He wanted the funeral to be very private, so even family on the West Coast did not attend, respecting his wishes."

For the rest of his life, Joe would never talk about Marilyn or allow her name to be mentioned in his presence. Dick Flavin recalls being the emcee at a fund-raising event organized by Emily that Joe attended. When Flavin said he had a story to tell the audience about Joe, a member called out, "Is it about Marilyn?" Flavin recalls, "Joe just stared down into his plate the rest of the night. It was like the air got sucked out of him."

While Joe was more private than ever as he carried the pain of Marilyn's death, he was not a recluse. He continued to play golf through the 1950s and '60s, before age and the aches of old injuries interfered with that pastime. The Presidio in San Francisco was a favorite course, and one of his regular partners was Louis Almada, who had played in the Pacific Coast League in the 1950s. "I could outdrive him a hundred yards," Almada told David Cataneo for *I Remember Joe DiMaggio*. "Joe just wanted to hit it straight, so he hit the ball easy. He just wasn't a natural golfer the way he was a natural, great ballplayer." Even when Joe asked for advice about a putt, "I wouldn't ever tell him how to play it. Because if it went wrong, he wouldn't talk to you for the rest of the game." After the round, Almada and any other playing partners "would sit down to have a bite or have a beer. Joe would just come in and not even say, 'See you fellas later. Good-bye.' He'd just come in and look at everybody there and just walk away."

When Joe turned 50 in November 1964, over 1,100 people packed into the Sheraton Palace Hotel in San Francisco to celebrate the milestone. Yankees broadcaster Mel Allen was the toastmaster, and among the salutes he read was a telegram from President Lyndon Johnson. People would have crowded the speakers' table anyway with Joe sitting at it, but what made this night special was that he was flanked by Tom, Vince, and Dominic, as well as Willie Mays, Mickey Mantle, Lefty Gomez, and Lefty O'Doul, who received a huge ovation when he was introduced. Hands tired quickly with all the autograph requests.

When it was his turn to speak, Joe stood and offered what for him was a Shakespearean soliloquy: "This night I shall always remember. I feel humble at the sight of this tremendous turnout and am also deeply grateful to those who traveled great distances to share this night with me. It's wonderful. It's heartwarming. How can I ever thank you? I'm proud to have been a Yankee, but I have found more happiness and contentment since I came back home to San Francisco than any man has a right to deserve. This is the friendliest city in the world."

Even there, though, it could be difficult to guard his privacy. A brilliant profile written by Gay Talese and published in the July 1966 issue of *Esquire*, titled "The Silent Season of a Hero," opened with Joe observing a young blond woman from the second-floor window of DiMaggio's Grotto. "He watched until she left, lost in the crowd of newly arrived tourists that had just come down the hill by cable car. Then he sat down again at the table in the restaurant, finishing his tea and lighting another cigarette, his fifth in the last half hour." Joe was nervous because "in the crowd was a man he did not wish to see," a man he suspected was a reporter or a memorabilia collector seeking an autograph.

"Sometimes tourists will walk into the restaurant and have lunch and see him sitting calmly in a corner signing autographs and being extremely gracious with everyone. At other times, as on this particular morning when the man from New York chose to visit, DiMaggio was tense and suspicious." When the man arrived, a nephew tried unsuccessfully to shoo him away. Finally, Joe confronted him. The man said he didn't want to cause trouble and he thought that Joe was a great man. "I'm not great," Joe replied softly. "I'm just a man trying to get along."

Joe was most comfortable at home on Beach Street, with his ever-doting sister Marie; in Massachusetts (and later Florida too) with Dominic and Emily; and at the restaurant at Fisherman's Wharf, with longtime male acquaintances. "They may wait for hours some-times," Talese wrote, " . . . know[ing] that when he arrives he may wish to be alone; but it does not seem to matter, they are endlessly awed by him, moved by the mystique, he is a kind of male Garbo."

Although he was never comfortable in public and was usually cold when approached by strangers, it was only in his last decade that Joe became completely intolerant of others. Until then, into the mid-1980s, Joe stayed in the news through special events, pitching products, and, still, baseball. In 1968 Paul Simon composed the song "Mrs. Robinson," which contained the enduring lyric, "Where have you gone, Joe DiMaggio? A nation turns its lonely eyes to you."

When he was 53, he agreed to become a vice president and coach with the Oakland Athletics, his first regular-season on-field baseball job since retiring from the Yankees in 1951. He traveled with the club when it suited him, went to spring trainings, and was a hit-ting consultant. When that job ended, he was welcomed back at the Yankees camp every spring, and he was the most popular attraction at the Old Timers' Days at Yankee Stadium. He insisted on being the last of the retired Yankees to be introduced—though in the 1970s and into the '80s Mantle was the more popular Yankee among a younger fan base—and on being described as the "greatest living player." Baseball writers had voted to give him that designation in 1969, and he wore it as a badge of honor. Not Mantle, not Mays, not Musial, and not Williams—the Big Guy would be the greatest as long as he breathed.

It helped him maintain his distance from others. "Joe was so aloof, you couldn't really get to him," says fellow Hall of Famer and Mets broadcaster Ralph Kiner. "He always had a gofer with him, some guy on hand to send on errands and look out for him. Joe always sat alone. We'd play in golf tournaments together, and he liked me for some reason, so that was nice. At any event, though, he always had to be the man. He had to be the last guy announced, even at Shea Stadium. Not sure if this makes sense, but Joe did not want the glare, but he did want the glory."

Joe had lucrative contracts with Bowery Savings Bank in New York and for national promotion of Mr. Coffee machines, and both enjoyed very successful campaigns with him as pitchman. When articles appeared about him, he was always described as distinguished, perfectly dressed, tan, fit, and trim. Pat Harmon, covering a charity golf tournament in Florida, wrote, "Joe is handsome, quiet, and modest. He is everything a hero should be." When Joe retreated from the public eye, he went home to San Francisco and took a spin on the 36-foot *Yankee Clipper*.

"DiMaggio had the good fortune to age well," writes Lawrence Baldassaro. "A full head of silver hair atop his still trim physique made him look distinguished rather than elderly. His good looks and his baseball fame opened the door to a lucrative second career as a television spokesman. He became a television celebrity to an entire generation that had never seen him play baseball."

Over the years, there was less time for Vince, who seemed to have gone off in a different direction. Joe's most enduring family relationships were with Marie and Dominic, on either coast. Whenever he was in San Francisco, he shared the house on Beach Street with his sister. On the East Coast, he saw his younger brother in New York or quietly visited him and Emily in Marion, across Buzzard's Bay from Cape Cod, where they had moved from Wellesley.

"One time I stayed overnight there, and there was another house guest," remembers Flavin. "Joe had come to play in the annual charity golf tournament that Dom and Emily organized." Flavin was master of ceremonies for the tournament. "I had a 'pinch me am I really here' feeling as I spent a good part of the morning in the kitchen with the two of them as they drank coffee and talked baseball. Joe was always open and friendly with me because I was Dom's friend, and he knew I was not a threat to use him or try to get close to him. If Dom said you were okay, you were okay with Joe."

* * *

In 1969 Dominic, Vince, and Joe had to say good-bye to an old friend. On December 7, the anniversary of the Japanese attack on Pearl Harbor, Lefty O'Doul, the man who almost single-handedly popularized baseball in Japan, died from a stroke, at 72. He had last managed the Seattle Rainiers in the Pacific Coast League, and by the time he retired to concentrate on golf (often with Joe), he had compiled a 2,094-1,970 record. Few men had been more popular in San Francisco. His restaurant on Geary Street (where Lefty's original Bloody Mary recipe is still served) was a favorite hangout for athletes and fans. Dominic lost a paternal figure who had saved his career. Twelve years after his death, when O'Doul was inducted into the San Francisco Bay Area Sports Hall of Fame, Dominic was the DiMaggio brother selected to present the award to O'Doul's family.

With business going strong—his company was grossing in the millions—Dominic could continue to be involved in the Red Sox. He still headed the Bosox Club, which was the most successful in the major leagues; the way it boosted attendance and fan participation was now being imitated by other teams. In 1970 Dominic proposed that there be interleague play to further spur interest in baseball, an idea that club owners thought was daft. Dabbling in politics, in 1976 he was named co-chair of Citizens for Ford, a group of Republicans and Democrats who supported the election of President Gerald Ford.

In July 1970, Tom Yawkey died, and his wife, Jean, became president of the trust that operated the Bosox franchise, which was put up for sale. Dominic made an offer. Jean Yawkey asked for time, and out of respect for her loss, he waited. Next thing he knew, a new ownership group, headed by the widow, was being introduced. It was also reported that when Jean Yawkey was asked about selling the team to Dominic, she replied, "Over my dead body."

"Dom was livid," says Flavin. "The statement that the team had been for sale was a sham. He not only had been used, he had spent considerable money putting together his team and the financing only to discover the Red Sox were not really for sale after all. He and Mrs. Yawkey stopped speaking, and he also stopped going to games or to spring training, where he had been an unpaid adviser to the players."

"He went into a shell after that," says Ted Lepcio, one of several Red Sox players who remained friends with Dominic. "He said literally, screw you guys, and you didn't hear from him for a long time. He divorced himself from the whole organization."

Dominic returned to family, philanthropy with Emily, and his business as top priorities. In family matters, he cast a wider net, becoming the liaison for the expanding clan. Elaine Brooks had married Donald DiMaggio, a second cousin to the DiMaggio brothers. When she was pregnant with her first child, she met Dominic at the funeral of a relative of her husband's; he was the only one of the four brothers to attend. "We had a lovely time talking, and I was very impressed with him," recalls Brooks, now remarried and living in Arkansas. "He had a 'head of the family' air about him. As we're all leaving he said, 'If you have a boy, will you name him after me?' I told him I sure would." A month later, Brooks learned she was to have twins. "As long as one was a boy, Dominic was the name. After my son was born, I called to tell him about the new Dominic DiMaggio. He was thrilled. We received cards from him and Emily for years after that."

Dominic would always be there for family events. Nieces and nephews and other relatives often wanted a word with him, to talk about business or baseball. Just a few minutes with Dominic made them feel better. "Everyone in the family always turned to Dad," his daughter says. "They all adored him and held him in the highest respect. Being his only daughter and attending Stanford, I was treated like royalty by Tom, Vince, and Joe as well as Marie when I visited my grandparents' house. It was filial love through and through."

Sadly, family matters also included making cross-country trips to arrange and attend the funerals of siblings. In September 1980, Tom died at age 75. Dominic would now run the family businesses in San Francisco from his company's headquarters in Massachusetts. Next to pass was Frances, the following year, at 70. Nelly, the only child of Rosalie and Giuseppe born in Isola delle Femmine, died at 84 in 1983. Now Dominic had Mamie, Marie, Vince, and Joe left.

He continued to steer clear of the Red Sox for years, a painful self-exile that included refusing invitations to Old-Timers' Games at Fenway Park. That ended in 1984. "At Joe Cronin's funeral, Dom saw Mrs. Yawkey standing outside of the church," Flavin says. "He approached her and said, 'Jean, life is too short to go on this way.' She threw her arms around him in thanks for forgiving her and relations with the team were restored." He would accept the invitation to the May 1986 game and be in a Red Sox uniform with Ted, Doerr, Pesky, and his brothers once again.

ADAPTING THE PAUL SIMON LYRIC, Edward Kiersh set off in the early 1980s to interview former major leaguers for a book titled *Where Have You Gone, Vince DiMaggio?* Some of the players were content with their lives, some had fallen on hard times, and some had found themselves in unusual circumstances, like baking doughnuts or whipping up clam chowder.

Kiersh found Vince to be "a quiet man content to live in the shadows of a legend, who at seventy-one [sic] is a Fuller Brush salesman in Los Angeles. Though a competent, .249 lifetime-hitting outfielder, he never enjoyed any fame, or the riches that usually go with it." The author also reported that Vince "often leaves work early to go fishing, tend to his garden, or to study the Bible in pursuit of 'the higher league.' Insisting that he's found inner peace, only one thing disturbs him. Except for a phone call every six months, or a fleeting glimpse of his brother on TV, Vince, like the rest of us, has been forced to wonder, 'Where have you gone, Joe D.?'"

Considering that this is the chapter that gave the book its title, Kiersh's interview with Vince is surprisingly brief and not especially insightful. But one quote caught readers' and his brothers' attention: "Joe's always been a loner, and he always will be. When the folks were alive we were a lot closer. But I guess in the last four years I've seen him two or three times. What can I do, I'm Vince, and he's Joe. He's always had a living style higher than mine, or higher than I cared to live. It's only a shame that we have gone such different ways. That's real sad. Family should stick together."

Dominic winced when he read it. He knew that it would not inspire Joe to pay more attention to his older brother—probably the opposite. As usual, Dominic was right.

Vince had one final comment: "The only pressure of being a DiMaggio was trying to convince people that I wasn't Joe. I've tried not to use it to get my foot in the front door. I want to do things on my own. But I guess no matter what I do, I'll always be under Joe's shadow. He was one hell of a star, and I was just an ordinary star." The book did prompt a few reporters to seek Vince out for "Whatever Happened to . . ." features. Dave Larsen of the *Los Angeles Times* found him "within a modest house on a quiet street," still in North Hollywood, "a gray-haired man who turned 70 a few months ago. He spends his time tending his backyard camellias, reading his Bibles, supplementing his Social Security by selling Fuller Brush products." His two distinctions, Larsen wrote, were that Vince had established the 134-strikeout single-season record and that he was the "forgotten DiMaggio."

In this interview, Vince came across as genial and contented. He told the story of getting Joe the job with the San Francisco Seals, and how Casey Stengel had called him when he thought his professional career was over. He described his Fuller Brush tasks, and Larsen wrote, "Spring training is upon us again. Vince DiMaggio wonders if he will have a good year selling brushes." It didn't seem to faze Vince that he was a DiMaggio yet still went door to door selling cleaning products to make a living.

Larsen observed about the DiMaggios, "An outsider gets the feeling it isn't a very close-knit family. Vince said he almost never sees Dom, that Joe is mostly on the road and that an occasional letter from a sister, Marie, who lives in Joe's house in San Francisco, is just about the only source of news."

Vince was still a Fuller Brush salesman up to the time he became ill with cancer, at 73. He had to have suspected something was seriously wrong, something God wouldn't take care of for him.

After the tests in Boston confirmed what Vince had been told, it would be left to Dominic to tell Joe that Vince was dying. The greatest living ballplayer could do nothing about it except, when the time came, attend his trailblazing brother's funeral.

As the 1986 Old-Timers' Day at Fenway Park approached, Vince kept changing his mind about going. He was finally persuaded to go by Dominic and the prospect of seeing his two surviving brothers. And there was another reason.

"He always loved the fans and was grateful to them," Joanne DiMaggio Webber says. "He played hard to not disappoint them. I remember one Sunday—he died the following Friday—a man and his son came to the door to see him and get an autograph. I told them my father, who was lying down, was too sick. Then I heard him say, 'Oh no, it's okay.' He got up and invited them in, having no idea who they were. He put on a Red Sox cap that Dominic gave him at the reunion. I took a picture of the three of them as they talked baseball. Here's a man who could barely make it to the bathroom, and he would have sung for them too if he could."

Many people were surprised that Joe agreed to the DiMaggio brothers' reunion that day in May 1986. He did it for Dominic, and to end his estrangement from Vince. He didn't know yet that Vince was dying. Maybe it was old familial instincts kicking in. Dominic's son Paul relates an anecdote from that day that sheds some light on Joe's mood.

"I was in the clubhouse with my father before the regular game, and it was full of reporters, photographers, players, retired players.

The place was packed," Paul recalls. "Dad and Joe were on the other side of the room, in an office. I figured I'd never get through to see them, so I left. I got outside and began walking around the stadium when a door suddenly opened and someone called to me, 'Mr. DiMaggio, Joe would like to speak to you.' I step in, and Joe was in the stairwell. He said, 'I saw you over there, leaving. I just wanted to say goodbye.' I was very touched by that, and to me it showed that my uncle was a gentleman and a guy with feelings."

Vincent Paul DiMaggio died at his home on October 3, a few weeks after his 74th birthday, with Madeline, Joanne, and Vicki there. He and his wife had been married for almost 54 years. He had enjoyed time spent with his four grandchildren and managed to live long enough to see two great-grandchildren born. He died with his belief in the Bible intact.

Predictably, obituaries identified him as Joe's older brother; sometimes Dominic was included. Most obit writers were tactful enough not to mention the strikeouts. A few months after he died, the *Sports Heritage* magazine published "Vince DiMaggio's Song," an appreciation by Jack B. Moore, who in 1985 had visited Vince. Moore was working on a book about Joe (published in March 1986), and Joe had refused an interview. Vince invited Moore to his home in North Hollywood to fill in some blanks about the early life of the DiMaggios. The 1987 tribute did not begin in a promising way: "It must not have been easy for Vince DiMaggio to go through life as the wrong DiMaggio." Vince spent as much time with Moore as he wanted, and when the interview was over, he and Madeline gave Moore a tour of their backyard garden. Then Vince played tapes he had recorded of himself singing arias and traditional Italian songs like "O Sole Mio." Moore was entranced. He concluded his piece: "He was a good singer, a gentle and loving person, a very good Fuller Brush salesman, a decent major leaguer, and a truly great Vince DiMaggio."

TWENTY-TWO

WHAT TOOTS SHOR had said in 1955 about Joe being a very lonely man remained true for the rest of his life, especially in his last decade, when he tried (with very aggressive help) to fill the void with money. While he stopped having flowers placed on Marilyn's grave in 1982—people were stealing them—and had relationships with other women, Joe remained too attached to her memory to find the kind of lasting companionship his brothers had found with their wives. A few friends remained, but others dropped away, died, or were frozen out because they had angered Joe in some way. He and Joe Jr. became estranged. He even showed little affection toward Dom when it was just the two of them left.

"I always had the sense when I was with him that he was a sad person," says Paul DiMaggio about his uncle. "And he was an unfortunate person, for all his fame. He was an incredibly shy, self-conscious guy for an American hero. It was hard to believe that he could last as long as he did with all those feelings stacked up inside him."

The last thing Joe sought in his seventies was headlines, but there he was in the news as a survivor of the earthquake that struck the Bay Area just after 5:00 P.M. on October 17, 1989, shortly before Game 3 of the World Series between the Oakland Athletics and San Francisco Giants. It was not nearly as devastating as the Bay Area quake that Giuseppe and Rosalie had felt in 1906, yet 62 people were killed by it.

Joe was spending the majority of his time in San Francisco, living on the top floor of the house on Beach Street, with the sister to whom he had always been closest, Marie, occupying the bottom floor. Once again, despite being in her eighties, she cooked and cared for Giuseppe Jr.

After the quake struck, Dominic couldn't reach Joe or Marie. It occurred to him to call Bob Sales, the sports editor of the *Boston Herald*, who had to have assigned a reporter to be in the Bay Area to cover the World Series. "I'm very worried about my brother and my sister," Dominic told Sales. "They have a house right where there was so much damage, and we can't get hold of them." Sales told his Series reporter, Stephen Harris, to find Joe.

As Harris told David Cataneo: "I got to the closest point to where his house was. His house was located on a street that was right at the point where some of the worst damage happened. There was a house right across the street that sort of pancaked down on top of itself, totally destroyed. Right on his corner, about three doors down, an eight-unit apartment building exploded because of a gas main. Several people got killed, I think." Joe emerged out of the chaos, telling Harris, "I'm looking for my sister. We haven't been able to find her yet. She's very old, and we're worried about her."

Marie was at a friend's house, shaken but uninjured. While Joe did use his hero status in the city to get contractors working quickly on his damaged house, he otherwise waited like everyone else on lines for food and water being dispensed at Red Cross stations. Perplexed and awed residents of the neighborhood would notice a tall, distinguished-looking gentleman they recognized as one of America's greatest sports heroes.

Between the earthquake damage, the dampness of the climate, and the taxes in California, Joe sought another home. He bought a place on a golf course in south Florida—ironically, in the town called Hollywood. He played there and stayed mostly to himself, though his adoptive granddaughters—Joe Jr. had married a widow and adopted her children—inspired him to establish a wing at Memorial Regional Hospital in his new hometown, the Joe DiMaggio Children's Hospital.

South Florida attorney Morris Engelberg met Joe in the mid-1980s and became one of the Clipper's few confidants. In 2003 he published a book titled *DiMaggio: Setting the Record Straight*, "a story of deep friendship, of unquestioned loyalty by a middle-aged man exhibiting a boyish devotion to a graying American idol." Much of the book was intended to repudiate how Engelberg had been characterized in some published accounts, especially Cramer's biography, as a money-grubbing leech who made millions on a sports hero he viewed as a cash cow.

It is indisputable that he helped Joe make a lot of money. Engelberg surveyed the landscape of a booming sports memorabilia market and realized that few if any autographs would be more valuable than the Great DiMaggio's. He came up with one scenario after another, and Joe, seeing how each one made more money than the last, became a willing actor in them. At an appearance in Atlantic City in 1988, you could buy Joe's autograph for $15. In 1993 he sold 1,941 bats on the QVC channel for $3,000 each. By the late 1990s, a signed DiMaggio baseball was worth $300. It could be argued that Joe, given the boom in sports memorabilia and collectibles late in his life, would have earned a lot of money anyway, but Engelberg made it easy for him.

Engelberg and his entourage enforced Joe's strict rules about what he would sign: no original art, books, round objects, bats, uniforms, advertising items, or anything to do with Marilyn. He wasn't being paranoid. A year after Joe died, there was an auction of baseball-related memorabilia. Apparently, Joe had been unaware when he scribbled his signature that he was affixing it to the cover of the first *Playboy* issue, which had devoted a few pages to Marilyn Monroe. It sold for $40,250.

Engelberg continued to wheel and deal, turning the Joe DiMaggio name into an ATM. To be fair, there were show promoters who were making Joe offers he couldn't refuse, up to $100,000 for an appearance. If you had the greatest living ballplayer, your event had to be top drawer. And such fees were perhaps the only way Joe had left, other than the once-a-year ovations on Old Timers' Day at Yankee Stadium, to measure the endurance of his fame.

Joe had to know that however much money he earned, he couldn't take it with him. That didn't mean, though, that Joe Jr. was going to get it. Joe had pretty much written his son off. He told hangers-on that he was ashamed of the bum.

Joe Jr. always had the odds stacked against him. He was the only child of one of the most famous sports stars the country had ever produced. His divorced parents had fought over him. At 12, he had gone to live with his father and Marilyn after they married, and then *they* were divorced. Marilyn died. His mother had divorced again and married again. (Dorothy Arnold would pass away in November 1997.) He himself had married and divorced and was estranged from his children. He seemed to have met none of his father's expectations, and his father made no secret of it. Junior had to think that was the reason his father spent less and less time with him as the years went on.

Joe Jr. and Marilyn, on the other hand, had genuinely hit it off. She tried to serve as a bridge between the boy and his reticent father. If she and Joe had been together longer, a lot might have turned out differently. For the rest of her life, she and Joe Jr. stayed in touch. The night she died they spoke on the phone; he said later there was no indication that she had only hours to live. While his childhood wasn't as awful as Marilyn's had been, Joe Jr. experienced his share of abandonment, often shuffled off to camps and boarding schools. He had gone to Yale, then dropped out and enlisted in the Marine Corps, but even that structured environment didn't help. He drank and drugged his way through the 1960s, '70s, and '80s. Joe Sr. said the hell with him.

Dominic, as was his way, tried to help. He had to know something of what life was like for Joe Jr., being always compared to the incomparable. When Joe Jr. was looking for a job after the Marines, Dominic gave him one at his plant in Lawrence. He also offered his nephew a room in his house, but Joe Jr. slept on a cot in the factory. He was diligent enough at his job that Dominic sent him to Baltimore, with a promotion, to help get a new factory there off the ground.

That factory was destroyed by a fire. Joe Jr. fell in love with a widow in Baltimore. He and Sue married, and Joe Jr. adopted her two young daughters, Paula and Kathie. Joe Sr. never warmed up to Sue, another reason for father and son not to see each other. However, Joe did embrace his new granddaughters. For the rest of his life, he spent as much time as he could with them and helped them financially after he had washed his hands of their adoptive father.

After Joe Jr. and his family moved to the West Coast, his drug use put a strain on the marriage it couldn't bear. When he and Sue divorced, he drifted away from his daughters, his eventual granddaughters, and especially his father. Every time Joe Sr. heard from his son he had a different address. Joe Jr. would occasionally accept money from his father, but he wasn't really interested in money. He wound up living in a trailer and working in a junkyard. That was where he was when he was told that his father was very sick.

Entering their eighties, one might think that Joe and Dominic, the only two sons of Giuseppe left, would want to be as close as they could be. Instead, Dominic was collateral damage as Joe's world contracted and he came to trust fewer people. And the avarice Joe displayed selling his signed memorabilia bothered Dominic.

"To my recollection, my father went to one signing when he kept the money, but otherwise he never took a penny for his autograph. Yet they weren't free either," says Paul DiMaggio. "For many years he had a standard letter that would be sent to anyone asking him to autograph a ball, photo, whatever, to send a check made out to the Association of Professional Baseball Players of America, which helped retired baseball players, especially those who played before there was a pension. I can't tell you how many of those letters I had to copy and send out. Then he would sign what people wanted and turn all those checks over to the organization."

For his part, it bothered Joe that his brother had such a Midas touch. Dominic had made a lot of money on commercial real estate in the Bay Area, including DiMaggio's Grotto, which wouldn't have existed without Joe's sweat and stardom. Dominic had it easy in other ways too: a long marriage, all three of his children were college graduates, and he wasn't always on his guard in Boston or at the vacation home in Florida. Pretty good life for a guy without a single World Series ring or MVP Award.

And there had been the Mamie situation. When their sister had gotten too sick to care for herself, "Joe was sitting in San Francisco, and he didn't lift a finger," wrote Richard Ben Cramer. "So Dominic had to fly across the country, to put her into a nursing home. Dom wasn't happy about that episode. And neither was Joe. Because Dom flying all that way to take care of Mamie—that shamed Joe. And shame was what he hated worst."

In his final years, Joe had little contact with his remaining brother. Even in Florida at the same time, they often stayed apart. "We saw Ted Williams more than we saw Joe," says Paul DiMaggio. "I really don't know what the problems between the brothers were. Joe was just a very unhappy guy, and it didn't take much for there to be a problem." The more Joe was involved with Engelberg and the unseemly chase for money, the more Dominic felt shut out. It was like his brother had become a captive of his own cult.

In his later years, Joe refused most honors, still shunning the spotlight and people—other than Engelberg—whom he thought were trying to make money off his name. He said no when the town of Martinez wanted him to dedicate Joe DiMaggio Drive and baseball fields within the city. He also said no to the ceremony dedicating *Joltin' Joe,* the speedboat he had been given by the Yankees in 1949, which Martinez officials had restored. (He didn't avoid Martinez itself. He sometimes went to Long Drugs there to chat with one of his granddaughters, and he'd stop for a meal at Amato's.) He did not pick up his honorary degree from the University of San Francisco. He did, uncharacteristically, serve as the grand marshal of the Half Moon Bay Halloween Parade in 1994, a few weeks before he turned 80.

The next year a San Francisco newspaper assigned a reporter to see if DiMaggio still spent time in the city. "It's an odd task, tracking the ghost of a man who is still alive and well, but Joe DiMaggio is more ghost than real guy," wrote Scott Ostler. "The man who packed and rocked Yankee Stadium for 13 years, who married Marilyn, who was San Francisco's No. 1 son and gift to the world, moves about quietly, slipping in and out of old haunts, barely rippling the water." Ostler reported that some of Joe's grade school buddies could be found playing cards at the Italian Athletic Club every afternoon, across the park from Saints Peter and Paul Church, where all the DiMaggio funerals had been, and "Dario Lodigiani, who played big-league ball for six seasons and still scouts for the White Sox, runs into DiMaggio now and then at a golf course in Napa."

Ostler concluded his article, "In every sighting of Joe DiMaggio, he is well-dressed, natty and dapper, coat and tie, shoes shined."

Until his health failed him, Joe continued to visit San Francisco from Florida. Arthritis and a pacemaker did not stop him from traveling. (The installation of the pacemaker in 1987 had caused him to miss his first Old-Timers' Day at Yankee Stadium in 35 years.) There were no fishermen left of his father's generation, of course, but some of the kids he remembered from the old neighborhood, as well as men he'd become acquainted with over the years, were still around. Lefty O'Doul's was an old haunt to visit, and Liverpool Lil's (now co-owned by Gil Hodges III). Joe might sip Pabst Blue Ribbon beer and chat about baseball. He was sometimes seen in his car parked by Fisherman's Wharf, reading his mail. He could no longer linger at the restaurant on Fisherman's Wharf. It had closed in 1986, after 50 years in business.

He remained close to Marie, who, despite health issues, plugged along through her eighties. (Mamie had died at 88 in 1992.) She turned 90 in July 1996, then, the following year, she was gone. She left behind her daughter, Betty, who lived in Los Angeles, and her two brothers. Dominic flew west, and they went through the burial process once again.

Joe would accept invitations to be at Yankee Stadium, and not just for Old-Timers' Games. George Steinbrenner, owner of the franchise since 1973, treated Joe like the Bronx Bomber royalty he was. In October 1996, the Yankees had just won their first world championship in 18 years (a drought unthinkable in the Yankee Clipper's day), and Joe accepted Steinbrenner's offer to ride in the first car in the ticker-tape parade through the Canyon of Heroes in Manhattan. On Old-Timers' Days, he'd see the few fellows left of his generation of Yankees—Berra, Rizzuto, Henrich, Silvera, Bobby Brown, a few others. He enjoyed seeing them, but he didn't linger with them. After the ceremonies, he was gone.

On Old-Timers' Day in July 1998, Bob Sheppard announced the last participant: "Ladies and gentlemen, please rise and welcome the greatest living ballplayer, the Yankee Clipper, Joe DiMaggio." Joe strode out in a dark blue suit, and the fans roared, though few at the Stadium that day had seen Joe play. Two months later, he was back in the Bronx for Joe DiMaggio Day and to celebrate the team's record-breaking 114-victory season. The highlight was being presented with replicas of his nine World Series championship rings, which had been stolen from a hotel room many years earlier. But

Joe looked frail, and word started to spread that the Big Guy was seriously ill.

Indeed, it was his last public appearance. Joe had lung cancer, but he didn't learn that until the following month when he checked into Regional Memorial Hospital in Hollywood to battle a bout of pneumonia. A cancerous tumor was discovered in his right lung. It was removed on October 14. There were more procedures during what turned out to be a 99-day stay in the hospital.

Joe did not go easily. Given that his dignity had always been so extremely important to him, it might have been a blessing if he had died suddenly. But the lung cancer that killed him took its time. His body betrayed him again—this time by being too tough to give in.

The surgery had come too late to prevent the cancer from spreading, and doctors were trying to fend off various infections as well. Joe's blood pressure sank so low on November 16 that a priest was called in to perform last rites, but Joe rallied. The day before his 84th birthday on November 25, Engelberg notified news outlets that Joe had lung cancer. "I want to get the hell out of here and go home," Joe begged doctors on December 3, but the next day he was wracked by a fever, intensifying congestion, and an intestinal infection. A week later he slipped into a coma.

But again, Joe didn't die. After 18 hours, he regained consciousness. According to the *New York Daily News,* Angelo Sapio, a friend who had also been Joe's barber for years, visited Joe in intensive care. He told Joe about recently meeting a man who said he was at the game in Cleveland in 1941 when "the fifty-eight-game hitting streak" came to an end. Joe tugged Sapio closer to him and rasped, "It's fifty-six."

People magazine reported, "Joe Jr. has yet to visit his father since he's been in a Florida hospital," in a short article titled, "Where Have You Gone, Joe DiMaggio Jr.?" When Joe Jr. was asked about staying away from his father, he responded, "If he wants me to visit, he can ask me." Joe didn't.

In January, the doctors conceded that his condition was terminal and allowed him to go home. A bed was set up for him on the first floor of his house where he could watch TV, and there was round-the-clock nursing care. Engelberg drew up a document making him the decision-maker on Joe's care, and Joe signed it.

In late January, NBC News reported that Joe DiMaggio had died. ESPN was about to go live with the news, but was wise enough to wait to get ahold of Dominic, who denied it. Something like a DiMaggio death watch was in place. Joe wouldn't accept that this was it. He had an invitation from the Yankees to throw out the first pitch on opening day, and a sign on his bed read, APRIL 9 YANKEE STADIUM OR BUST.

Engelberg also became the gatekeeper, deciding who could visit, which was almost no one. Steinbrenner was allowed. So were Joe's adoptive granddaughters, Paula and Kathie, and their husbands. (Joe liked their spouses a lot more than he had liked Joe Jr.'s.) In February, Dominic showed up at Joe's home. Engelberg didn't want him there, but Joe had asked for him, so Dominic, who had just turned 82, drove up from his Florida home. He would appear more often as Joe became more frail.

The two brothers reminisced—the house on Taylor Street, the Horse Lot, other kids in the neighborhood, Giuseppe and Rosalie, Marie and their other sisters and Tom and Mike who died too young, Vince with his wonderful voice and how his rebellion opened the door to baseball for the youngest DiMaggios, selling the *Call-Bulletin* on street corners, the Seals and Lefty O'Doul, and those glorious years of roaming center field in New York and Boston and not giving a damn thing to each other—every hit, run, game, and championship had to be earned. With every visit, Dominic watched his last link to the DiMaggios of Martinez drift away.

"Whatever their problems were, and yes, they weren't buddies those last years of Joe's life, but when the chips were down, would they go to bat for each other? Absolutely," Paul DiMaggio says.

"Once my father got in to see his brother, he was there to help. He had doctors flown in from Boston to see if anything could be done. Unfortunately there wasn't, other than be there for his brother, even with that lawyer interfering."

On March 1, hospice care was provided. Five days later, Engelberg made the decision to let Joe die by turning off the breathing machine. Dominic was there and exclaimed, "You're killing him!" The machine was turned back on, and Joe breathed again. Dominic was not there the next night. Kathie was, along with Paula's husband, Engelberg, and the nursing attendants.

Joe DiMaggio missed opening day at Yankee Stadium by a month. He died shortly after midnight on March 8, 1999. There were published accounts, including one in Cramer's comprehensive biography, that immediately after Joe died Engelberg pulled the 1936 World Series ring off his finger. In Engelberg's version of events, Joe had given him the ring for safekeeping when he entered the hospital, and the lawyer was trying to return it.

Immediately after news outlets reported Joe's passing, the tributes came. "He was the very symbol of American grace, power, and skill," said President Bill Clinton. In an extensive obituary, the veteran *New York Times* sportswriter Joseph Durso described Joe as "a figure of unequaled romance and integrity in the national mind because of his consistent professionalism on the baseball field, his marriage to the Hollywood star Marilyn Monroe, his devotion to her after her death, and the pride and courtliness with which he carried himself throughout his life." He quoted the writer Wilfrid Sheed: "In dreams I can still see him gliding after fly balls as if he were skimming the surface of the moon."

Dominic took over the arrangements for his brother's funeral. He had Joe's body flown to San Francisco, where, as with the rest of the family, his funeral mass would be conducted at Saints Peter and Paul Church, where Joe had been baptized, received his first communion, and been married.

There were no more than 60 people at the funeral on March 11. Dominic knew his brother wouldn't want it to be a spectacle. He invited nieces and nephews and a few other family members. Bud Selig, the commissioner of Major League Baseball, was there, as was Gene Bundig, who had succeeded Joe's former teammate Dr. Bobby Brown as the American League president, but there were no former players. Engelberg was there, wearing the 1936 ring. Joe Jr. was there, sporting a gray ponytail and a new suit. A cousin had staked him to a new set of teeth. Joining Joe Jr. and Engelberg as pallbearers were Joseph DiMaggio, Mike's son; Joe Nacchio, who had known Joe for decades; and his granddaughters' husbands, Roger Stein and James Hamra. Officiating was Rev. Armand Oliveri, who had grown up with the youngest DiMaggio brothers in the North Beach section.

Dominic gave the eulogy. He told the mourners that his twice-divorced brother had everything in his great baseball career except the right woman to share his life. Clearly, his divorce from Marilyn and her subsequent death planted in Joe a loneliness and need for isolation that couldn't allow him to be happy in a lasting relationship and affected his relationship with others. Dominic concluded his candid, heartfelt eulogy by praising Joe's efforts to help children with the wing at the Florida hospital.

Joe was buried in the Holy Cross Cemetery, joining his family. Dominic and Paula and Kathie requested that donations in his name go to the Joe DiMaggio Children's Hospital.

In his will, Joe left his son a trust fund that would pay him $20,000 a year. Much of the rest of the estate went to his two granddaughters. On August 7, only five months later, Joe Jr. died of a sudden heart attack. He was 57. His body was cremated and his ashes scattered in the Pacific Ocean.

After Joe's funeral, his niece Joanne Webber reflected on how her uncle Dominic had seen to every detail and made sure it was the kind of funeral he thought his brother would have wanted. That was what Dominic did—take care of the family. She remembered that when she had been stuck in a bad marriage for a long time and finally called Dominic to cry on his shoulder, he not only cheered her up but sent money so she could hire a top divorce attorney. Dominic had also come across the country to take care of the funeral when Madeline passed away.

"He was always there, always taking care of people," Joanne says. "With a problem, he listened and figured out what to do and made it happen. After Joe's funeral, I went up to Dominic and told him, 'You're like the Godfather.' He smiled and nudged Emily and said, 'You hear that? I'm the Godfather.' He thought it was funny, but it was true. He was the head of the family."

TWENTY-THREE

THOUGH HE HAD BEEN businesslike in taking charge of the funeral arrangements, Joe's death deeply hurt Dominic. "When he came home from the West Coast, he said, 'I've buried all my siblings,'" Paul DiMaggio recalls. "And he had. He was there for every one of them, and he took care of Joe last. 'The only one left is me,' he said. It affected him a lot."

But Dominic's final years were not to be ones of unhappiness and grief. Quite the opposite—he savored the decade he had left to live not so much because he was a self-made man, the son of immigrants who had achieved what is thought of as the American Dream, but because in relishing his accomplishments he could try to share them with family and friends.

All three of Dominic's children graduated from college. "He mentioned to me on more than one occasion that when he served on corporate and charitable boards of directors, he always felt a little self-conscious that he was not educated like his fellow board members were," says Paul DiMaggio. "It seemed to bother him that he did not have that formal degree, not realizing that he had educated himself well beyond the basic requirements for a baccalaureate. My father was determined that his kids and his kids' kids would never feel inadequate in the area of education. He set up trusts for each of his grandchildren to have the funds to go to college. An education is revered in this family, thanks to Dad. But he also imparted to each of us that a person who lacked an education should never be looked down upon. We all learned his lesson in humanity and humility."

Paul and Peter went to work for the Delaware Valley Corporation, and eventually Dominic was able to turn over the running of the business to his sons. His daughter, Emily, went into the media field, working for various publications, living for a time in Manhattan. When old rival Bobby Brown was president of the American League, his office was in a building next to the one where Emily lived. "We would see each other often when he visited his daughter," Brown remembers. "I enjoyed seeing Dominic because he was a great guy, and the pride he had in his daughter made it obvious how much family meant to him."

With work responsibilities much diminished, and being able to afford to do what they wanted, Dominic and Emily divided their time between two homes, the house in Marion on the water near Cape Cod and the winter home in Ocean Ridge, near Palm Beach. He played golf every Wednesday with friends, and on many weekends with his wife. He stopped in at the office once a week to check up on things, and he had a home office where he managed his real estate holdings.

"There wasn't a week that went by when Dom and I didn't have lunch together," says Dean Boylan Sr. He and Dominic met through their wives, who saw each other in the 1950s when their children attended the same school. Dominic and Boylan, whose son took over for him as owner of Boston Sand and Gravel, became very close friends. "We used to talk business, and Dom became a director in our company. He was a huge, huge help in guiding us through difficult times, making decisions. When I saw Dom during the week, not the director's meeting, but during the week, he and I would talk about it. His advice was very valuable as well as generous."

In both personal and professional relationships, people were drawn to Dominic. He could be a confidant, a pillar of support, or simply a sounding board. "He had a calmness under duress, and he was strong and intelligent, he could think things out, and he was loving," Emily explains about her husband. "I think he developed the reputation as a wise counsel because he had these gifts, and he had a kindness and feeling for others when they were hurting."

"He was a very sincere person," Boylan says. "As you got to know him, you thought he was terrific. When you had something to talk about or were going through an experience, Dominic made you feel like you were the only person who counted. And when he told you something, that was his word and it was a 101 percent reliable. He would never waver from it."

Baseball friends remained very important to Dominic—especially Ted Williams. Ted had about the same luck as Joe in marriage. He was divorced twice and had rocky relationships with his three children—a son, John Henry, from his second marriage, and daughters Bobby-Jo and Claudia, one from each marriage. After he resigned as skipper of the Washington Senators—which had become the Texas Rangers—he stayed in Florida. There would be the occasional trips north for Red Sox events and for Dominic and Emily's charity efforts, and to the Hall of Fame in Cooperstown, where he had been inducted on the first ballot in 1965, with 93 percent of the vote. (Why not unanimous? Maybe there was still a bit of lingering press bias.)

He especially loved the Florida Keys, where he indulged his passion for fishing. As he aged, he became more content with life. He would always have rough edges, but much of the anger was gone and there was more warmth. "Ted actually became a happy individual, his happiest years were in his sixties and seventies," Dick Flavin says. "He mellowed out and was more appreciative of what had happened to him in life and the affection people had for him, while

Dominic's brother became more eccentric. If someone had asked me many years ago who would be the crazy, unhappy old man, Ted or Joe, I would have said Ted because he's crazy and unhappy now. But it turned out the other way around." He even fell in love again, with Louise, a woman he had known as a friend before and during his second marriage.

In anticipation of the fiftieth anniversary of the 1941 season, Dominic collaborated with the sportswriter Bill Gilbert to write *Real Grass, Real Heroes.* Ted Williams wrote an especially warm and gracious introduction. And when the publisher and Dominic threw a book launch party at Tavern on the Green in Manhattan, Joe wasn't there, but Ted flew up from Florida to attend.

Ted campaigned for Dominic to join him and Bobby Doerr in the Hall of Fame. Dominic had not been elected in the 15 years following his 1953 retirement. He was not one to speak up himself about it, but Ted was less reserved. "Ted was really passionate about Dom being included in the Hall of Fame," remembers Yogi Berra, who also served on the Veterans Committee. "He was pretty persuasive. But others didn't see it that way."

Dominic's Cooperstown credentials were viewed as borderline. Yet during the seasons he played, he was surely a Hall of Fame–caliber player. As a center fielder, he holds the American League record for most chances accepted per game (2.99), and he is one of only five outfielders in baseball history to record 500 or more putouts in a single season. On the offensive end, during his ten full seasons Dominic totaled more base hits than any other major leaguer. He was behind only Ted in runs scored. He averaged almost 105 runs scored per year; the only two other players to do so in the 20th century were his brother Joe and Lou Gehrig. He was a seven-time All-Star in ten seasons. And certainly Dominic's character and integrity, and the time he volunteered to serve as the American League representative, merited strong consideration.

The Veterans Committee didn't agree. There is no doubt Dominic suffered from being overshadowed by Joe. When the center fielder Richie Ashburn was inducted into the Hall of Fame in 1995, Ted told whoever would listen that Dominic was not only a better ballplayer statistically, but "if the game was on the line and you needed a clean hit or a hard-hit ball, he was as good as anybody."

Dominic didn't lose sleep over it. In a 2007 appearance on the show *Red Sox Stories,* when he was asked about the possibility of still being voted in, he replied, "It's too late. I'd rather see the spot go to a younger man who would enjoy it more. I had my chance."

While Ted campaigned for Dominic's entry into the Hall of Fame, Joe did not. Dominic was fine with that. "I know that when people used to ask him who was the best defensive center fielder he ever saw, he would say, 'My brother Dom,'" Dominic told *Sports Illustrated* in 2001. "But he would never say, 'Dom belongs in the Hall of Fame,' because if he had said that and I had gotten in, he knew people would have said, 'Dom's only in because Joe pushed for him.' We're not that kind of people." He also told the writer, "I've had a tremendously fulfilling life."

He had no problem being elected to the Boston Red Sox Hall of Fame in 1995. Among the others in that institution's freshman class were Joe Cronin, Doerr, Ted, Johnny Pesky, Babe Ruth, Carl Yastrzemski, and Tom and Jean Yawkey. Teammates Jimmie Foxx and Mel Parnell made it in two years later, Boo Ferriss in 2002, Billy Goodman in 2004, and Ellis Kinder and Vern Stephens in 2006. Jimmy Piersall got the nod in 2010.

Ted was distraught when Louise suddenly died in 1993. But he had long-lasting friendships. Until age made travel more troublesome, he saw Pesky, Doerr, and Dominic as often as he could. When they were at their Florida home, Dominic and Emily visited with Ted. Otherwise, there were notes, cards, phone calls. As with his family members, Dominic was consistently in touch with friends by phone, including many former teammates, whether they had been stars like Doerr and Pesky or not.

"He was the best friend I ever had in baseball," states Babe Martin. "Both of us old guys, we must have called each other every week, one called or the other one did. Once a week, we would call one another. If Emily answered, I sure enjoyed talking to her too, she's a sweet lady. Dominic was a marvelous guy, the kind who could make you feel like a brother."

Red Sox players of the 1940s and '50s especially enjoyed the 1999 All-Star Game at Fenway Park, where the special guests were players nominated by Major League Baseball to an All-Century team. As each of the 33 living nominees came out on the field, actor Kevin (*Field of Dreams*) Costner introduced them: Henry Aaron, Willie Mays, Bob Feller, Sandy Koufax, Yogi Berra. Dominic and Emily were there to see Ted, four months after Joe's death, finally be recognized as "the greatest living ballplayer." He threw the ceremonial first pitch, a strike to Carlton Fisk, and the crowd cheered at an ear-splitting level, giving Ted the adulation and love that had often been withheld during his career.

Ted had a keen interest in Joe's health in the late 1990s. "[Dominic] had become closer and closer to Williams through the years, closer at the end than he was to his brother Joe," wrote Leigh Montville in his biography of Ted. Joe was "the one man who knew the complications of Williams's life better than any other man on the planet. Never close, friendly enough, but never friends, the two superstars had been forced to deal with the same adulation, the same attention, the same artificial sainthood. They were the two lead characters in the same myth. Could anyone else understand what that had been like? Joe and Ted, they understood best the demands of each other's lives."

The two had also shared difficulties with their only sons. But while Joe wrote off Joe Jr., Ted and John Henry kept trying. John Henry's management of his father in the sports memorabilia business was a strong bond between them.

"This was not necessarily the healthiest thing—a young man

who had a difficult time finding his own way, and who was the son of a singularly famous and iconic father, making a living directly off his father's fame," wrote David Halberstam in *The Teammates*. "The world of baseball appearances and memorabilia is not a particularly genteel one, but even so a number of serious people in the world deeply disliked dealing with John Henry Williams, and in time some of Ted's oldest friends felt they were being kept away from Ted because they had been critical of what they felt was John Henry's growing exploitation of his father."

Maybe it was because he genuinely cared for his former rival's well-being, or he felt a special kinship with him as the best players of their era, or he felt for Dominic losing the only brother he had left. Or maybe for all of these reasons, Ted kept calling Dominic asking for updates as his brother battled cancer. When Joe died, he felt the loss deeply.

Ted's own health deteriorated rapidly. When he had quadruple bypass surgery in 2000, Dominic flew to San Diego to visit him and encourage him to get better. By the time he turned 83 in August 2001, Ted had suffered two strokes, a valve in his heart leaked and doctors couldn't fix it, the once-robust Splendid Splinter was down to 130 pounds, and he was confined to a wheelchair. Dominic called him every day and then relayed their conversation to Doerr and Pesky. "Dommie, you're the only one I have left," Ted would say when his spirits were low.

"Ted realized what Joe did—that Dominic was a much more complete man than they were in terms of he had a successful family life, children, grandchildren around him," says Flavin. "He had this whole business that he made. He didn't trade on his name. He worked hard and made a go of it and became a captain of industry as well as a big donor to charity. He was a much more successful man than they were. The difference was, Ted honored and loved Dominic for it and Joe resented him for it."

There was no avoiding the fact that Ted had only months to live.

In October 2001, Dominic said to his wife and Flavin during dinner that he had to go down to see him. Because of 9/11 the month before, he preferred driving. Emily was aghast that at age 84 he was proposing to drive from Marion, Massachusetts, to Hernando, Florida.

"I was sipping my second—okay, maybe third—glass of wine when this came up," recalls Flavin, who in addition to emceeing many Red Sox events—where he would often recite his composition "Teddy at the Bat"—was an Emmy-winning commentator on Channel 4 in Boston. "Suddenly, I found myself suggesting that I drive south with him. Emily felt better about that."

They tried to enlist Doerr from Oregon, but his wife, Monica, still hadn't recovered from two strokes of her own two years earlier. However, Pesky, a spry 82, agreed to go along. Flavin, only 64 then, would share the driving with Dominic, with Pesky in the backseat. They set off on October 20. There was a stop along I-95 so Dominic could be the guest at a Philadelphia Athletics Historical Society event, then it was back on the road.

Ted rallied when he saw his three friends and enjoyed reminiscing about the Red Sox days one more time. He laughed, with the old twinkle in his half-blind eyes. But at one point he became despondent and began to weep. Only Dominic could get him out of it. "You're having a bad time, but you've got to play the hand that's dealt you," he told Ted. "All the other hands you've been played, you played them so well. You made yourself a hero, and you're an American hero in two wars." Ted calmed, and the visit that day turned fun again.

On the second day of the visit Dominic, channeling his brother Vince, sang an Italian love song, which Ted so enjoyed that he asked Dominic to sing it again. He did, then Flavin sang, "I'll Take You Home Again, Kathleen." There could be no encores, as Ted was tiring.

Ted weakened that winter. It was a surprise that he was still alive at all when the 2002 season began. Dominic called him every morning that spring to describe the previous day's Red Sox game, "and it was hard for Dominic to tell whether he was still there at the end of the line, because sometimes he would slip out of consciousness in the middle of a call," Halberstam writes. "There had been one final call when Dominic had called in and sensed a silence at the other end and he had asked, 'Teddy, are you still there,' and Josh, Ted's attendant, had said, 'No, he's fallen asleep.' 'Well, please tell him I called,' Dominic said, and the next day Ted died."

Dominic had one more funeral to attend in July 2002.

As Dominic approached 90, he was reasonably healthy—though there were still pains from the Paget's disease—and he remained active in charity work, sometimes in collaboration with his aging former teammates. In May 2004, he and Doerr and Pesky were honored by the North End Community Health Center and the North End/West End Neighborhood Service Center with a new award named for Dominic. The following year the three were honored again, this time for their 50 years of support (and Emily's) for the Dana-Farber Institute, which treats and seeks a cure for pediatric cancers.

In between, there had been a long-awaited triumph—a Boston Red Sox world championship, the first since 1918. In the 2004 World Series, the Sox swept the St. Louis Cardinals. "That first time the Red Sox won the World Series, President Bush invited all the players to the White House, and Dominic and I went with them," Jimmy Piersall recalls. "And the president said, 'I'm really glad to see DiMaggio and Piersall here.' Dominic was thrilled by that. And I was thrilled to be sitting next to him. He was a wonderful man, and he had a tremendous wife."

He and his tremendous wife were "absolutely inseparable," says Flavin.

"It was rare for my parents to not go somewhere or do something together," agrees Paul. "They were pretty much inseparable."

Dominic turned 90 in February 2007 and received birthday

wishes not only from his three children and six grandchildren but from what had become a widely extended DiMaggio family. "I'm the last one of the 11 DiMaggios of Taylor Street," he said in a radio interview. "We all must go. I luckily survived. I've had a truly fabulous life. I have no complaints." He said that he played bridge, followed the stock market, and managed money for his grandchildren. "I'm having a problem moving around, and I'm trying to stay as close as I can to home. I have good days and bad days. After all, at 90 you can't expect to feel good every day. After being so active, you feel it. You start slowing down. You've got to give in a little bit."

When asked if he was still contacted by people wanting information about Joe DiMaggio, Dominic replied, "Every once in a while." He continued: "If I had to be the brother of somebody, I couldn't think of a person I would like to be the brother of other than Joe." Asked if he had any goals, Dominic said, "Reach 91."

Later that year the Red Sox won another world championship. Dominic did not get to Fenway Park much anymore, preferring to watch games on television from home. When he and Emily were in Florida, he went to spring training games when he felt up to it. The last one he attended was with his friend Dean Boylan in February 2009, when he turned 92.

Later that month, his health faltered. He developed pneumonia. It was decided that he and Emily should head up to Marion to be near their children and his doctors in Boston. He couldn't shake the congestion and felt weaker and weaker. Eventually, as with Joe, the doctors decided Dominic would be most comfortable at home, where he wanted to be. Emily was always there, as were nurses when he became too weak to get out of bed. Children and grandchildren visited, always bringing a smile to his face.

On the night of May 7, 2009, a Thursday, Paul had just conducted a business seminar. Before heading home across the border in New Hampshire, he called his wife, who was with his parents at the house in Marion. She asked him to come down and stay the night there. Dominic was in and out of consciousness, watching the Red Sox against the Cleveland Indians at Fenway Park.

"I said, 'Sure, I'll be there as soon as I can,'" Paul remembers. "I wasn't that tired, and I wanted to see all of them anyway."

When Paul arrived, Dominic was propped up in the bed in the den, with a view of Buzzards Bay. The game was over, a 13–3 thrashing by the home team, but a replay had just begun. Paul sat down to watch it with his father. He could hear Dominic acknowledge every Boston tally on their way to victory. As the game was drawing to a close, the nurse on duty that night checked on Dominic and said, "I think he stopped breathing."

"I went upstairs and got Mom," Paul says. "We bent over and kissed him. He was gone."

The last of the DiMaggio brothers had died peacefully at home, with family.

INDEX

Aaron, Henry, 299
All-Century team, 299
Allen, Mel, 271
All-Star Games: (1933), 67; (1936), 66–68, 80; (1937), 85; (1938), 97; (1939), 109; (1941), 132; (1942), 150–51; (1943), 162–63; (1944), 164; (1946), 172, 177–78; (1949), 219; (1950), 231; (1951), 238–39; (1999), 299
Almada, Louis, 43, 55, 271
American Dream, 9, 19, 92, 267, 294
Anderson, Dave, 218, 222
Andrews, Mike, 267
Appling, Luke, 68
Arizona-Texas League, 36
Ashburn, Richie, 298
Association of Professional Baseball Players of America, 22, 286
Auker, Elden, 108
Averill, Earl, 31, 85, 110–11

Babe Ruth Story, The (film), 204
Babich, Johnny, 131
Baer, Arthur, 32
Bagby, Jim, 134
Baker, Frank "Home Run," 268
Baldassaro, Lawrence, *Beyond DiMaggio: Italian Americans in Baseball*, 105, 274
Banks, Ernie, 165
Barath, Steve, 55
Barney, Rex, 197, 226
Barrow, Ed, 53, 57, 86, 93, 94, 108, 109, 128–29, 146, 151, 154, 160
Barsochinni, Reno, 256
Baseball Hall of Fame, 268, 297–98
Baseball Writers of America, 145, 151, 268
Bassler, Johnny, 53
Batts, Matt, 225
Bauer, Hank, 221, 223, 231
Baum, Spider, 31
Beazley, Johnny, 152

Bendix, William, 204
Benedetti, Dante, 39
Benswanger, Bill, 135
Berg, Moe, 118
Berra, Yogi, 171, 187, 197, 201, 214,
    221, 233, 240
  and All-Star Games, 231, 299
  and Dom, 218, 297
  and Joe, 234
  and Old-Timers' Day, 288
Bevens, Bill, 196–97
Bilko, Steve, 261
Bodie, Ping, 31–32
Bosox Club, 266, 275
Boston Bees, 3, 77–79, 80–81, 85,
    89–90, 99–100
Boston Braves, 56, 77–78, 159,
    206–7, 211
Boston Patriots, 266, 267
Boston Red Sox:
  American League championships
    (1946), 2; (1967), 268
  and Dom, see DiMaggio, Dominic
    Paolo
  Fenway Park, 119, 121, 201
  50th anniversary of, 236
  and Old-Timers' Day (1986), 1–6, 279
  ownership of, 267–68, 275–76
  and player rights, 170
  postwar season of, 172–73, 186
  Red Sox Hall of Fame, 298
  trades, 199, 236
  and wartime games, 158
  and Williams, see Williams, Ted
  and World Series (1946), 179–81;
    (1967), 268; (2004), 302
  and Yankees, 96–97, 103, 111, 117, 121,
    122, 127, 130, 137, 170–71, 185–86,
    199–200, 209–11, 218, 221–22
Boudreau, Lou, 134, 174, 205–6, 236,
    246, 250, 251, 253–54

Boylan, Dean Sr., 295, 296, 303
Braddock, Jim, 91, 145
Branca, Ralph, 1, 196, 225
Brannan, Sam, 11
Brecheen, Harry, 180
Brillheart, Jim, 229
Brooklyn Dodgers:
  move to Los Angeles, 261
  playoff game (1951), 2
  and Robinson, 161
  World Series (1941), 141–42, 197;
    (1947), 196–98; (1949), 225–26
Brower, Frank "Turkeyfoot," 34
Brown, Bobby, 171, 187, 206, 211,
    214, 219, 226, 248, 257, 288,
    292, 295
Brown, Les, and His Band of Re-
    nown, 139, 202
Bundig, Gene, 292
Burdette, Lew, 233
Burr, Harold, 106
Busch, Noel F., 104
Bush, George W., 302
Byrne, Tommy, 171, 233

Cabrera, Miguel, 1
California:
  baseball in, 21–23
  fishermen in, 12–13
  Governor's Cups, 30, 71, 88, 98,
    99, 175, 177, 198, 261
  history of, 11–12, 16
California League, 22–23, 203–4
California Ship Building Corpora-
    tion, 163–64
Camilli, Dolph, 31, 141
Campanella, Roy, 219, 225
Cancro, Larry, 5
Cannon, Jimmy, 80–81, 145, 203,
    209, 238
Casey, Hugh, 141–42, 197

Cataneo, David, 94, 282
  I Remember Joe DiMaggio, 25–26,
    39, 44, 45, 55, 271
Caveney, Ike, 41, 43
Chadwick, Henry, 118–19
Chandler, Happy, 231
Chandler, Spud, 171, 187
Chapman, Ben, 61, 62, 63, 95, 159
Cincinnati Reds, 65, 85, 99, 114, 118,
    120
Cincinnati Red Stockings, 22
Clinton, Bill, 291
Cobb, Ty, 38, 55, 57, 60, 120, 268
Coleman, Jerry, 214, 224, 226, 231
Collins, Eddie, 103
Conigliaro, Tony, 267
Considine, Bob, 90–91, 145
Cooper, Mort, 152
Coscarart, Joe, 62
Costner, Kevin, 299
Cramer, Doc, 95, 120
Cramer, Richard Ben, *Joe DiMaggio:*
    The Hero's Life, 51, 56, 144, 171,
    207, 269, 283, 286, 291
Cronin, Joe:
  and All-Star Game, 132
  funeral of, 277
  as general manager, 199, 214, 232,
    236, 251, 252
  as manager, 53, 113, 118, 121, 139–
    40, 150, 161, 163, 170, 173, 187
  as player-manager, 85, 95, 97, 130,
    141, 148, 158
  and Red Sox Hall of Fame, 298
  resignation of, 195
Crosetti, Frank, 38, 50, 59, 60, 63,
    69, 83, 89, 187
Culberson, Leon, 180

Daley, Arthur, 162, 164, 168
Daley, Bill, 133

Daniel, Dan, 62, 108, 128, 144, 145,
    165, 188
Danning, Harry, 73
Daresta, Louis, 26
Deal, Cot, 200, 201
Dean, Daffy, 137
Dean, Dizzy, 67, 84, 85, 137
Delaware Valley Corporation, 253,
    295
Delock, Ike, 245, 252
Dempsey, Jack, 84
Devine, Joe, 71, 107
Dickey, Bill, 131, 160
  and All-Star Games, 85, 97, 109
  as catcher, 63, 97, 142, 153, 171,
    214
  as hitter, 73, 98, 99
  as manager, 172, 179
  and World Series, 89, 142
DiMaggio, Adrianella [Nelly] (sister),
    15, 18, 277
DiMaggio, Dominic Paolo, 90, 250
  aging, 5, 237–38, 246, 302–4
  and All-Star Games, 132, 150, 172,
    177–78, 219, 231, 239
  and baseball, 49–50, 64–66, 87
  birth and childhood, 15, 18, 26, 29
  and business, 253, 255, 260, 264,
    267, 275, 277, 286, 295, 300
  career achievements of, 252–53
  as center fielder, 50, 69, 81, 87, 98,
    102, 112, 123, 124–25, 168, 178,
    187, 206, 207, 216–17, 252, 253,
    297, 298
  compared with Joe, 2, 122, 128,
    139, 145, 208, 216, 217, 252,
    285, 298
  death of, 304
  determination of, 186, 207, 217
  Dominic DiMaggio Day, 123
  and Emily, *see* DiMaggio, Emily

DiMaggio, Dominic Paolo (*cont.*)
    and family, 3, 6, 75, 86–87, 115,
        126, 254–55, 260, 265, 276–77,
        278, 285, 286, 288, 290–93,
        294–95, 303
    final years of, 294–96, 302–4
    at Galileo High, 49–50, 119
    and hitting, 82, 99, 102–3, 112, 123,
        129, 131, 137, 138, 159, 189, 194,
        205, 207, 211, 219, 225, 231, 247,
        252, 297
    and income, 170, 179, 214
    injuries to, 107, 119, 120, 180, 190,
        250
    in Japan, 242–43
    and Joe, 3, 4, 57, 122–23, 124–25,
        133–34, 137, 173, 201, 210,
        219–20, 222, 239, 272, 274, 281,
        285–86, 290–92, 303
    as the "Little Professor," 120, 127,
        159, 188, 194, 200, 217
    and media, 107, 113, 120, 122–23,
        130–31, 137, 138, 252
    as mentor, 124, 188–89, 217, 233,
        247
    and military service, 143, 149, 153,
        157–59, 253
    and MVP awards, 115, 216, 233
    as newspaperboy, 27, 218
    and O'Doul, 82, 87, 98, 102, 112–13,
        275
    and Old-Timers' Day, 1, 2, 4–6, 277,
        279
    and Paget's disease, 266, 302
    and players' rights, 4, 95, 169–70,
        200, 251, 263, 286, 297
    popularity of, 2, 4, 130–31, 177, 178,
        200, 252–54, 296
    and postwar season, 169, 172–73,
        177–78
    Real Grass, Real Heroes, 18, 49, 297

    and Red Sox, 113, 117, 118, 126–27,
        137, 141, 152–53, 167, 170,
        187–90, 201–2, 214, 216–20,
        223, 231–33, 236, 237, 245–47,
        267–68, 275–76, 277
    and restaurant, 191, 213, 216, 253,
        260, 286
    and retirement, 251–53, 264–66,
        276
    and Seals, 65–66, 74, 79, 81–82,
        87–88, 94, 98–99, 106–7
    wearing glasses, 29, 57, 87, 95, 122,
        130, 189, 194, 209, 253
    and Williams, 3, 88, 117, 133–34,
        137, 140, 194–95, 266, 286, 296,
        297, 298, 300–302
DiMaggio, Dominic Paul Jr. [Paul]
        (Dom's son):
    birth of, 231–32
    and business, 295
    and his father, 220, 243, 259, 265,
        267, 286, 290, 294–95, 302,
        304
    and Joe, 259, 279–80, 290
DiMaggio, Dorothy Arnold (Joe's
        wife), 84, 96, 110, 125, 143, 249,
        268
    death of, 284
    and divorce, 156, 166, 172
    and marriage to Joe, 115–16,
        144–45, 146, 151, 154, 166
    remarriage of, 191
DiMaggio, Emily (Dom's daughter),
        255, 265, 276, 295
DiMaggio, Emily (Dom's wife), 293,
        298, 299
    and charities, 265–66, 276, 296,
        302
    and children, 231–32, 260
    courtship and marriage of, 192–93,
        195, 207, 209, 211–12, 243, 302

and Dom's illness and death, 303,
304
and family, 4, 213, 228
and Marilyn, 250, 268, 270
DiMaggio, Frances (aunt), 14
DiMaggio, Frances (sister), 15, 18,
277
DiMaggio, Giuseppe (father):
and baseball, 23–24, 29, 35–37, 42,
48, 73, 86–87, 90–91, 99, 119,
133, 179, 210–11, 216
death of, 215–16
emigration to U.S., 9–10, 12, 17
and family, 14, 19, 24–27, 29
as fisherman, 9, 13, 15, 16, 18, 19,
23, 24, 36, 74
and Great Depression, 35–36
and homemade wine, 53, 155
and media, 99, 133, 211
and retirement, 132–33, 213
and sons' wives, 96, 115, 166, 195
and wartime restrictions, 146
DiMaggio, Joe (Giuseppe Paolo Jr.):
aging, 5, 178–79, 185, 187,
202–3, 204, 208–9, 224, 226,
230–31, 233–34, 238, 240,
241–42, 271
ailments and injuries, 51–52, 53,
62–63, 79–80, 105, 107, 111,
113, 121, 128, 129, 139, 156, 157,
166, 172, 178–79, 186, 193, 198,
202–3, 204, 205, 208–9, 211,
214–15, 221, 234, 238, 244, 259,
285, 288–90
and All-Star Games, 66–68, 80,
85, 97, 109, 132, 150, 219, 231
and baseball, 21, 25–26, 38, 39–41
birth and childhood, 15, 18, 24–27
broadcasting, 249, 258, 259
career credentials, 244
comeback of, 171–72, 218–19

comparisons with, 2, 79, 80–81,
100, 103, 106, 120, 122, 128, 139,
145, 164, 190, 208, 216, 217, 252,
278, 285, 298
death of, 290–91
and Dom, 3, 4, 57, 122–23, 124–25,
133–34, 137, 173, 201, 210,
219–20, 222, 239, 272, 274, 281,
285–86, 290–92, 303
and Dorothy, see DiMaggio,
Dorothy
and earthquake, 281–83
and family, 3–4, 229, 254, 258–59,
271, 274
and fans, 66, 96, 98, 108, 133, 151,
165, 211, 218, 222–23
50th birthday, 271–74
and golf, 229, 271, 273, 274, 275
as "greatest living ballplayer," 4,
273–74, 284, 288
as hitter, 83, 89, 103, 111, 139, 151,
187, 188, 202, 211, 219, 234,
252
hitting streaks, 46–48, 131–32,
133–35, 136, 139
in Japan, 242–43, 257
Joe DiMaggio Days, 222–23, 288
as loner, 3, 5–6, 21, 43, 55, 83, 183,
201, 208, 215, 239, 240, 270,
272–73, 281, 287
Lucky to Be a Yankee, 16, 24, 39, 53,
67, 152, 166, 171
and Marilyn, 247–50, 255–59,
268–71, 281, 284, 291, 292
and media, 60, 61, 62, 63–64, 66,
68, 84, 94, 104–5, 108, 121,
128–29, 133, 138, 146, 193, 209,
214, 218, 230, 238–39, 240
mentors to, 55–57, 62
and military service, 143, 151, 154,
155–57, 165–67

DiMaggio, Joe (*cont.*)
  and money, 40, 41, 42, 50–51,
    56, 57, 73, 93–95, 96, 98, 104,
    113, 117, 128–29, 146, 156, 166,
    172, 191, 198, 214, 215, 283–84,
    285–86
  as MVP, 115, 143, 145, 146, 195, 198
  as newspaperboy, 27, 214, 218, 290
  and nightlife, 144–45, 191–92, 258
  as number 5, 80, 244
  and Old-Timers' Days, 1, 2, 3, 4–6,
    273, 279, 288
  as outfielder, 69, 82–83, 102,
    110–11, 193
  and product endorsements, 3, 244,
    258, 273, 274
  and retirement, 3, 229, 238, 244,
    245, 260, 268–74, 281–84,
    287–90
  and Seals, 4, 28, 41–44, 45–49, 52,
    53–54, 278
  at spring training, 59–62
  and stardom, 74, 79, 96, 109, 115,
    131–32, 133, 166, 168, 171, 207–8,
    214, 229, 233, 244, 248, 268,
    269, 278, 288
  stoicism of, 68, 80, 94, 197
  and teammates, 139, 193, 203,
    207–8, 222
  and Vince, 21, 25, 28–30, 43, 79
  and World Series (1936), 72–73;
    (1937), 89–92; (1938), 99; (1941),
    142; (1942), 151–52; (1947), 196–
    98; (1949), 226; (1951), 241–42
  and Yankees, *see* New York Yankees
DiMaggio, Joe Jr., 154, 166, 172, 179,
    215, 222, 240, 270, 283, 289
  birth of, 143, 144
  death of, 292
  and father's death, 292
  odds stacked against, 284–85, 299

DiMaggio, Madeline (Vince's wife),
    44–45, 263–64, 280, 293
DiMaggio, Mamie/Mae (sister), 15,
    18, 277, 286, 288
DiMaggio, Mary/Marie (sister), 3,
    213, 256, 258, 272, 279
  birth and childhood of, 15, 18
  death of, 288
  and earthquake, 282
DiMaggio, Michael Michelli (broth-
    er), 57
  birth and childhood of, 15, 18
  death of, 254–55
  as fisherman, 19, 23, 24, 74, 91,
    116, 133
  and restaurant, 171, 191
DiMaggio, Peter (Dom's son), 260,
    295
DiMaggio, Rosalie (mother):
  and baseball, 72, 87, 179, 210,
    222–23
  in California, 9–14, 17
  cooking for guests, 53, 88, 155, 213
  and her children, 19, 23–24, 25, 74
  illness and death of, 236–37, 254
  and sons' wives, 96, 115, 166, 195
  and wartime restrictions, 146
DiMaggio, Salvatore (uncle), 14
DiMaggio, Thomas Gaetano (brother):
  and baseball games, 72, 90, 222
  birth and childhood of, 15, 18
  as businessman, 24, 74, 91–92,
    267
  and contract negotiations, 42, 50,
    57, 65, 66, 93–95, 128, 146, 154,
    169
  death of, 276–77
  and family, 115, 216, 237, 256
  and fishing, 19, 23, 24
  and restaurant, 91, 133, 143, 146,
    163, 171, 191, 216, 263

DiMaggio, Vicki Rose (Vince's daughter), 191, 255, 263, 280

DiMaggio, Vincent Paolo:
and All-Star Games, 162–63, 164
and baseball, 20–21, 23–24, 25–26, 27, 28–30, 36, 57, 78, 161–63, 185
birth and childhood, 15, 18, 25–26
born-again, 263–64, 277, 280
and Boston Bees, 3, 77–79, 81, 85, 89–90, 99–100
and Cincinnati Reds, 114, 118, 120
compared with Joe, 2, 79, 80–81, 85, 100, 106, 120, 128, 145, 164, 190, 208, 278
death of, 280
end of baseball career, 2, 229, 245, 255
eyesight of, 95–96
and family, 3–4, 5, 115–16, 254, 255, 263, 278, 280
and fans, 163, 279
as fielder, 79, 90, 98, 101, 102, 128, 135, 154, 162, 190, 204
and fishing, 228
health of, 5, 90, 154, 155, 279
as hitter, 81, 85, 90, 105–6, 113, 125, 136, 162, 165, 191, 198
and Hollywood Stars, 48–49, 52–53, 57, 64
ignored by the public, 167, 229, 262, 277
impersonation of, 264
income of, 102, 200, 216
and Kansas City Blues, 102, 105–6, 113–14
and Madeline, 44–45, 263–64, 280
and media, 3, 80–81, 90, 100, 106, 120, 138, 190
and military service, 143, 147, 155, 163–64
as newspaperboy, 27, 218, 290

and New York Giants, 174–75
and Oakland Oaks, 190–91, 198
and O'Doul, 78, 175–76
and Old-Timers' Day (1986), 1, 2–6, 279
personality of, 148, 162, 176–77, 203, 224, 228
and Phillies, 164–65, 168, 174, 175
and Pittsburg Diamonds, 216, 223–24, 227–29
and Pittsburgh Pirates, 120–21, 125–26, 128, 135–36, 148, 153–54, 162
as rebel, 20, 78
and restaurant, 228
and retirement, 262–64, 274, 277–79
and reunion (1956), 260–62
and San Diego Padres, 64
and Seals, 4, 27, 28, 30, 35, 41, 43–44, 45, 49, 175–77, 190, 278
as sporting goods salesman, 190, 203, 228
and Stockton Ports, 203–4, 216
and strikeouts, 40, 96, 100–1, 165, 177, 278
tenor voice of, 20–21, 27, 147–48, 224, 228, 280
and Tucson Lizards, 36, 41
Vince DiMaggio Night, 223
"Vince DiMaggio's Song," 280

DiMaggio brothers:
best in the game, 210, 217, 219
distance between, 262–63, 274, 278–79
and O'Doul's funeral, 275
and Old-Timers' Day (1986), 1–6, 277, 279
Seals reunions (1956), 260–62; (1962), 270
songs and poems about, 138–39, 202, 273, 277, 280
and vaudeville tour, 73–74

DiMaggio Digest, 86–87
DiMaggio family:
　children, 15, 18–19
　family background of, 9–11
　family home of, 92, 96
　family life of, 18–19
　and Joe's 50th birthday, 271, 272
　postwar years, 171
　at weddings and funerals, 115–16,
　　210–11, 213, 215–16, 237, 254–55,
　　256–57, 270, 276–77, 288
DiMaggio's Grotto, San Francisco,
　3, 91, 116, 133, 143, 146, 163, 171,
　191, 213, 216, 228, 253, 260, 263,
　272, 286, 288
Dobson, Joe, 173, 236
Doby, Larry, 201, 219
Doerr, Bobby:
　and All-Star Games, 132, 162, 178,
　　231
　and DiMaggio family, 53, 210
　and Dom, 187, 217, 302
　in Hall of Fame, 297, 298
　and military service, 158
　and Old-Timers' Day, 1, 277
　and Red Sox, 95, 117, 127, 130, 137,
　　141, 177, 189, 214, 222, 223, 224,
　　225
　and retirement, 237–38, 245
　and Ted, 88, 301
Dressen, Charlie, 225, 249
Dropo, Walt, 214, 231
Durocher, Leo "The Lip," 67, 68, 97,
　141, 142, 241

Eagle Base Ball Club, 21, 22
Eckhardt, Oscar "Ox," 54
Effrat, Louis, 242
Elliott, Bob, 125, 207, 239
Engelberg, Morris, 283–84, 287,
　289–91, 292

Erskine, Carl, 196, 225
Etten, Nick, 191

Fagan, Paul, 175–76
Fain, Ferris, 176
Fanning, Skeeter, 31
Far West League, 227–29
Feller, Bob, 143, 147, 151, 157, 170,
　178, 198, 208, 241, 299
Ferriss, Dave "Boo," 2, 161, 173, 178,
　179, 180, 193–94, 199, 213
Finney, Lou, 122
Fisher, Mike, 23
Fisk, Carlton, 299
Fitzsimmons, Fred, 73, 141
Flavin, Dick, 250, 251, 253, 271, 274,
　275, 296, 300, 301
Ford, Gerald R., 275
Ford, Whitey, 232, 233, 240
Foxx, Jimmie, 55, 85, 97, 126, 127,
　130, 132, 141, 165, 298
Fremont, John, 11
Frisch, Frankie, 125, 126, 135, 148,
　163, 164, 268
Fuchs, Emil, 78
Furillo, Carl, 196, 197, 225

Galan, Augie, 41, 48, 67, 163
Gehrig, Lou, 60, 103, 240, 297
　and All-Star Games, 68, 85, 97, 109
　and ALS, 105, 108–9
　death of, 131, 204
　diminishing powers of, 89, 96, 98,
　　99, 104, 106
　income of, 93, 94
　in Japan, 54, 55
　Lou Gehrig Day, 108–9, 206
　and number 4, 80, 244
　and World Series, 73
　and Yankees, 34, 57, 61, 63, 66, 69,
　　82, 111, 114

Gehringer, Charlie, 68, 85
Gernert, Dick, 245, 247, 251
Gibson, Sam, 38, 98, 107
Gilbert, Bill, 18, 297
Gionfriddo, Al, 197–98
Gomez, Vernon "Lefty," 121, 129, 151
  and All-Star Games, 85, 97
  in Japan, 55
  and Joe, 83, 84, 271
  and Seals, 35
  and World Series, 69, 73, 89, 99,
    152, 160
  and Yankees, 63, 86
Goodman, Billy, 223, 224, 251, 298
Gordon, Joe, 93, 99, 109, 142, 153
Goslin, Goose, 69
Gowdy, Hank, 147
Graham, Billy, 263
Graham, Charlie, 42, 53
Great Depression, 27, 33, 35–36, 45,
  46, 49, 92
Greenberg, Hank, 85, 89, 97, 110,
  129, 147, 149, 151
Gross, Milton, 239
Grove, Lefty, 54, 67, 85, 97, 137

Hadley, Bump, 86
Hagen, Walter, 84
Halberstam, David, 168, 180, 253,
  266
  Summer of '49, 205
  The Teammates, 146, 207, 300, 302
Hamey, Roy, 114
Haney, Fred, 53
Harris, Bucky, 186, 193, 196, 200,
  210, 211, 214, 233
Hartnett, Gabby, 67, 268
Hawkins, Frankie, 87
Hecht, Ben, 248, 256
Hegan, Jim, 205–6
Heilmann, Harry, 31

Hemingway, Ernest, 7, 145
Henrich, Tommy "Old Reliable," 86,
  214, 222, 224, 288
  aging, 171, 187, 230
  and All-Star Game, 231
  and Joe, 110, 208, 230
  and military service, 160
  and World Series, 142, 196, 197
Herman, Billy, 67, 68
Hermanski, Gene, 225
Higbe, Kirby, 141
Hoag, Myril, 69
Hodges, Gil, 196, 225, 239
Hofmann, Fred, 41
Hollywood Stars, 34, 45, 48–49,
  52–53, 57, 64, 156, 177
Hornsby, Rogers, 55
Houk, Ralph, 187, 222
Howard, Lee, 147–48
Hubbell, Carl, 67, 72
Huggins, Miller, 33, 109
Hughson, Tex, 2, 162, 173, 189, 199,
  224
Hutchinson, Fred, 99, 157

Isola delle Femmine, Sicily, 9–10, 13,
  19, 262

Jackson, "Shoeless" Joe, 55, 60, 62
Japan, baseball in, 23, 54–55, 235,
  242–43, 257, 275
Jethroe, Sam, 161
Joe DiMaggio Children's Hospital,
  Florida, 283, 292
Johnson, Earl, 149
Johnson, Lyndon B., 271
Johnson, Magic, 267
Johnson, Roy, 86
Joiner, Roy, 45
Jolley, Smead, 52, 53
Jolly Knights, 39–40

"Joltin' Joe DiMaggio," 139
Jones, David, 166
Joost, Eddie, 47
Jordan, Michael, 267
Jorgensen, Spider, 197, 225

Kahn, Roger, *Joe & Marilyn,* 116, 249, 257
Kansas City Blues, 102, 105–6, 113–14
Keeler, Wee Willie, 131, 132
Kell, George, 246, 251
Keller, Charlie, 108, 142, 214
Keltner, Ken, 134, 174
Kiersh, Ed, *Where Have You Gone, Vince DiMaggio?,* 3, 277–78
Kinder, Ellis, 199, 220–21, 224, 237, 246, 298
Kiner, Ralph, 232, 239, 273
Kluttz, Clyde, 174
Knickerbocker, Billy, 66
Kofoed, Jack, 51
Koufax, Sandy, 299
Kramer, Jack, 199, 210, 221
Krichell, Paul, 62
Kuzuru, Makoto, 235

Landis, Kenesaw Mountain, 163
Lane, Bill, 52, 64, 71, 88
Lardner, Ring, "You Know Me Al," 31
Larsen, Dave, 190, 278–79
Larsen, Don, 31
Lavagetto, Cookie, 197
Lazzeri, Tony, 34, 50, 59, 63, 66, 69, 83, 89, 93, 99
Leiber, Hank, 72
Lemon, Chet, 206
Leonard, Dutch, 138
Lepcio, Ted, 245, 252, 276
Lewis, Buddy, 206

Lindell, Johnny, 196, 214
Lodigiani, Dario, 25, 27, 39, 47, 56, 157, 191, 287
Lombardi, Ernie, 31
Lopat, Eddie, 226, 233, 240, 243
Lopez, Al, 153
Los Angeles Angels, 45, 48–49, 53, 198, 261
Louis, Joe, 115, 157
Lumber Leagues, 29–30, 40
Lyons, Ted, 268

MacFayden, Danny, 81
Mack, Connie, 77, 108, 202
MacPhail, Larry, 160, 172, 179, 186, 198
Maglie, Sal "The Barber," 242
Mailho, Emil, 47
Mails, Walter, 66
Major League Baseball Players Association, 200
Manhattan Merry-Go-Round (film), 84, 110
Mantle, Mickey, 107, 238, 240, 242, 271, 273
Mapes, Cliff, 224
Marion, Marty, 200
Maris, Roger, 147
Martin, Babe, 210, 217, 239, 299
Martin, Billy, 231, 233, 243
Martinez, California, 11–13, 216
Martinez, Don Vicente, 11
Martinez, Don Ygnacio, 11
Masterson, Walt, 131
Mayo, Eddie, 73
Mays, Willie, 271, 273, 299
McCarthy, Joe:
  drinking problem, 171, 172, 199, 232
  and Red Sox, 199–200, 201, 211, 224, 225, 231, 232

and Yankees, 53, 60, 61, 62, 63, 68,
    69, 86, 96, 97, 104, 108, 109,
    111, 129, 131, 139, 151, 172, 186,
    196, 214, 233
McClure, Harry, 158
McCormick, Frank, 97
McDermott, Mickey, 246
McGraw, John, 72
McKechnie, Bill, 135
McKinley, William, 17
Meany, Tom, 166
Medwick, Joe "Ducky," 67, 141, 163
Mele, Sam, 124, 186, 187, 188–89,
    190, 201, 206, 214, 217, 223
Metkovich, Catfish, 158, 161, 169, 180
Meusel, Bob, 34
Miller, Arthur, 269
Mills, Howard, 83
Minafo, Bat, 39
Mission Red A's, 41
Monroe, Marilyn, 247–50, 254,
    255–59, 268–71, 281, 284–85,
    291, 292
Montville, Leigh, 170, 299
Moore, Jack B., 280
Moses, Wally, 188, 206
Muir, John, 12
Murphy, Johnny, 60, 142
Murray, Arch, 230
Musial, Stan, 148, 152, 162, 163, 219,
    239, 252, 273

Nacchio, Joe, 292
Ness, Jack, 47
Newcombe, Don, 196, 219, 225, 226
Newsom, Buck "Bobo," 47, 49, 63,
    187
New York Giants:
  Vince traded to, 174–75
  and World Series, (1936), 72–73;
    (1937), 89–92; (1951), 241–42

New York Yankees:
  and contracts, 93–95
  and Joe, 50–51, 53, 56–58, 82–83,
    86, 89, 93–98, 103–5, 113, 114,
    121, 122, 146
  "Murderers' Row," 34, 72
  ownership of, 160
  postwar season, 173
  and Red Sox, 96–97, 103, 111, 117,
    121, 122, 127, 130, 137, 170–71,
    185–86, 199–200, 209–11, 218,
    221–22
  spring training camp, 59–62
  and World Series (1928), 35; (1936),
    69, 72–73; (1937), 89–92; (1938),
    99; (1939), 114; (1941), 141–42,
    197; (1942), 151–52; (1943), 160;
    (1949), 225–26; (1950), 235;
    (1951), 241–42
  and Yankee Stadium, 82–83, 112,
    123, 137
  the "Yankee Way," 61, 199–200
Norella, Tony, 131
North Beach Merchants, 65
Nowlin, Bill, 88

Oakland Athletics, 273
Oakland Oaks, 35, 71–72, 176, 177,
    190–91, 198
Oana, Henry "Prince," 39, 41
O'Doul, Francis Joseph "Lefty," 31,
    33–34, 71, 116
  and baseball in Japan, 54–55, 235,
    242–43, 257, 275
  death of, 275
  and Dom, 82, 87, 98, 102, 112–13,
    275
  and Joe, 55–57, 58, 62, 83, 94, 229,
    242, 256, 271
  and Padres, 243
  and PCL playoffs (1947), 198

O'Doul, Francis Joseph (*cont.*)
  records set by, 54, 55
  and Seals reunions, 261, 270
  and Vince, 78, 175–76
O'Francis, James, 217
Old-Timers' Day (1986), 1–6, 277, 279
Oliveri, Rev. Armand, 292
O'Malley, Walter, 261
O'Neill, Steve, 232, 246
Orlando, Johnny, 95, 180
Ostler, Scott, 287
Ott, Mel, 72, 174, 175, 268
Owen, Mickey, 142, 197

Pacific Base Ball Convention, 21, 22
Pacific Base Ball League, 22
Pacific Coast League, 28, 30, 32–35, 45–49, 64, 71, 87, 98, 115, 117, 156, 175–76, 198, 261
Page, Joe, 171, 172, 223, 233
Parker, Dan, 68
Parnell, Mel, 173, 220–21, 224, 236, 243, 246
Paul, Gabe, 266
Peacock, Johnny, 119
Peery, Charles, 257
Pellagrini, Eddie, 188, 194
Pennock, Herb, 164
Perry, Ray "Little Buffalo," 223
Pesky, Johnny, 88, 137, 301, 302
  and military service, 153, 159, 160
  and Old-Timers' Day, 1, 277
  and Red Sox, 148, 152–53, 169, 177, 178, 180, 187, 194, 214, 220, 222, 223, 224, 236, 238, 245, 246
  and Red Sox Hall of fame, 298
Petrocelli, Rico, 267
Philadelphia Phillies, 164–65, 168, 174, 175

Piersall, Jimmy, 233, 245, 247, 298, 302
Pinelli, Bob, 31
Pippen, Henry "Cotton," 69, 103
Pittsburg Diamonds, 216, 223–24, 227–29
Pittsburgh Pirates, 120–21, 125–26, 128, 135–36, 148, 153–54, 162
Pool, Harlin, 47
Povich, Shirley, 63, 84, 109, 130, 135
Powell, Jake, 97
Priddy, Jerry, 106
Prohibition, 32

Quinn, Bob, 90

Raimondi, Bill, 45
Raschi, Vic, 171, 187, 220, 221, 224, 231, 233, 240
Red Sox Stories, 298
Reese, Pee Wee, 118, 141, 142, 196, 225
Rego, Jimmy, 94
Reiser, Pete, 141, 142, 197
Reynolds, Allie, 187, 196, 221, 223, 225, 226, 231, 233, 240, 241
Rice, Grantland, 138–39, 145
Rickey, Branch, 161
Rizzo, Johnny, 120, 125, 135
Rizzuto, Phil, 129, 160, 211, 214, 221, 224, 230, 231, 288
  and Blues, 113
  as MVP, 234
  and World Series, 142, 152, 196–97
Robinson, Jackie, 161, 196, 219, 225
Roe, Preacher, 225
Rolfe, Red, 63, 85, 109, 142
Rooney, Mickey, 248
Roosevelt, Franklin D., 62, 72, 85, 127
Rosalie D. (boat), 10, 16, 29

Rosen, Al, 266
Rosen, Goody, 174
Rossi Olive Oil team, 40
Rowland, Clarence "Pants," 107
Ruffing, Red, 60–61, 86, 97, 99,
    103, 109, 114, 152, 156, 171
Rumill, Ed, 193
Ruppert, Jacob, 53, 56, 63, 93, 94,
    104, 109, 160
Russell, Rip, 180
Ruth, Babe, 32, 33, 66, 86, 131
    The Babe Ruth Story, 204
    and Braves, 56, 78
    and cancer, 201, 204
    comparisons with, 60, 84, 103, 108,
        162–63
    and "Curse of the Bambino," 185
    death of, 204–5
    and exhibition games, 34–35, 55,
        159
    income of, 146, 198
    and number 3, 80, 244
    records held by, 89, 192, 242
    and Red Sox, 179, 185, 298
    and Williams, 112
    and Yankees, 73, 185

Sabie, Ezrulle, 264
Sacramento Solons, 48, 99
St. Louis Cardinals, 151–52, 179–80,
    268, 302
Salt Lake City Bees, 31, 34
San Diego Padres, 64, 69, 71–72, 88,
    103, 243
San Francisco, 16–19
    baseball in, 21–22
    earthquakes (1906), 17, 30; (1989),
        281–83
    Italian immigrants in, 10–11, 12–14
    Recreation Park, 30–31, 35, 54
San Francisco Giants, 30

San Francisco Missions, 41
San Francisco Seals, 30–35, 198, 235
    and Dom, 65–66, 74, 79, 81–82,
        87–88, 94, 98–99, 106–7
    and Joe, 4, 28, 41–44, 45–49, 52,
        53–54, 278
    reunions (1956), 260–62; (1962),
        270
    Seals Stadium, 35, 38, 41
    and Vince, 4, 27, 28, 30, 35, 41,
        43–44, 45, 49, 175–77, 190, 278
Sapio, Angelo, 289
Scarsella, Les, 177
Schalk, Ray, 268
Schulte, Frank "Wildfire," 165
Schumacher, Hal, 72
Schwartz, Alan, 219
Scott, Frank, 223
Scott, George, 266
Seattle Rainiers, 98–99, 275
Selig, Bud, 292
Selkirk, George, 60, 63, 86, 109
Sewell, Rip, 153
    and "eephus ball," 178
Sheed, Wilfrid, 291
Sheehan, Tom, 46
Sheehy, Pete, 80, 208
Shellenback, Frank, 49
Sheppard, Bob, 288
Shite, Ernie, 152
Shor, Bernard "Toots," 83, 125, 145,
    146, 157, 191, 215, 220, 249, 258,
    268, 281
Silvera, Charlie, 217, 288
Simmons, Al, 158
Simon, Paul, "Mrs. Robinson," 273,
    277
Sisler, George, 131
Skolsky, Sidney, 248
Slapnicka, Cy, 147
Slaughter, Enos, 152, 180

Smith, Al, 134
Smith, Red, 188, 195
Smith, Reggie, 267
Snider, Duke, 196, 225
Solotaire, George, 254
Souchok, Steve, 211
Spahn, Warren, 1, 207
Speaker, Tris, 62
Spence, Stan, 205, 206
Spreckens, Al, 203–4
Stanky, Eddie, 197, 207
Steinbrenner, George, 288, 290
Stengel, Casey, 69, 249, 278
  and Boston Bees, 99–100
  and Oakland, 177, 190–91, 198
  and Yankees, 214, 219, 222, 223,
    225, 226, 230, 233, 234, 239,
    240, 244
Stephens, Vern, 199, 205, 211, 214,
    220, 223, 224, 236, 251, 298
Stewart, Ed, 43
Stobbs, Chuck, 221
Stockton Ports, 203–4, 216
Strenzel, John T., 12
Sturm, Johnny, 142
Sullivan, Joe, 53
Sunset Produce team, 40–41

Tabor, Jim, 127, 158
Tacoma Tigers, 229
Taitt, June, 45
Talese, Gay, 183, 272–73
Taylor, Harry, 196
Tebbetts, Birdie, 188, 224, 236
Terry, Bill, 72, 73, 113, 268
Thayer, Ernest, "Casey at the Bat,"
    22
Thomson, Bobby, 2, 241
Throneberry, Faye, 245
Tobin, Maurice J., 159

Topping, Dan, 160, 192, 230, 244
Travis, Cecil, 151
Truman, Harry S., 173
Tucson Lizards, 36, 41
Tunney, Gene, 147

Umphlett, Tom, 251
Updike, John, 1

Vance, Dazzy, 268
Vander Meer, Johnny, 97
Van Robays, Maurice, 125
Vaughan, Arky, 162
Vaughan, Porter, 140
Venezia, Frank, 39
Vernon, Mickey, 179
"Vince DiMaggio's Song," 280
Vincent, Fay, The Only Game in
    Town, 23, 36, 86, 108, 137, 177
Vosmik, Joe, 95, 118

Wagner, Charlie "Broadway," 107–8
Wagner, Hal, 158
Walker, Dixie, 60, 61, 141, 142, 163
Walker, Harry, 60, 180
Walsh, Ed Jr., 47
Waner, Lloyd "Little Poison," 31, 34,
    125, 137
Waner, Paul "Big Poison," 31, 34, 125,
    137
Warneke, Lon, 68
Webb, Del, 160
Webber, Joanne DiMaggio:
  birth of, 78
  and Dom, 292–93
  and family, 155, 163, 191, 254
  and her father, 5, 19, 30, 78, 126,
    176, 190, 228, 255, 262–63, 279,
    280
  marriage of, 262, 263

and Rizzuto, 113, 129
and school, 147, 176, 255
and Ted, 88
Wedge, Will, 215
Weiss, George, 214
Whalen, Jimmy, 30
White, Sammy, 245
Williams, Bobby-Jo, 296
Williams, Claudia, 296
Williams, Dick, 266
Williams, Doris Soule, 160
Williams, Gus, 100
Williams, Joe, 80, 118, 136–37
Williams, John Henry, 296, 299–300
Williams, Louise, 297, 298
Williams, Marvin, 161
Williams, Ted, 54, 124, 273
  and All-Star Games, 132, 178, 219, 231, 239
  batting stance of, 71, 103–4
  birth and background of, 69–71
  death of, 302
  and Dom, 3, 88, 117, 133–34, 137, 140, 194–95, 266, 286, 296, 297, 298, 300–302
  and fans, 112, 121, 136, 150, 299
  and fishing, 88, 95, 265, 296
  and Hall of Fame, 296, 297–98
  hitting, 1, 103, 107, 111–12, 130, 136, 137, 138, 139–41, 153, 159, 173–74, 177–78, 189–90, 205–6, 209–10, 223, 234, 252, 265
  income of, 117, 170, 198
  injuries to, 122, 130, 138, 201, 232
  in left field, 120, 194, 206
  and media, 103, 136, 145, 195
  and military service, 149–50, 153, 159–60, 245, 246, 250–51
  and MVP, 143, 145, 153, 179, 195, 225, 231
  My Turn at Bat, 70, 132, 194
  and Old-Timers' Day, 1, 3, 4, 277, 299
  and Padres, 69, 71–72, 88
  records set by, 140–41, 221
  and Red Sox, 88, 95, 103, 111–12, 121, 127, 130, 153, 192, 193, 194–95, 214, 238, 265
  and retirement, 265–66, 296–97, 300–302
  Ted Williams Day, 246
  and Triple Crown, 153, 195
  and World Series, 180–81
Woodling, Gene, 234, 240, 241
World Series:
  (1914), 77
  (1928), 35
  (1936), 69, 72–73
  (1937), 89–92
  (1938), 99
  (1939), 114
  (1941), 141–42, 197
  (1942), 151–52
  (1943), 160
  (1946), 179–81
  (1947), 196–98
  (1948), 206–7
  (1949), 225–26
  (1950), 235
  (1951), 241–42
  (1956), 31
  (1967), 268
  (1989), 282
  (2004), 302
World War I, 18
World War II, 117–18, 127, 142, 143
  and baseball, 146–51, 157–58, 160, 167, 169
  postwar seasons, 168–69

Wright, Tom, 224
Wrigley, Phil, 261
Wyatt, Whit, 141

Yankee Clipper (boat), 256, 274
Yastrzemski, Carl, 1, 267, 298
Yawkey, Jean, 275–76, 277, 298

Yawkey, Tom, 101, 103, 117, 126–27, 148, 170, 192, 199, 252, 267, 275, 298
York, Rudy, 178, 189
Young, Cy, 268

Zanuck, Darryl F., 258
Zarilla, Al, 223, 224, 236